Beyond
the
Indigo
Children

"P. M. H. Atwater's pioneering work has paved the way for a new way of being and living. Now in *Beyond the Indigo Children* she beckons us to drop our fears and dogmas and grow into the conscious, spiritual beings that we are. Certainly consciousness has a plan, and she is the guide."

WINTER ROBINSON, AUTHOR OF *A HIDDEN ORDER*

"Drawing from her many decades of research and multitudinous sources, Atwater explains the New Children: who they are, why they are here, and how to recognize them. She further explains how human evolution is taking increasing quantum leaps with each wave of children, particularly with regard to their level of intelligence, which is far beyond what anyone might imagine. She provides practical and very helpful suggestions for recognizing, parenting, and enabling these New Children to adjust to and cope with their environment."

ROGER PILE, PH.D., PARAPSYCHOLOGIST AND FORMER DIRECTOR OF THE CENTER FOR GNOSTIC EDUCATION

Other Books by P. M. H. Atwater

Beyond the Light

Children of the New Millennium

Coming Back to Life

*The Complete Idiot's Guide to
Near-Death Experiences*

Future Memory

Goddess Runes

The Magical Language of Runes

The New Children and Near-Death Experiences

*We Live Forever: The Real Truth
about Death*

Beyond the Indigo Children

The New Children and the Coming of the Fifth World

P. M. H. Atwater, L.H.D.

Bear & Company
Rochester, Vermont

Bear & Company
One Park Street
Rochester, Vermont 05767
www.InnerTraditions.com

Bear & Company is a division of Inner Traditions International

LIBRARY OF CONGRESS CATALOGING-IN-PUBLICATION DATA

Atwater, P. M. H.
    Beyond the indigo children : the new children and the coming of the fifth
world / P.M.H. Atwater.
        p. cm.
    Includes bibliographical references and index.
    ISBN 1-59143-051-8 (alk. paper)
    1. Children—Psychic ability.   I. Title.
BF1045.C45A89 2005
133.8'083—dc22

                                                                    2005021062

Printed and bound in the United States by Lake Book Manufacturing, Inc.

10   9   8   7   6

Text design and layout by Virginia Scott Bowman
This book was typeset in Sabon with Garamond and Avenir as the display typefaces.

To send correspondence to the author of this book send a first class letter to the
author c/o Inner Traditions • Bear & Company, One Park Street, Rochester, VT
05767, and we will forward the communication to the author.

~

*This book is lovingly dedicated to
my grandchildren:
Richard Balin Coiner
Sara Ann Coiner
Micaela Annie DeGennaro
Aaron Stone Huffman
Myriam Renee Huffman (in spirit)*

*and to all the new children now being born,
who come to help our world move out of its
own "childhood" into times of greater maturity,
tolerance, and reason.*

I am forever humbled by and thankful for the countless opportunities I have had to study, share, and play with children. Flowing with their stream of consciousness has enabled me to focus on what is important and what is not in the larger scheme of things.

I am also grateful in the writing of this book to:
Terry Young Atwater
William G. and Jeanie Reimer
Robert Silverstein
Joan Brannigan
Joseph Chilton Pearce
Tobin and Mary Hart
Linda Silverman
John Van Auken
Carol Parrish-Harra
Susan G. Keavney
Glenn Mingo
Stephanie Wiltse

and a host of parents and professionals who graciously put up with seemingly endless questions and probing.

Contents

Introduction

Life is what happens to you while you are busy making other plans.

JOHN LENNON

I have been studying children since I was a child myself—wondering how words that were spoken resulted in what followed, watching movements, intentions, feelings, noting any changes that occurred when love entered the mix. This "laboratory of life" took on added significance for me when I birthed three and in my middle years miscarried three. I was a hands-on mother, active in Girl Scouts, Boy Scouts, and as a Sunday school teacher; baker of prize-winning goodies, instigator of spontaneous adventures, protestor of the politically absurd. I worked a full-time job in those days and then came home to another full-time job, as well as tended a garden that supplied what food could not be bartered. Intensely curious, I pursued every source of information I could find about the reason and purpose for human existence, our place in the universe, and the soul. This led me to initiate Inner Forum, Idaho's first nonprofit, metaphysical–spiritual corporation dedicated to exploring the facts and fantasies of inner and outer worlds of being. The probing I did as a child and continued in adulthood translated into programs that involved thousands of people throughout the northwest. The more experiences I had, the more I learned, the greater my curiosity . . . until I died.

My three bouts with death, each time I experienced the near-death phenomenon, turned my life upside down. Afterward, and for more

1

than a quarter of a century, I conducted first-hand research, investigating every aspect of near-death states. Seven books chronicle my findings, and some of my observations have since been clinically verified in prospective studies. During my fieldwork, I kept noticing not only how child experiencers of the phenomenon were changed by it, but also how similar these "altered" youngsters were to children born since the early eighties, and especially to those coming in around the millennial marker. In my book *Children of the New Millennium*,[1] later expanded and renamed *The New Children and Near-Death Experiences*,[2] I compared near-death kids with these new kids. Matches between these two groups concerned unusual sensitivities to taste, texture, touch, and smell, and to light and sound. They also shared intuitive enhancements and a greater intellect and sense of knowing, and were less competitive, more group oriented—with an almost empathic ability to understand another's feelings and needs. They became creative problem-solvers who were more attuned to things future and to the spiritual than to paychecks and bank accounts.

In this book I will go much deeper than in the previous one . . . because the new ones, those somehow "different" from the moment of their birth, bear all the earmarks of an evolutionary shift in the human species, that fabled quantum leap said to be our destiny at this time in history as our galaxy completes a 25,920-year rotation around what is regarded as the universe's Great Central Sun. Subjective and objective views will be treated equally throughout the pages that follow, for we have as much to learn from our mystics and shamans as we do from our scientists and educators. And I will share some of my own visions and revelations given to me while in prayer. The voice that emerges from this book is meant to be a little sassy, 'cause that's the way the new kids are. Brilliance aside, the new ones are a bit irreverent.

For beleaguered parents and puzzled employers, this book should be a godsend in helping you deal with today's children. For everyone else, I hope what you find here is a new perspective, a context for understanding our rapidly changing times in relation to the heightening of consciousness throughout the human family.

*Evolution is speeding up, not time.
Consciousness is evolving, becoming
aware of itself as creation's mentor.*

*Children are evolution's front edge.
They push at boundaries, challenge
the status quo, irritate convention.*

*That is their job . . . to set free all
that sullies the human heart and
blinds the mind to the relationship
between the Creator and the Created.*

The Mayan Gateway

The consciousness of each of us is evolution looking at itself
and reflecting upon itself.

TEILHARD DE CHARDIN

I have a story to tell you—a really big one. Although it's about the new children—those born since 1982 and continuing to be born—it is also about creation and consciousness and the challenges we currently face as a people. A new age is afoot, a time when science and spirituality complement each other, when predictions and prophecies say the same thing, when truth is finally recognized as the two sides of one view. In the spirit of storytelling, I will begin at the beginning. But be forewarned, I have every intention of throwing you a few curves.

For starters, our cosmos is thought to have been birthed when a pinpoint of compressed potential hurtled outward at unimaginable speed. Had this explosion been slightly less violent, the universe's expansion would have been too slow to sustain itself. Had it been slightly more violent, the universe would have dispersed into a thin soup. If the ratio of matter and energy to the volume of space at that moment of the big bang had been one quadrillionth of one percent less than ideal, creation wouldn't have happened. We wouldn't be here. It's as if the universe consciously desired the life it would one day cradle.

The genesis of stars began in nurseries of towering dust and gas. Life as we know it arose from the waters of a "cook's kitchen," nurtured by experiment after experiment until the right combinations occurred for producing the forms that, through the process of incarnation, would enable intelligence to expand. Humans crowned the list, with bodies sculpted as exquisitely as the universe itself. The eminent French scientist LeComte du Noüy observed, "From the very beginning, life has evolved as if there were a goal to attain, and as if this goal were the advent of the human conscience."[1]

This goal, the greater plan undergirding creation's story, was defined and mapped by native peoples the world over who knew what the goal was and passed on this knowledge through the prophecies, rituals, and relics they left behind. The most famous of these sacred legacies is carved into the Aztec–Mayan sun stone, completed in 1479 c.e. by astronomer-priests. Among the different calendrical systems they devised was the long count, calculated specifically for detailing immense passages of time—literally charting creation from the big bang to the year 2012 c.e. Commonly referred to as the Mayan calendar, this mathematical masterpiece is so accurate that modern astronomers are at a complete loss to understand how it was done. It is imagery-based, and an important key to decoding the symbolic glyphs is the way the number thirteen is used in conjunction with the orbit of planet Venus. Certain numbers found in the Book of Revelations also appear in the calendar, such as 144,000 (here representing days in a Baktun cycle, not the biblical number of saved souls).

Let's take a few moments to investigate this marvel. Chief among the many surprises it holds, at least as near as anyone can tell, is its purpose: to track the development of consciousness as creation unfolds. And it does this through the depiction of nine progressive growth stages or levels.

Here's a brief summary of how scholars interpret the calendar's nine levels:[2]

Cellular: From the big bang up to the origins of one-celled

organisms, begins 16.4 billion years ago (consciousness of
action and reaction)

Mammalian: Covering the emergence of larger and more compli-
cated life-forms, begins 820 million years ago (consciousness of
stimulus and response)

Familial: Interrelationships, independence, and the advance of
early humans, begins 41 million years ago (consciousness of
individual stimulus and response)

Tribal: The use of fire, tools, shelter, and the spread of social
groups, begins two million years ago (consciousness of awareness, similarities and differences)

Cultural: Creative invention, art and magic, agriculture, domes-
tication of animals, larger structures and societies, begins 102
thousand years ago (consciousness of reason)

National: A breakout in written languages, record keeping,
metals, manufacturing, the trades, banking, cities, religion
as an institution, begins 3115 B.C.E. (consciousness of law)

Planetary: Industrialization, machinery, compulsory education,
higher learning, entertainment, vast distribution networks,
global communications, digital technology, the Internet, begins
1755 C.E. (consciousness of power)

Galactic: Photonics, nanoseconds, unique forms of multitasking,
apocalyptic plagues and Earth changes, the harnessing of light,
alternative energy sources, ecological issues, begins 1999 C.E.
(consciousness of ethics)

Universal: Recognition of consciousness and intent as driving
forces, emphasis on religious and spiritual matters, awakening to life-form interconnections, corporate stewardship,
the global village, fading of borders and boundaries, begins
2011 C.E. (consciousness of co-creation)

The long count ceases December 21, 2012. (The end date is actually
October 28, 2011, but because of math complications, the 2012 date is
used.)

Notice how evolution speeds up with the passing of each stage. Evolution, not time! Contrary to the overwhelming sense of rush we've all felt of late, the scientific measurement of time has not increased enough to account for what we've been experiencing. It is not time that is accelerating so much as creation itself, as it shifts and re-shifts to accommodate finer frequencies of vibration brought on by the expansion of higher states of consciousness. The difference is perceptual—evolution playing leapfrog with our minds.

The time buffer and the protections we once enjoyed because of it—ample time to correct our follies, adjust to changing conditions, and integrate what we've learned—is virtually gone, as the distance between events and their consequences has dramatically shortened. The Internet, text messaging, cell phones, computers, digital cameras, TV, fax, lasers, fiber optics, and robotics all bring the world to our doorstep instantaneously. "How can I slow down, make sense of this?" is a question that strikes at the heart of each of us. We feel as if our entire planet is having a nervous breakdown.

Yet on December 21, 2012, the center of our galaxy will rise with the morning sun, completing another 25,920-year journey around the great wheel of the zodiac (known astrologically as a "cosmic year"). On that date, though, more than simply an astrological year will close in readiness for the next. Mayans described creation as consisting of five worlds or "suns" (eras). Each sun is shown ending in catastrophe, a transitory period of crisis and upset we recognize, thanks to the modern-day study of chaos, as necessary for new forms and new growth to emerge. This "death of the old, birth of the new" echoes the idea of the phoenix rising from the ashes of destruction, ensuring by its flight not only a fresh start but a world better than the one before. The Mayan fifth sun or fifth world is slated to end in 2012.

End?

More to consider here is that the spiritual levels of the Jewish kabala, the cycles called yugas in Hinduism, and the time-keeping traditions of the Hopi, while eerily similar to the Mayan calendar's suns, also predict the fifth world as soon to come. This galactic alignment that heralds the start of the fifth world can be found in most sacred traditions, including Mithraism, Vedic astrology, Islamic astrology, European sacred geography, Christian religious architecture of the Middle Ages, and in various hermetic traditions, to name a few.[3] Incan lore masters named the period to come *pachacuti*, meaning "the time beyond time when the Earth turns over." Ancient Egyptians knew it as the onset of the "flight of the fifth phoenix." A Hopi prediction says that the Blue Star Kachina (a sky being) will dance for the first time in the plazas of their pueblos when the fifth world arrives.

Another prediction for a blue star as herald for the rising of a fifth world was given by modern-day futurist and intuitive Gordon-Michael Scallion. In his newsletter, *Intuitive Flash*, he declared that the blue star was the comet Hale-Bopp, the cosmic spectacle that zoomed across the skies of planet Earth in 1997.[4] Comet Hale-Bopp was indeed stunning. The last time human eyes gazed upon the comet was during the days of construction, when the great pyramids of Giza neared completion. Throughout history, sky phenomena such as this have been regarded as harbingers of great or dire things to come. They still are.

No one can doubt that the time in which we are currently living truly is unlike anything else in memory or of record, and not just because of the incredible "toys" we have, which are supposed to make our lives easier, or the progress we have made as a society. That's a given. Yet, the era we live in—where rapid change has become the norm—was foreseen, mapped, detailed, and described thousands of years ago by our forebears, people who understood the difference between the evolution of creation and consciousness and the passing of hours and days. They recognized *purpose*, that the human family was no accident upon this Earth, that there was a plan created by a Source above and beyond things visible and invisible.

Not enough remains of these ancient cultures, especially that of the Mayans, to tell us more about what they knew. What we can be absolutely certain of, however, is that the closing date depicted on the Mayan calendar is not doomsday. It illustrates a gateway we will cross through—like a time-space portal into new ways of living, new worlds of opportunity.

Consider our passage a birth, if you will; as with all births, there exists now and will continue to be pain and discomfort, loss of innocence, challenges that sweep us off our feet and slam us on our butts. We will change because we have to. The year 2004, when this book is being written, is a watershed year for everyone. The world around us has turned upside down while a new world steadily approaches. And—don't you love it?—there is another wrinkle to this scenario.

Ancient traditions reveal that the birthing we are now going through will also produce the birth of another life stream or "root race." Not a race in the sense of skin tones and physical characteristics, necessarily, although that too may occur, but a root race in the sense of rootstock—the human gene pool. The psychics and mystics who predict this also claim that the ones now entering are "fifth root race types."

Fifth?

To attempt an answer to this question, we must open Pandora's Box, that fabled receptacle of the strangely wonderful that will not close once opened. That box is our mind, flinging wide to accommodate news about the fifth root race, the fifth world, the fifth dimension, the fifth chakra. All of this is necessary to know, like groundwork, really, before we can even begin to understand the pressures we all feel today and the immense challenges we face raising our newest crop of kids, kids who defy categorization . . . new kids for a new world.

2

The Fifth Root Race

*Great numbers of children will be born who understand
electronics and atomic power as well as other forms of
energy. They will grow into scientists and engineers of a new
age which has the power to destroy civilization unless we
learn to live by spiritual laws.*

EDGAR CAYCE

Admit it. Textbooks used throughout our halls of learning are, for the most part, hopelessly out of date, especially as concerns what is known about our primordial past and our possible future. Today's scientists are actually rewinding history's clock, and establishing as they do timelines and scenarios much different from what we previously learned. New discoveries are happening so fast that even our brightest can hardly keep up, let alone the hierarchy of scholarship designed to preserve what is "acceptable."

For example, the radiocarbon dating of Paleo-Indian sites in the Americas has been found to be in error. Those sites could actually be tens of thousands of years older than anyone thought. The last ice age on our planet was not a continuous deep freeze that gradually thawed. New evidence proves that the weather then whipped back and forth between the extremes of warm–wet and cold–dry–windy, and that the transition time from one environment to the next *happened in as little as three to twelve years!*[1]

More new evidence suggests that the body type we have today did not evolve from early proto-humans. Our Cro-Magnon ancestors "emerged," males around six-and-a-half feet tall, females up to the males' shoulders.[2] And they were talkative, intelligent, sleek of body, and immensely creative. Among their inventions was the sewing needle with a hole in it for thread, which they used to make tailored clothes complete with decorated tunics and leggings, parkas, collared shirts with cuffed sleeves, and boots and moccasins. They built most of their dwellings facing south to take advantage of solar heat, fashioned ingenious cobblestone floors that were sturdy and dry, preserved food year-round in cold caves, ate diets so healthy we moderns would be wise to emulate them, crafted clever tools, separated living spaces for greater efficiency, and eventually took to the water in boats for better fishing.

Their cave art enthralls anyone lucky enough to see it, especially the recently discovered paintings in caves near Combe d'Arc, about 260 miles south of Paris, France. These stunning rock galleries depict half-human–half-animal figures and extinct European cousins of African beasts, lending credibility to the theory that a land bridge must have once connected the continents, and that the entire world's population might indeed have descended from one group of pioneers who started out from Africa.

Yet how this happened, how humankind went from being virtual naked apes to folks who led the way to what became a "breakout" or sudden development of civilization, that missing link to the greatest story evolution could ever tell us is still missing. We don't know. Maybe our seed came from the stars or other planets; maybe we were designed and created by a godlike race to be their worker-bees; maybe we were souls still in spirit who helped fashion the bodies we would one day inhabit from what was available on Earth so we could descend from the spirit world into matter as co-creators with the Creator—committed to what is known in esoteric traditions as "the human experiment:" This recognizes the human form as a vehicle for transformation that is sufficient enough to refine the power of the soul while the soul itself serves as steward for creation's continuous unfoldment.

We may never know the actuality of this, but we can entertain some other intriguing clues to our origins that are just as valuable as what science tells us.

> *Clue number one.* Missing from general discourse are teachings from the "mystery schools" . . . a collection of revelations gained from dreams, memories, channelings, psychic guidance, and otherworldly encounters. This wellspring of inner wisdom about the beginnings of all beginnings and the purpose undergirding existence has spread across the generations via oral history traditions, storytelling, rituals, vision quests, and shamanic-style initiations. All religious thought and all mystical knowings are based at their core on the validity of these mysteries as spiritual truth.
>
> *Clue number two.* When one considers this mystical counterpoint to knowledge, the missing link in the story of evolution shifts to become *the story of involution*—the descent of the soul from realms of spirit into involvements and entanglements with matter.

Certainly life evolves. Even small changes in the weather can have a significant impact on the environment and the life-forms it supports, including the human family. Yet today's science is telling us evolution does not occur the way we were once taught—genes can jump around, and new forms can manifest quickly and in ways we never before imagined. These scientific discoveries are very similar to the ancient wisdom teachings—the mystical half of the equation—especially with regard to species-wide mutations that advanced humankind.

From wisdom or mystery teachings, for example, we learn about the comings and goings of "life streams" or "life waves." Many of the visionaries and prophets of the last several centuries have used the term *root race* or *rootstock* to describe a foundational gene pool that makes up the human race. The understanding given is that a progression of seven root races (life streams) are necessary to provide the soul with enough leverage to develop its potential and perfect human form as it seeks to return to Source. Further, each root race is said to facilitate a global period of readjustment as it advances, so new growth and change can occur throughout the planet.

One famous revelator of material like this was Helena Petrovna Blavatsky, founder of the Theosophical Society of America, an organization dedicated to religious, spiritual, and social pursuits founded in 1875 and still flourishing today.[3] Other voices of revelation in the society were that of C.W. Leadbeater, who wrote at length about cycles in the development and refinement of humankind in his book *The Masters and the Path*,[4] and Colonel Arthur E. Powell with *The Solar System*.[5]

Powell explains, "Each of these Root Races, or stages of development, is divided into seven sub-races, or seven sub-stages; and again each sub-race is further divided into seven smaller units, variously known as branch-roots, or nations."

Leadbeater and Powell categorized the progression of root races in this manner:

First root race: Etheric, begins 18 million years ago (the entry of spirit into matter)

Second root race: Hyperborean, begins 8 million years ago (early physical forms and gender differences, centered in the Arctic and northern climes)

Third root race: Lemurian and Mu, begins one million years ago (full flowering of genders and racial groupings with the introduction of darker skins, movement to southern regions, Indian and Pacific Oceans)

Fourth root race: Atlantean, begins 85,000 B.C.E. (lands now lying beneath the Atlantic Ocean, the Azores; progenitor of modern body types supposedly with the first "Adam")

Fifth root race: Aryan, begins 10,000 B.C.E. with right-brained megalithic cultures from 10,000 to 3000 B.C.E. and left-brained modern cultures from 3000 B.C.E. to the present (consciousness separated into two hemispheres, east and west—now fusing back together, a global leap in species refinement)

Sixth root race: Originally unnamed but now called Aurorean, begins around 2400 to 3000 C.E. (centered in North America and Europe, fuses all global patterns into one planetary consciousness)

Seventh root race: Unnamed, begins 7000 to 8000 C.E. (centered in South America, graduation away from the necessity for earthplane "schools," perhaps etheric in nature with a different means of reproduction and growth)

This rendition differs somewhat from the nine levels of consciousness/creation development as detailed in the Mayan calendar, however the correlations between both views are fascinating.

To help us gain a better grasp of the subject of root races, the Reverend Carol Parrish-Harra offered to comment on this early theosophical material. She is founder and spiritual director of the intentional community Sparrow Hawk Village in Oklahoma, and is a dean at Sancta Sophia Seminary (a modern-day mystery school that is fully accredited as a degree-granting institution).[6] One of her goals is to return to Christianity its esoteric heritage, free of doctrine or adornment. Of her ten books, the second edition of *The New Dictionary of Spiritual Thought* is especially useful.[7] It contains the drawing (shown on page 15; used with permission), of the seven root races appearing as life waves as they descend from the etheric or spirit realms into physical incarnation on the earthplane (involution), and then ascend back to Source after completing their growth cycles (evolution).

Here are some comments from a letter Reverend Parrish-Harra wrote to me about her understanding of root races.

"We recall that spiritual science calls you and me the fifth sub-race of the fifth root race of humanity, or fifth stage of human consciousness to develop on the planet, and look at today's children from that perspec-

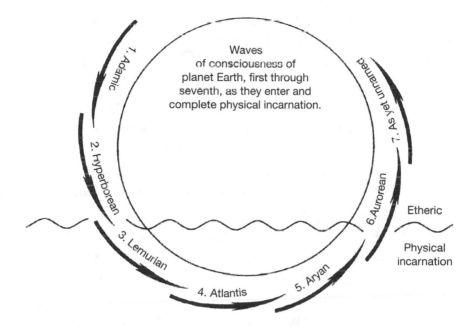

Waves of consciousness of planet Earth, first through seventh, as they enter and complete physical incarnation.

1. Adamic
2. Hyperborean
3. Lemurian
4. Atlantis
5. Aryan
6. Aurorean
7. As yet unnamed

Etheric

Physical incarnation

tive. Theoretically the teachings say humanity will pass through seven great stages. Each stage is called a 'root race,' because it develops out of itself seven great flowerings called sub-races. Think of 'race' as the human race and 'root' as a foundation for a wave of souls forming new and expanded capabilities of human potential.

"As humanity passes through these consecutive stages, the human lifestream evolves. These progressive periods of dominant cultural complexes or peoples are centered in geographic areas where the stream of divine sparks converges into expression. We call this a 'root race.' While a somewhat complex theory, it gives us a way to look at what is happening worldwide.

"If we recognize that each period of time has its own impetus and demands, we see there were long periods of time when the building of the physical body was of primary importance, then the gradual build ing of the emotional nature became dominant. In due time, we began stages of mental body-building —the assignment to which current humanity has been responding."

Another viewpoint on this subject comes to us from the psychic readings given by Edgar Cayce during the first half of the twentieth century. Cayce lived from 1877 to 1945. He grew up on a farm near Hopkinsville, Kentucky, married, became a photographer, and one day lost his voice. In an altered state, instructions came "through" him for how to cure the problem. That first psychic reading surprised everyone, including Cayce, and led to his becoming one of the most documented and accurate psychics in history. The Association for Research and Enlightenment (A.R.E.), an organization dedicated to the preservation and study of Cayce's readings, is very active worldwide and offers many services to its membership.[8]

The monthly newsletter *Ancient Mysteries*, produced by John Van Auken, Lora Little, Ed.D., and Greg Little, Ed.D., is one of the A.R.E.'s many publications. For those interested in the latest findings related to archaeology and anthropology and how they compare to esoteric studies and material from the readings of Edgar Cayce, the newsletter is a gem.[9] One particular issue (August 2002) featured an article entitled, "Origin of the Races: Oneness in Diversity." I was so impressed by the article that I obtained permission from the authors to carry it here (sidebars that accompanied the article were edited out for brevity's sake). I think you will be as fascinated as I was in reading the piece.

ORIGIN OF THE RACES: ONENESS IN DIVERSITY

The Bible tells us that we are all descended from Noah, who was in turn descended from Seth, a son of the first couple, Adam and Eve. Traditional biblical chronology traces this first couple back to about 4004 B.C. Sometime later, Noah's three sons are assumed to have differentiated into the various races of man we know today. However, recent genetic studies indicate that the ancestry of all currently living human beings can be traced back to a single woman. Dubbed "Mitochondrial Eve" (ME), this woman supposedly lived in Africa about 200,000 years ago. Does this mean that biblical history as outlined in the book of Genesis is merely allegorical? And if mankind can be traced back to the same mother, why are we divided into such seemingly dissimilar groups or races? In addition, with whom did this first woman mate?

Scientists have several, mostly conflicting theories, including the discovery of "Y Chromosomal Adam," who appears to have originated several thousand years *later* than his female counterpart, ME. To further complicate matters, recent analysis of ancient DNA obtained from 60,000-year-old Australian bones yielded no linkage whatsoever to ME. Fortunately for us, the history of humanity as outlined by the Edgar Cayce readings is not only able to account for the biblical story, but may even clarify what seems to be incompatible scientific evidence. But to explain the differences in (and the oneness of) the races of humanity, we must start at the beginning of creation.

In the Beginning: What the Bible Tells Us

Most Bible scholars agree that Genesis provides us with two different creation stories. The first, with which the Bible begins, tells us of the creation of the world in six days by a plural God who the Hebrews call the Elohim (Gen. 1:1–4). On the sixth day of this first creation story man is created: "And God said, let us make man in our image after our likeness . . . So God created man in his own image, in the image of God he created them; male and female created he them" (Gen. 1:26–27).

The second creation story begins with Chapter 2 of Genesis and tells the familiar story of Adam and Eve in the Garden of Eden. In this version Adam is "formed of the dust of the ground" not by a plural God, as in the previous creation, but by an individualized "Lord God" (Gen. 2:7).

The Arc of Ascending and Descending Evolution

According to the Cayce readings, these seemingly conflicting stories are included in the Bible for a reason. They form a highly condensed version of the full story of creation, which began many billions of years ago and is still playing out. The readings describe an arc of spiritual and physical devolution followed by an evolutionary return to a state of oneness with the Father ([Cayce] Reading 3003–1). As the readings put it: "All vibration must eventually, as it materializes into matter, pass through a stage of evolution and out. For it rises in its emanations and descends also. Hence the cycle, or circle, or arc, that is as a description of all influences in the experience of man" (Reading 699–1).

Throughout this arc, there have been key turning points, which have involved changes in the spiritual and physical bodies of the human race. In theosophy these points are referred to as the "seven root races," which W. H. Church (*Edgar Cayce's Story of the Soul*) believes correspond to Cayce's "seven stages of man's development" (Reading 281–25). The term *root race* is actually mentioned in only three readings. In one reading we are told that the next evolutionary step for humanity—the fifth root race—will coincide with the future opening of the Atlantean Halls of Records (Reading 5748–6). Both this reading and 5750–1 indicate that this opening, and thus the entrance of the next root race, may be imminent!

Cayce on Multiple Creations and Root Races

According to the readings, then, the first biblical creation story refers to an initial creation of mankind as spiritual, free will companions to the Father. At this point, man was an androgynous spiritual being ("male and female he created them") in full communication and oneness with the Creator. Sometime later, many of the entities began to get curious about the workings of the rest of creation. They then used their free will to project themselves into the denser world of matter. This turning point is what Church and John Van

Auken *(The Lost Hall of Records)* call Cayce's first root race.

Originally, the idea was to observe and learn, but eventually these very fluid and ethereal beings decided to draw closer into material form by creating and occupying humanoid life-forms of a lower vibration. This was the second root race. At this point, they were still androgynous and could move in and out of their earthly bodies. They began to form communities on earth, and many resided in the landmasses centering around the Pacific Ocean, which Cayce called Mu or Lemuria.

One individual was told in a reading that her cave drawings, made 10 million years ago in Lemuria, could still be found in the American Southwest (Reading 2665–2).

Over millions of years, this group became increasingly focused into their earthly creations until they lost even more of their connection with the Creator. They could no longer come and go into matter at will. Still androgynous, they retained some of their spiritual powers and were able to live thousands of years. However, they were using their abilities primarily for selfish reasons. One of the worst examples was their creation of "things," to serve as slaves. These creatures were materialized thought projections in the form of animal-human or plant-human hybrids. This period coincides with the origins of Atlantis, about 200,000 B.C., and is considered to be the third root race.

As a result of this continued devolution, the Christ Spirit developed a plan to rescue these souls so that they could regain their rightful spiritual heritage. About 108,000 B.C., Amilius, the Atlantean Christ incarnation, and a group of other spiritual beings incarnated into Atlantis, where they, too, eventually became enmeshed in matter. Amilius was one of the first to separate into two sexes, when his female half projected out as Lilith. Sometime later, Amilius determined that a new physical body would need to be developed for mankind in order for evolution out of the earthplane to occur. The physical form of the Priest Ra-Ta, an earlier Atlantean incarnation of Edgar Cayce (about 50,000 B.C.), was one of the forerunners of this new body (Reading 294–19). However, the final perfected version—the fourth root race—was not unveiled until about 12,000 B.C. (Reading 294–150).

The Fourth Root Race and the Five Adams and Eves

And this is where we first encounter Cayce's story of the origin of the races, the stage which he also identifies with the second creation story in Genesis (Reading 364–7). Once the fourth root-race-body was ready, the Christ Spirit incarnated as Adam and Eve in five different races and in five separate areas on the earth *simultaneously.* The red race incarnated in Atlantis (and North America), among the racially chameleon-like third-root-race Atlanteans. The white race incarnated near Mt. Ararat, the Carpathians, and Iran. The other three races incarnated in the Gobi area of China (yellow), the African Sudan and Egypt (black), and the Andes area of South America (brown) (Reading 364–13). Interestingly, Cayce emphasized that skin color was not the important differentiation for these five groups: "For He hath made of one blood the nations of the earth" (Reading 3976–24 and Acts 17:26). Instead, he asserted that the colors actually symbolized an inner law or thought pattern which involved one of the five senses. The yellow race he described as "mingling in the hearing," while the white and red were specifically connected to vision/sight and feeling/touch, respectively. The black and brown races were not so clearly identified with a specific sense, but some Cayce scholars, such as Church, have interpreted the readings as assigning taste to the black race and smell to the brown race (Reading 364–13). Souls could incarnate into each of the races in order to focus on the spiritual issues associated with the corresponding sense.

The Oneness of All Races

Cayce indicated that there has been much intermixing since the projections of these five races. Also, he seems to reinforce a recent scientific finding regarding the importance of environment in influencing the amount of the color-producing pigment, melanin, present in the skin.

"For they are all one; there's no races, they are all one—they either have enjoined or have separated themselves, and as has been indicated from times back the environmental influences have made for changes in the color, or the food or the activity has produced those various things . . . " (Reading 1260-1). "Would snow be the place for the black? Or the sun the place for the white? Or the desert and the hills for either the white or black? As were partakers of those things that brought about those variations in that which enters, or becomes as the outer presentation, or the skin, or the pigment that is presented in same" (Reading 364–9).

Was Mitochondrial Eve an Atlantean?

Since ME is believed to have lived about 200,000 B.C., could she perhaps have been one of the androgynous Atlanteans— even the unseparated Amilius/Lilith soul? According to the readings, the feminine side was often dominant, which could have caused the projected earthly body to contain only female characteristics. If so, this may explain why Chromosomal Y Adam appears later in our genetic heritage, since in Cayce's story the split into separate sexes occurred sometime later. And what about the 60,000-year-old Australian DNA that could not be linked with ME?

Cayce indicates that even as each new root race was developing, the previous one did not immediately die out. Scientists have seen this very pattern in the co-existence of Neanderthal and Cro-Magnon Man.

Are We Still Evolving?

In 1939 Cayce was asked, "What will the Aquarian Age mean to mankind as regards Physical, Mental, and Spiritual development?" He responded that we would gain "the full consciousness of the ability to communicate with or to be aware of the relationships to the Creative Forces and the uses of same in the material environs."

Cayce further notes that "ONLY those who accept same [the influence of the vibratory influences] will even become aware of what's going on about them!" (Reading 1602–3). Thus it appears that we are moving in the direction of regaining abilities we had during the era of the third root race. If so, racial divisions would become less relevant, since skin color for that root race could be changed at will based on the environment.

So Cayce does confirm that we are on the upward or more spiritual side of the arc of evolution, and that our choices affect that direction. We evolve through "suffering, patience, and understanding," as shown to us in the pattern of the Christ through his many incarnations from Adam to Jesus (Reading 5749–14). As the readings often state: "The spirit is life; the mind is the builder; the physical is the result" (Reading 349–4).

Although Cayce had little to say specifically about root races, this study by Van Auken, Little, and Little places what he did offer in context with modern science. Its implications about how the human race began and how we may have evolved as a species are stunning.

3

The Fifth World

Only as recently as the late twentieth century have scientific developments advanced our understanding of nature to the point that now, for the first time, we are able to perceive in myth the outlines of a physical science remarkably similar to what theorists are just now beginning to develop. Far from being crude tales devised by primitives, certain ancient myths record a sophisticated cosmological science of exceeding brilliance, one that rivals the contemporary big bang theory in its predictive accuracy and is in many ways more aesthetically pleasing.

PAUL A. LaVIOLETTE, PH.D.

If you keep up with the latest in scientific findings, you will encounter what I've only briefly touched upon—that, although early life-forms were primitive and of lower consciousness, the presence of intervening forces—missing links to the emergence of "modern" humans who looked and acted a lot like us—goes way back in time.

By the way, did you catch the parts about half-human–half-animal beings in the last two chapters?

Cayce spoke at length about this, the entanglements souls wound up in when they messed around with early life-forms while trying to

23

assist in the process of co-creating a better body. The pleasures of sex, for instance, produced surprises with offspring that mixed animal and human forms in unique and sometimes grotesque ways. Cave paintings the world over depict this offspring "departure." Just two years ago some statue-like carvings made from mastodon tusks were found in southwestern Germany. Dating between 30,000 and 35,000 B.C.E. the discovery included a horse, a bird, and a half-man–half-lion dubbed "lion man." Scientists are excited about this, as they say it represents the earliest example of symbolic imagery that can be authenticated. At least, they think it's symbolic.

Mayan legends tell of "molders" who fashioned humankind from life-forms already available, what you and I would call proto-humans. Interestingly, hominid bones recently unearthed in Ethiopia date back 6 million years, while a skull found in Chad is estimated to be 7 to 8 million years old.

Most of the ancient creation stories that still exist, and there are thousands of them around the world, describe eras or ages of dramatic change that significantly altered the landscape and livability of what remained, shifted the climate, and scattered beings and beasts. Each one emphasizes the existence of "Noahs"—survivors to seed the next cycle. In the table on page 25, John Van Auken compares two Native American versions and their symbolic depictions to the Cayce material (I've done some editing for brevity).[1]

Consider now a chart of the Mayan calendar's five worlds or suns (see page 26), along with some of the mythology attributed to them. The version I offer is summarized from numerous legends and research studies. There is a rhythm to how this occurs, a pulse beat, that is beyond what science can either confirm or deny. This type of rhythmic motion and the "motive" ascribed to it (Source inspired) are typical of early calendars. By the way, early calendars were not designed to have additional eras tacked on just to accommodate the advances of time-shifts (a linear approach). They were made to recycle what they contained and continue to do so, for as long as Earth's creation and the development of consciousness continued to interact with one another (an abstract approach).

ANCIENT LEGENDS

HOPI	ALGONQUIN	EDGAR CAYCE
FIRST PEOPLE/WORLD Lived in endless space, forgot original commandment, misled by the Talker and the Handsome One; the chosen were called	*FIRST AGE* Great Spirit creates life	*FIRST AGE* MU—ethereal, semi-physical
SECOND PEOPLE/WORLD Out of the anthill; obey the plan/desire things not needed, thread runs out	*SECOND AGE* Wind of change, as a Spirit speaking to spirits	*SECOND AGE* MU—material, two groups; physical/semi-physical; self-seeking worship of Belial versus ever-hopeful Law of One
THIRD PEOPLE/WORLD Advanced quickly—Flying shields, Spider Woman, song in their hearts, sail away on boats	*THIRD AGE* Serpent in Paradise, secretly an evil rose in paradise; Great Flood, Turtle Island—the Earth dries, fear and hardship abound	*THIRD AGE* Atlantis—high culture, prototypes, logos enters, falling away from spiritual truths, floods/quakes, migrations to new lands in small groups with records, some wisdom and power
FOURTH PEOPLE/WORLD Tops of their heads emphasized; island-hopping to new world, world complete	*SEARCHING FOR FOURTH AGE* A time of migration across Beringia, find land of spruce pines, enter Snake Lands—first peace then war, white people helped, and will return (Inca, Maya, Aztecs have same legend)	*FOURTH AGE* Re-people the earth; the long haul to Egypt, Maya, Inca, China, India, etc.

THE FIVE COSMOGONIC EPOCHS OF THE MAYAN CALENDAR

FIRST WORLD   *Jaguar/Ocelot Sun*
Earth element, feminine energy
A time when giants lived (created by gods). They lived in caves, ate what was available, were attacked and eaten by jaguars [bones found of pre-diluvian animals in deep ravines under dense layers of strata]. Devastating winds and long periods of darkness. Fire.

SECOND WORLD   *Winds Sun**
Air element, masculine energy
Human race in danger of being destroyed by hurricanes, so gods transformed them into apes so they could hold on better and not be carried away [the reason humans and simians resemble each other]. Huge forests flattened by cyclones. Winds. Hurricanes. Darkness.

THIRD WORLD   *Rain of Fire Sun*
Fire element, feminine energy
Destruction by rains of lava and fire. Humans were transformed into birds, thus were saved from cataclysm [evidence of humans buried under layers of lava and ashes]. Volcanoes erupting. Darkness. Ice.

FOURTH WORLD   *Water Sun**
Water element, masculine energy
Everything perishes because of terrific storms, torrential rains, floods reaching nearly to mountain tops [gods changed people into fish to save them]. Time of the elders. Materialism. Dark side has a lot of power.

FIFTH WORLD   *Earthquake/Movement Sun*
Ether element, fusion of masculine/feminine energy
World ends with huge shifts, movements, earthquakes, perhaps a pole shift (magnetic/geophysical). The age of modern humans. Began 3114 B.C.E. and ends 2012 C.E.

---

*There is disagreement about the second and fourth suns: many metaphysical and mystical writers claim the second sun is water and the fourth is wind; professionals in the field, however, and especially folklorists, usually say just the opposite. In this rendition I went with the latter.[2]

Tradition has it that after the year 2012, there begins a period of 5,200 years during which the natural order returns—a time of wisdom, peace, harmony, love, and various states of higher consciousness. A few modern voices have interpreted this to mean that a sixth sun is on the horizon.

Sixth sun?

There is no evidence on the sun stone to suggest a sixth sun in the Aztec–Mayan cosmology. Not even a hint. Instead, there is every indication that, as a "calendar round," the Mayan calendar will recycle, repeat itself for another turn around the wheel once the cycles it predicted have come to fruition. In other words, nothing ends. The ascension or descension of creation's story continues, and in league with shifting energy currents.

Almost all of the time measurements I am aware of, be they based on myth, story form, tradition, or actual calendrical calculations, point to this present time in the history of the human family as the beginning of the fifth world. And you can include Mayan sun legends in this, because, on December 21, 2012, the original vibration of the fifth sun ends *as a higher octave of the same sun begins*—at another level of existence, another plane of potentiality. What we haven't realized yet, what the Mayan calendar has been illustrating all along but few have noticed, is that at this particular shift of eras when the fifth sun ends—true to design—creation-consciousness folds on itself, rolling back over the same sun but at a greater ratio of energy vibration than before. During the first and last cycles of *any* early calendar, folding energy alters the experience of time. This either slows available potential, or accelerates it.

So guess what is happening at this shift of cycle enfoldment?

> *The fifth world is spiraling into ascension!*
> *With it, potentiality is skyrocketing!*

Those who cannot keep up with the acceleration of change now occurring, those who refuse to grow, are screaming at those who can, screaming for attention and love in the only way they know how—with anger. Consciousness is actually becoming self-aware . . . a global mind has formed. Russian scientist V. I. Vernadsky and French theologian Teilhard de Chardin predicted this and named it the *noosphere*, envisioning a mental envelope that would one day encompass Earth like a threaded fabric, connecting all minds, all consciousnesses together in a web of luminescence. This spiritlike or etheric web of sparkling light is often seen by meditators, those in prayer or in ecstasy, near-death experiencers, and people who have undergone transformations of consciousness.

Many say that the Mayan calendar reflects the end of history as we know it, a world based on duality and separation, and the birthing of a golden age of enlightenment during which it will be possible to attain unity consciousness, oneness. A return to the natural order is predicted, in the sense that respect, honor, cooperation, tolerance, understanding, and peace are instinctive in the human family and will resurface if given a chance. (Warlike responses are representative of *learned* behavior.)

The various traditions of fifth world cosmology carry essentially the same message, and feature this same basic revelation: the return of a Christlike being, either as a single soul or through a "Christed" state of consciousness that anyone can achieve. ("Christ consciousness" is an awareness of being anointed by love and grace as one surrenders to the Godhead or Source. It is a state of forgiveness and blessedness in a life dedicated to the service of a higher or spiritual calling.)

An important but seldom mentioned aspect of creation myths is that invariably, each sun or world so described is said to produce its own Adam, its own messiah, and its own Noah. The modern times in which we live offer no exception. The version of the fifth world now ending will produce its Noah, a type of survivor with the consciousness needed to seed the next level, just as happened at the closing of the other eras. And the heightened version of the fifth world soon to arrive will have its own Adam; its own messiah (perhaps the Second Coming of Jesus Christ, or of Quetzalcoatl, or some other figure of such stature); and, eventually, its own Noah, as the ascended fifth world blends into the next level of development on Earth and the fuller expression of the sixth root race.

Adams, messiahs, Noahs . . . each new world is a microcosm of the macrocosm, another step up the ladder of a grander scheme to a greater purpose.

The Fifth Chakra

*The universe is a self-organizing system engaged in the
discovery and realization of its possibilities through a
continuing process of transcendence.*

DAVID KORTEN

I've noticed that the messiah of each era sets the body type and state
of consciousness for that era. This individual (actually a series of individuals born in different places around the world yet modeling the
same pattern) is a progenitor of what is to come. Such holy ones have
disciples or students they teach about the mysteries of life and death,
about Deity (revealed as sacred knowledge or "Holy of Holies"). They
inspire, motivate, and uplift, then leave, either dying as a martyr or
mysteriously disappearing. Those so influenced by these masters are
admonished to continue doing as they have been taught, "and more
also."

The idea of a progenitor, a first-born, is part of every cultural myth on
our planet. Many prophets and scholars believe that Jesus Christ was the
messiah figure for the fifth world. Buddha, Mohammed, and Bahá'u'lláh
are often included in that patterning as well.[1] With the lesser fifth world
quickly fading and an ascended version of the same era about to launch,
we can't help but question: Is the Messiah coming back? My answer:

Absolutely yes! Only this time, I expect that second coming to be larger than life.

Why would I say that? Well, in ascended states, everything expands, enlarges, and accelerates—it becomes more of itself. Several modern examples illustrate this principle. Consider the moviegoers who flocked to see Mel Gibson's *The Passion of the Christ,* then consider the impact this one movie had on people globally. You could say in a sense that the Second Coming of Christ is happening right now, not only at your local cinema and in movie houses across the world, but in how the film affected viewers personally. Look at church parishioners and people of faith everywhere who are finally willing to accept the biblical injunction that states we are each "gods in the making," capable of far more than we were taught once we spiritualize (ascend in consciousness, expand) and live accordingly. This injunction puts the possibility of messiah-hood in everybody's lap, along with the responsibilities that implies, welcome or not.

As we move further into the ascension of the fifth world, we will encounter oversized pressures and stresses as well. You could call it "overwhelm." That's because we're facing more of everything, coming faster and from every corner. Our fail-safe, a solution that works, is a return to the natural order. Ascended states are natural states. The soul-filled qualities of compromise, tolerance, cooperation, and compassion are instinctive. So is the desire to attain ever-higher states of consciousness. This is modeled for us by our messiah-figures as a way to help us jump-start our own potential—the role they fulfill is that of way shower.

And challenges skyrocket with each year that passes. Various mystery school traditions teach that with each advance of a root race, challenges specific to the wave of energy that group represents will accompany it. These energy waves correspond to particular *chakras*—the seven organizing centers in our bodies that receive, assimilate, and transmit life energies. Each of the seven root races is said to have the "job" of fully developing the power of its corresponding chakra throughout the populace, thus energizing those particular qualities, activities, and challenges within the social structures of the time. Accordingly, when all seven root races have completed their evolutionary journey, all seven chakras will operate as one, both within the individual and throughout society itself. (Root races are said to recycle, too; everything does, as the human family continues to spiral in grand sweeps of development and experience, until it reaches its goal of awakened companionship with the Creator.)

Right now we're dealing with a whopper—the last stages of fifth chakra unfoldment, which centers on will power. *Chakra* is a Sanskrit term meaning "spinning wheels of light." I regard each of these "wheels" (and I see their light both inside and over each center) as a kind of generator that enables us to function in a healthy manner. A blocked chakra plugs up the energy in that area of our body and throughout the attitudes, feelings, and life experiences we have that correspond to that area. An open chakra enables the energy in that part of our body and makeup to flow easily and effortlessly, so we feel better, perform with greater confidence, and are able to accomplish more.

The book *Anatomy of the Spirit: The Seven Stages of Power and Healing,* by Caroline Myss, Ph.D., offers an in-depth exploration of the seven chakras in the human body, how they function, and the influence each has in the outworking of our life's potential.[2] What follows is my rendition of the chakras, their functions and associations, based on my own research and experiences. (Some of my discoveries differ slightly from those of Myss.)

First (root chakra): Associated with body support, elimination, legs, bones. Tribal power and group identity. Survival issues. The material world; Earth.

Second (relationship chakra): Associated with sexual organs, hips and pelvis. Need for relationships, pleasure, and sex. Desire issues. World of creativity.

Third (personal power chakra): Associated with stomach, adrenals, pancreas. Standing up for oneself; fight or flight. Personality issues. Energy world.

Fourth (emotional chakra): Associated with heart, lungs, breast, thymus gland. Forgiveness, compassion, love. Intimacy issues. Emotional world, feelings.

Fifth (willpower chakra): Associated with throat, thyroid,
   neck, mouth, nerves. Expression, communication, the will.
   Domination issues. World of ideas.

Sixth (mind/imagination chakra): Associated with brain, pineal/
   pituitary glands. Reason, vision, and knowledge. Mental issues.
   The world of insight, spirit.

Seventh (spiritual chakra): Associated with major body systems
   and the skin. Devotional, inspirational, transcendent. Trust
   issues. The world of faith.

Face it. Fifth chakra energy—issues of will and domination—has
commanded headlines for as long as there have been headlines. And as
the fifth root race moves into its final stages of development (remember,
it's been around for several thousand years and is only now reaching
numbers significant enough to herald a major shift in global population characteristics), so too does the fifth chakra. Everything moves in
rhythm with evolution's urge. To maintain that rhythm, the different
parts of the whole need to move in sync with the whole, or the process
will slow down or detour. You and I help or hinder by the choices we
make. Daily. That makes us important. And here's why.

Fifth chakra issues center around the use of willpower. How do you
express the power of your will? Do you seek to empower others or over-
power them? These questions strike at the very core of the basic need for
self-expression we all have—the need to be heard and acknowledged, to
contribute ideas and thoughts in a way that allows goals to be achieved.
The challenge of the fifth chakra is one of domination itself. Who's in
charge? Are outcomes and lifestyles to be strictly controlled, or can room
be made for the diversity that becomes possible through negotiation and
compromise?

The challenge of "power over" or "power to" is the crux of each war
currently being fought on the earthplane, each abuse of human rights,
each government and each religion that refuses to address its own short-
sightedness. Only individual choices, made one person at a time, can
make a meaningful difference where issues of personal will are concerned; leadership cannot.

Are we ready for the futuristic sixth root race and the sixth chakra? Maybe as individuals, but not as a society. Still, it's clear to me that our present mix has already been spiced by an early wave of sixth root race types—those who seem to have no "skin" in terms of their sensitivity and how otherworldly they are in whatever they see, think, and do. Wait around another four to six hundred years and there will be a lot more of them. Perhaps you and I will even be among them, should we reincarnate at a time when they proliferate.

To help us gain a better grasp of the relationship between root races and chakra development, I prepared a table, shown on page 34, that condenses the basic teachings on the subject from mystical (esoteric) traditions. The column titled "Level of Energy" corresponds with root races and the color of their overall vibratory pattern, and "States of Awareness" corresponds with chakra development. "Types of Consciousness" covers basic drives and planes of operation.

The fifth root race (previous, present, and ascended) is by all accounts the "blue race," blue in the sense of the vibratory resonance it maintains and further develops from the potential existent within the consciousness it holds. The color blue does not necessarily indicate that a fifth root race type of individual has a blue aura (the energy field that surrounds and fills us, that we emit). Claims in this regard, that the color of a person's aura is the determinant of which root race they belong to, are misleading.

Still, there are stories told today of people being born with a bluish cast to their skin who have certain characteristics in common. Gordon-Michael Scallion, the futurist, speaks of this in his writings. Also, Mata Amritanandamayi, called the "Mother of Immortal Bliss," is reported to have had blue-colored skin at birth.[3] Such individuals tend to have exceptional awareness, are highly developed intellectually *and* intuitively, and are comfortable with ambiguity and complex challenges. They have sensitive digestive systems, a susceptibility to allergies, differences in eyesight, and heightened faculties; a noticeable sensitivity to foods, light, sound, and energy fields; plus an amazing ability to function with extremely low levels of stress during difficult situations.

ESOTERIC TEACHINGS OF SOUL EVOLUTION
THROUGH THE AWAKENING OF THE HUMAN MIND

COLOR / LEVEL OF ENERGY	STATES OF AWARENESS	TYPES OF CONSCIOUSNESS
Red	Physical	Physical plane; earthly manifestations. Survival issues, the collective, tribal power with the emergence of individual power
Orange	Astral	Etheric plane; invisible "blueprints." Creativity and the imaginal worlds, inner guidance and heightened senses
Yellow	Mental, concrete	Mental plane; body-mind energy. Decision making and personal will, the need for recognition and invention, active
Green	Mental, abstract	Buddhic plane; awakening to spirit. Initial enlightenment, enlarged worldview, embracing the diversity of people and places
Blue	Higher intuition	Atomic plane; self as an individual. Emphasis on both education and knowing, wisdom and the higher aspects of intuition
Indigo	Inspiration	Monadic plane; fully individuated. Sense of separation from the indivisible whole dissolves, greater insight and perception
Violet	Spiritual	Divinity plane; aligned with soul power. Surrender to God's will, dedication to higher and more involved opportunities for service

The pattern of characteristics just given, however, is *not* exclusive to people purported to have a bluish cast to their skin. Not at all. Further, this pattern *exactly* matches what I kept finding with child experiencers of near-death states, and I discussed this discovery in two of my books, *Children of the New Millennium*[4] and its follow-up, *The New Children and Near-Death Experiences*.[5] What I recognized consistently for over a quarter of a century as I researched the near-death experience is that for *both* adults and children, the episode seems to expand, enlarge, and accelerate whatever potential is present within the individual before the incident occurs . . . as if they were caught up in the energy of ascension.

Let me be more specific about the implications of what I just said.

The characteristics of ascended fifth root race types are the same as those of people who undergo any type of momentous or impactive transformation of consciousness, no matter how caused, whether through a near-death experience, another significant event, or even by being born that way. The overall effect caused by all these individual transformations can be observed throughout populations at large.

As the fifth world moves into ascension, so too does the fifth root race and the spreading of fifth chakra energies and challenges. We are expanding, enlarging, and accelerating, as a people and as a society and as a planetary body of governments, economies, ideologies, and religions that, for the most part, is only recently beginning to realize the import of what it means to share space on a round ball in a sky full of light globes.

Our five senses are expanding in function, too. What was once called "psychic" is now called normal, as we edge closer to a "science of intuition." What's more, we're moving into the fifth dimension. The first three dimensions have to do with the laws of time and space, the fourth with the astral or etheric plane, and the fifth—well, that's the one that frees us from time and space dynamics while enabling us to weave our intentions directly into the fabric of what we want to manifest. Nothing is hidden in the fifth dimension; all is revealed. Can we handle that? We can . . . eventually.

Joseph Chilton Pearce, an expert on what affects the development of a child's brain and how that plays out in society and with the evolution of the human family, has written his most electrifying and important work, *The Biology of Transcendence: A Blueprint of the Human Spirit*.[6] In this seminal work he suggests that the human being actually has five "brains." He describes the brain proper as consisting of four main structures: the hind or "reptilian" brain, the middle or limbic brain, the forebrain or neocortex, and the prefrontal lobes. Then he goes on to state that, thanks to the emerging science of neurocardiology, we can say there is a fifth brain—the heart. Far more than a blood pump, researchers have discovered that 60 to 65 percent of all heart cells are neural cells, identical to those in the brain; that the heart is actually the major glandular structure of the body, producing hormones that profoundly affect the operations of the body, brain, and mind; and that the heart produces two-and-a-half watts of electrical pulsation with each beat, creating an electromagnetic field in and around us that is identical to that of the Earth.

Yes, we have a fifth brain—one that scientific evidence now confirms is more powerful and extraordinary than we ever imagined. No wonder transplant patients who receive the heart of another report connecting to bits and pieces of the other's memories and personality traits. They didn't just receive a donor organ that possesses cellular memory, they got a brain! (Research to support the claim of cellular memory and the amazing intelligence of the heart is growing. Refer to *The Heart's Code* by Paul Pearsall, Ph.D.[7] and the work of the HeartMath Institute.[8])

Isn't it incredible that the fledgling science of intuition has shown us that our five senses are being triggered to perform higher functions, at the same time the new science of neurocardiology has established that we have a fifth brain . . . all during the time of the ascension of the fifth world, and the fifth root race, and the fifth chakra?

All those fives. Patterning like this, nature's way of bringing order and cooperation to what seems to be disorder and chaos, is explained by yet another new science, the science of synchrony.[9] No kidding! The idea that "birds of a feather flock together" can now be proven, on every level of existence—from traffic to fads, from fish to fireflies, from births to evolution itself. Patterns. We know from the study of chaos that this is true—that as order disintegrates into chaos, that very chaos gives birth to a new order.[10] Life utilizes random unpredictability to ensure continued advancement. Yet, what seems random is part and parcel of an underlying order.

Can you stomach one more five?

The number 5 in numerology and as a mystical symbol means "change." It has other meanings, like progress, growth, communication, travel, education, the fun of sex, leadership, the will to achieve and accomplish, science, discovery, adventure, insight. Everything turns and alters under the influence of five energy. It is action-oriented and signifies forward motion. Five also refers to the five-pointed star, the star of man in relation to God, Jesus as Messiah, Christianity.

FIVE . . . the number of change, the energy pattern that best clarifies what is overwhelming our world and implanting itself into our children.

Forget the Ritalin, parents. Give the kids more wiggle-room, more puzzles to solve, and more challenges to wrap their brains around. You won't keep these youngsters quiet, at least not for long.

5

The March of Generations

The highway of life—always under construction.

FRANK AND ERNEST (CARTOON BY BOB THAVES)

Root race advancements do not always correspond with the beginnings and endings of eras. This time they do. Along with the crossover, a major shift has occurred in our culture that affects the march of generations. Some say this shift was caused by the conflicts over the Vietnam War, which took us from postmodernism to new ways of thinking; others claim it was the arrival of the third millennium in 2000–2001. Each is a part of what happened, but much more is involved here than what seems obvious. By taking a look at this, we can gain a glimpse of how the larger schemes of creation's story translate into the shorter lengths of human life—what appears at eye level when we gaze across the table or down the block.

After all, evolution is not some abstract idea. It's you and me, Grandma Tillie and Uncle Fred, and what's reflected back to us from seemingly minor lives lived in obscurity. I've already said we're all important. We really are. The great plan couldn't work without us.

So what do I mean by the march of generations? I am referring to groups of people who come and go in waves of intent and purpose, one group after another, within a sweep of time. Each wave is marked by an

imprint or pattern of energy, a type of consciousness that distinguishes
the wave's members from those who came before and from those who
will follow. Similar to the motion of ocean waves, each generation rolls
in, spreading across the many shores of our planet in response to the
unique forces that propel it. Cyclic in nature, these waves can be studied
and charted. Information gained from doing this is useful in the field of
predictive forecasting and for interpreting the impact change has on the
human spirit. Two researchers who excel in generational studies in the
United States are Neil Howe and William Strauss. Their initial tome,
Generations: The History of America's Future, 1584 to 2069, is a seminal achievement.[1] (It is their typing that I build from in my own work.
Other demographers disagree on dates, but I've found Strauss and Howe
to be the most accurate.)

Flipping pages in a dictionary reveals that, technically, a "generation"
is the span of years, accepted as the average period, between the birth of
parents and the birth of their offspring. A group of like-minded people
of the same approximate age who act in concert with each other over a
period of time also constitutes a generation. (For example, our current
body of justices in the U.S. Supreme Court see themselves as the protectors
of federalism, state sovereignty, and the First Amendment. High court attitudes and opinions, like the ones I just listed for you, change about every
thirty years, generally the equivalent of what is said to be a generation.)

Tradition is more specific, pegging a generation at thirty-three years—
also said to be the length of years Jesus lived. If we consider astrology in this, and it is fair to do so, then the span can vary (thanks to
the elliptical orbit of Pluto, the generational planet) from twelve years,
when Pluto is in the sign of Scorpio, to thirty-two years, when the planet
is in the opposite sign of Taurus. It fascinates me that today's experts
on generational research vary the time increments too, somewhat the
way astrologers do. Most seesaw between fourteen to twenty-six years
in defining generations, depending on the impact of historical events;
but when making projections, they tend to rely on arbitrary figures like
twenty-two years.

So, how does this relate to fifth root race types and, more specifically, to the new children coming into the world now? You're going to love this. The generational spread that gives us the best opportunity for understanding where and how our children fit, at least in our own country, stacks up in the following manner:*

1901–1924, G. I. Joes (builders), estimated at 6 percent of our population

1925–1942, Silents (caregivers), estimated at 11 percent of our population

1943–1960, Boomers (rebels), estimated at 27 percent of our population

1961–1981, Generation X (survivors), estimated also at 27 percent

1982–2001, Millennials (fixers), estimated at 29 percent of our population

The newest of the new can now be added to the spread. I categorize them as:

2002–2024, 9/11 Generation (adapters), percentage unknown

A deeper look at each generation on the list will both surprise and amaze you, especially how the patterns reflect the human response to shifts in societal pressures. Since Pluto represents generational changes in the human family, I'll include some interpretive astrology as an interesting extra. Here goes.

1901–1924, G. I. JOES (BUILDERS)

This has been dubbed the "greatest generation" in recognition of their sacrifices and achievements during the entirety of the twentieth century. Toughened by the Great Depression and two world wars, they came

---

*Population percentages based on 2002 statistics.

to possess a practical, down-to-earth discipline that enabled them to tackle any problem with "can-do" confidence. Uncommon valor was their common virtue. Long-term commitments, patriotism, and a strong faith in God motivated their actions and defined the way they thought. They built big businesses, big governments, big churches, big entertainment ventures, and they did things together, as if they were a community of doers who possessed "the right stuff." Doggedly persistent, they were masters of invention, design, and construction. And they were dutiful parents, creating organizations like Boy Scouts and Girl Scouts for their children. They had unstoppable energy (Superman and Super Hero Comics came from this group) and upheld the power of authority, of tradition, of "the greater good." They fulfilled the American dream as no other group before or since, and won two-thirds of the Nobel prizes awarded to Americans in doing so, with many amassing tremendous wealth.

As you might imagine, they were also known for being tight-fisted and downright stingy sometimes, hoarding more than they needed, and making excessive demands to get a job done "the way it should be." Their inventiveness concerned the physical, what they could see, hear, and touch. Frivolity did not interest them, nor did sexual or emotional excesses or deviations. Life was conditional; you got what you deserved or earned. Astrologically, the generation splits between Pluto in Gemini from 1901 to 1913 (the sign of experimentation, invention, ideas, communication, restless energy, and the desire to initiate new projects), and Pluto in Cancer from 1914 to 1924 (the sign of motherhood, food, protection, defense, traditions of hard work and loyalty, ownership, sentimentality, and the need to stabilize energy).

1925–1942, SILENTS (CAREGIVERS)

Sandwiched between the heroes of World War II and the rebels who would come after them, this is best known as the generation of broken dreams, faithful workers who were either forgotten or unappreciated or skipped over or ignored. Theirs has always been the responsibility since childhood of taking care of others, especially their parents, as if they were somehow designated the consummate helpmates. Lacking a cohesive core of motivational leadership (no U.S. President ever emerged from their ranks), they developed an alone-in-the-crowd mentality that depended more on a systems approach to life than on individual enterprise. No great cause or challenge defined them. Considered withdrawn and uninteresting overall, they matured devoid of any distinctive qualities that readily set them apart.

Yet this is the generation that gave us civic and social concern, and they accomplished this by plumbing the inner depths of self. They gained in the process a keen sense of how and why human beings fall short of fulfilling their ideals, and of the passages, seasons, and turning points everyone grows through in life. The sexual revolution and the divorce epidemic that followed originated with these people, along with the recognition of psychiatry and psychoanalysis as important fields of study. They produced some of the best comedians and songwriters in history, as well as a long list of people who excelled in the helping professions. Virtually every major player in the civil rights movement can be traced to this one generation, as can the birth of the Peace Corps and a host of advocacy movements. Often pegged as either bureaucrats or company players, organization and management were their forte, retirement nest eggs a common bonus.

Pluto's influence during this time span is divided between two signs: 1925–1937 under the aegis of Cancer (described earlier), and 1938–1942 with Leo (the sign of rulership, the boss, dramatic flair, expansive worldview, generosity, open-heartedness, gourmet preferences, gambling, and the tendency to expect more than can be delivered).

1943–1960, BOOMERS (REBELS)

What began as self-examination with the silents evolved into a "me first," narcissistic mentality with the boomers that quickly resulted in a youthful upheaval of furious and powerful proportions. This is the generation that broke all the rules. They were the victory babies, so large in number that they burst through the seams of every entitlement imaginable: schools, housing, medical care, government programs, employment opportunities, and (soon on the horizon) retirement. True "yuppies" (demanding more than they can afford to pay for by themselves), they seemed blessed from their very beginnings with largesse, the best their parents could provide. Visionary idealists who followed their bliss, they expanded the sexual revolution into an orgy of free love, pill-popped psychedelics, and rock 'n roll. They produced huge concerts ("If you can remember Woodstock you weren't there"), huge protests ("Stop the war in Vietnam" and "Shut down the nuclear power plants"), huge gatherings ("We stand beside the workers of Poland"), and huge movements ("This is the dawning of the Age of Aquarius"). Theirs was a new consciousness, new values.

And they possessed a spiritual euphoria unmatched by any other generation, jumping from drugs to religious revivals to Jesus saves to evangelism to new age–new thought groups to mythology to Eastern mysticism to gurus, to prophecy and psychic phenomena and a veritable explosion in pop therapies, self-help books, yoga, and meditation classes. They also spawned the most active era of church formation in the twentieth century.

Their arrogance and creative independence fostered a revolution in the entertainment industry and the media, in technology and communications, in literature and fashion, and in the development of space shuttles and leading-edge explorations. Declaring their fathers emotionally insensitive and their mothers their best friends, this group eventually moved from self-absorption to self-destruction. A vast array of ills followed, such as the AIDS epidemic, drug addictions, and alcohol abuse. In an effort to avoid fighting in Vietnam, some became dodgers and drifters, awash in failed expectations and colossal bankruptcies and foreclosures.

The years 1943 through 1957—most of the time frame covered by this generation—saw Pluto in the sign of Leo (described earlier). It wasn't until the last couple of years, 1958–1960, that Pluto's orbit took it into Virgo (the sign of harvest, efficiency, practicality, health matters, virtue, detailed analysis, criticism, withheld emotions, caution, propriety, and a nervous, sometimes self-deprecating energy).

1961–1981, GENERATION X (SURVIVORS)

This, our nation's thirteenth generation, has been labeled the "lost generation," a star-crossed bunch challenged by poverty, drugs, and parental neglect. Alienated from society because of the Vietnam conflict, skyrocketing divorce rates, mass corporate takeovers driven by "greed is good" attitudes, ethical impropriety in government, the failure of religious relevancy, and a school system unable to do its job, they turned primitive and tribal in nature. If you don't believe me, just take a gander at their body piercings and tattoos, and notice their penchant for creating their own families via gang loyalties or tight clan-clusters of like-minds.

Theirs is the most aborted generation in history, which left them with a fear that children are unwanted and commitments are a waste of time. Couple that with the instant gratification that defined their world—fast food, fast copies, drive-through banks, hundreds of television channels to surf—and you begin to understand their show-it-to-me-now, shortened attention span. It's no wonder they developed a brooding, dark cynicism. Called "the generation with no name," they originated the crimes of identity-theft, computer viruses, and piracy raids on "secure" Web sites.

Music, they claim, is more important to them than sex, money, or power. And what music! Popular preferences include acid rock, punk, rap, and the birth of vulgarity as an art form. Anarchy appeals to them, so does sexual deviance and androgyny. Theirs is the only generation in this spread to be less educated than their parents. A "signature" (particular trait or characteristic that undergirds the generation's energy) of depression and suicide is part of their makeup, yet a strong instinct for survival prevails. You can recognize this in their talent for entrepreneurship—not careers, specifically, but the skill of forming start-up companies and independent businesses based on the network approach, then clocking hours like a workamaniac. They possess an almost missionary zeal to cut through rhetoric, filter out noise, and institute practical truths. Proven allegiances and tested relationships mean more to them than wealth. Some live like "adultolescents" (those who, in their twenties and thirties, still reside with and are supported by their parents) or share duties and debts in co-housing projects. Here, Pluto divides almost evenly between Virgo (already described) from 1961–1971, and Libra from 1972–1981 (the sign of marriage, relationships, partnerships, diplomacy, the court system, justice, clever perversions, vanity, the arts, and the "mask" of smiling when in doubt, appearing in control while crying inside).

1982–2001, MILLENNIALS (FIXERS)

Society breathed a collective sigh of relief with the emergence of this dynamic group of new traditionalists, who see themselves as "generation fix," here to repair the excesses of their forebears in the Boomer Generation and the cynicism of those in Generation X. Their capacity for innovative thinking, abstraction, intuitive knowing, and spatial reasoning, their high IQ scores and wisdom beyond their years run smack into the reality of a shrinking middle class with predominately single-parent households. (Refer to *Millenials Rising: The Next Great Generation,* by Neil Howe and William Strauss.[2]) Volunteer-minded and dedicated to the return of ethics even at very young ages, they support causes like Habitat for Humanity, biodiversity, sustainability movements, renewable resources, and excellence in education.

Loyal to whatever family they may have, they are slow to commit, pragmatic, and self-reliant. It is commonplace to see both males and females training in judo and karate as well as a broad span of sports and endurance tests. The ones born earlier in the cycle favor the radical middle in politics and tout the advantages of electronic democracy and tax reform. These older Millennials are gung-ho about business ventures and wealth building. They thrive on challenges, yet operate best in small groups, smart mobs, and coalitions. Authority figures do not impress them. Thus far, younger Millennials seem to be following the same trend.

Overall, they exude a snappy confidence that has all the earmarks of an underlying anger—specifically against anything inauthentic, phony, or a con. Females tend to be aggressive; males willing to share duties and pleasures on a more equal basis. Many of the older ones are bisexual and practice oral sex. Even though they tend to mature early, they lack a sense of spelling and grammar—probably because electronic multitasking requires no such skills. They are so used to swapping music, copying videos, and downloading images that to pay an individual for the work required to perfect talent is somehow foreign to their thinking. In spite of the great energy they possess, obesity is increasingly a problem, as are a plethora of attention disorders and coping difficulties. Real-time coverage of the September 11 attack on America awakened in them a new patriotism and a strong resolve, similar to that of the G.I. Joes after Pearl Harbor.

Pluto passed through three signs during the millennial generation. From 1982–1983, Libra concluded its influence (described earlier). Then, from 1984–1995, Pluto made a fast trip through Scorpio (the sign of transformation, "death of the old, birth of the new," legacies, taxation, other people's money, life extremes, sexuality and birth as political issues, sacredness, magic, secrets, and the swing between ego and soul). From 1996–2001, Pluto moved into Sagittarius (the sign of humanitarianism, philosophy, religion, law, foreign countries and foreign interests, travel, higher learning, science, sports, quick tempers and sharp tongues, honesty, and an infectious enthusiasm for progress).

2002–2024, 9/11 GENERATION (ADAPTERS)

Only conjecture about this generation can be offered at this point, as the newest of the new are just arriving. There's a signature of fear with this bunch, although at first they may appear to be fearless. It is my sense, intuitively and through my study of astrology, that safety, security, monetary policies, fiscal responsibility, and restructuring will become big issues for them. Initially, though, the clash of cultures that underscores the unrest on our planet will be their primary focus—and they will be ready to tackle such a challenge, as the needed skills will be inborn, stamped on their very souls. The world as we know it will change under their watch. So will borders and boundaries, social services, trade, governments, and individual opportunities for advancement. Excitement about the task ahead of them may cool somewhat as the enormity of it sinks in. They will almost certainly be filled with spontaneous surges of creativity and spirituality, but this could backfire on them if they forget to protect themselves and institute strong defensive measures. Because of that, a streak of conservatism and caution will be necessary, as well as heavy dollops of patience.

Many predictions have been made by various psychics, channelers, and visionaries about the years of this generation's emergence; I've made a number of them myself. A few to consider are:

2004: Major challenges in the operation of the World Bank and International Monetary Fund.

2004 and 2012: Venus passes between Earth and sun, a rare sky event heralding the final preparatory period before passage through the Mayan gateway.

2007: The war of Armageddon, as predicted by Christian fundamentalists, is supposed to begin.

2012–2013: The fifth world ascension begins as predicted by a consensus of spiritual traditions.

2017: The United States is "reborn" with new thinking and new vigor after a series of major miscalculations in foreign policy, economic reform, and political leadership.

Also during 2017: Astronomers suspect that the last full solar eclipse may occur, as our moon is slowly spiraling away from Earth. It may be too distant after that to cover the sun completely.

Astrologically, Pluto will remain in Sagittarius from 2002–2008 (already described). For the bulk of the time, 2009–2024, Pluto will be in Capricorn (the sign of governments, rulers, authority figures, conservatism, social services, status, investments, career, controls and manipulations, awards, achievements, dedication, practicality, austerity, perfectionism, protectionism, and the reigning-in of emotion).

The majority of astrologers believe that the Age of Aquarius finally dawns in the year 2025, when Pluto enters that sign and marks the generation that is born under its influence. A commonly held prediction is that the next great avatar or messiah will be born on February 18, 2080, when seven planets cluster in the sign of Aquarius, especially Jupiter and Saturn (duplicating the unique alignment of these two planets at the birth of Jesus). I have no doubt that spectacular events will follow such a birth. In the years 2133 and 2134 Halley's comet will make its thirty-third fly-by, heralding the ascendency of Aquarian energy. The world as we know it today won't exist then. Changes will be that dramatic.

The generation that ushers in the Aquarian Age (a 2,160-year "month" in the cosmic year) will in all probability cover the years 2025 through 2043. I name them the Aquarians, because those years span the entirety of Pluto in Aquarius. Aquarian energy is striking in its ability to envision and create, and is so innovative, free thinking, eccentric, wide open, and freedom-loving that I doubt that any other patterning could share space with it. So I add to the march of generations that of 2025–2043, Aquarians (universalists).

I've mentioned *signatures* on several occasions while exploring generational imprinting. Allow me to explain myself. Signatures are particular traits or characteristics of an energy patterning that undergird its cycle. Positive and negative signatures for the generations I've covered in this chapter are summarized in the table on page 49.

The energy shifters that tilt the human family toward a radically different consciousness, more egalitarian and spiritual by nature, are the millennials. During the course of their generational cycle, Pluto changes signs three times. With three very different vibratory energies operating in just one generation, "tug-o-wars" can happen and already are occurring, pitting optimistic problem-solvers against amoral or resentful controllers who act out. This situation, one of far-ranging extremes in behavior and intent, reflects the twin urges of evolution *and* devolution happening simultaneously. Historically, patterning such as this accelerates available energy to almost unimaginable proportions while diversifying population groups in unpredictable ways. (For instance, the massive youth bulge throughout the Muslim countries, where more than half the population is under the age of twenty-five, is threatening to destroy culture, theirs and ours, in flames of terrorism. Young men and boys untrained in critical thinking, many awash in suffocating poverty, are falling prey to maniacal clerics who preach intolerance and hate. The backlash created by this could lead to World War III. You could term the phenomenon a "youthquake" based on how it tends to split off the latter part of Generation X and all the Millennials from the wise counsel of elders and educators. The pressure created by evolution/devolution [construction/destruction, progress/regression] could render diplomacy useless.)

GENERATIONAL SIGNATURES

GENERATION	POSITIVE SIGNATURE	NEGATIVE SIGNATURE
G. I. Joes (1901–1924)	Perseverance	Stubbornness
Silents (1925–1942)	Compassion	Disillusionment
Boomers (1943–1960)	Enthusiasm	Selfishness
Generation X (1961–1981)	Resourcefulness	Suicide and depression (self-condemnation)
Millennials (1982–2001)	Tolerance	Anger (a peculiar impatience)
9/11 Generation (2002–2024)	Adaptability	Fear (insecurity)
Aquarians (2025–2043)	Humanitarian	Instability (crisis)

In the United States, schools have already been hard-hit financially by the demands of a diverse young population. Having to modify curriculums and teaching styles to accommodate an almost unbelievable range of immigrants now enrolled has strained budgets to the breaking point.

The historical flow of generational change is compromised by this—too much stress in too short a time.

It is the Millennials who are the pivot group in this scenario. No study of them, however, in any country accurately identifies the range of potential they possess. Since each generation must reinterpret truth in their own terms, we will be challenged again and again by this one. Their task as the pivot group is to reinvent and redistribute energy and resources. They reset the stage on which human drama is acted out so the 9/11s and Aquarians can "write" a better script. *They are the shift generation in the age of shift. As our nation's fourteenth generation, they are a five!* In the practice of numerology, you add the digits in numbers to arrive at symbolic meanings. Thus, fourteen, one plus four, equals five. Here we go again . . . .

See what I mean about the new children? For good or ill, they are leading us places we have never been before.

Blues or Indigos: Challenging the Labels

Let us think again about what we are doing in labeling these "new children." I believe this is the new sub-race of individuals for which our fifth collective has been preparing. It corresponds to new growth on an old tree—the family tree.

REV. CAROL PARRISH-HARRA, PH.D.

I've noticed that as cycles change and new streamers of consciousness roll in, invariably there are a rash of "sightings"—revelations from psychics and visionaries, claims and counterclaims from sensation seekers, skeptics, investigators—all with the goal of bringing to the public's attention what is or is not true about the phenomenon at hand. This flurry of activity serves to awaken us. In the spirit of being one of the bell-ringers, I want to add my voice to the growing chorus about the new kids. The question before us is: Which root race are the new ones? Blue or indigo (fifth or sixth)?

The new children have been variously described as Indigos (because of the supposed color of their auras), Star Kids (because of their purported origination from other worlds), Crystal Children (because some say they are highly developed), and so forth—none of these claims hold up in the face of research, whether via scientific observation or by studying mystical/esoteric traditions or through summarizing visionary revelations. "Indigo" and the other labels are now subject to serious challenge.

Professionals in the field of child development and education, parents, even the kids themselves, are having problems with the idea that certain character traits are the province of so-called "Indigos" (or "Crystals," "Star" or "Sky" kids), when, in fact, the majority of today's children match those traits—without evidencing anything like a purple aura, or being a hybrid from another planet, or possessing "god-like" wisdom. Being supersensitive, confident, highly intelligent, creative, nonconformist, extraordinarily psychic and spiritually aware, impatient, empathic, great at problem-solving, yet difficult to parent or educate—these characteristics are typical to fifth root race energy as it intensifies.

Children born since around 1982 really are different, like no other generation of record. If the hype about Indigos makes this point and no other, it has done the world a favor and hopefully will help to engender an overall transformation in how we regard and teach children. Surely it will inspire a forum whereby the children themselves can speak and be heard. . . for our youngest citizens truly have something important to say that is worth hearing.

What is happening now with our children, within ourselves, and in the world around us, is tied together as synchronized movements in the same evolutionary leap. In order to help you understand this and learn how to recognize what has value and what may not within the general discourse on the new children, I'd like to explore a few of the other offerings on the subject.

POPULAR NOTIONS TO CONSIDER

In their popular book, *The Indigo Children: The New Kids Have Arrived*, Lee Carroll and Jan Tober state that the new kids are indigos (sixth root race) because they have purple auras.[1] They write about how technologically oriented the new youngsters are, how highly intuitive and creative, confident, strong, and nonattached they are, with quick, sharp minds.

Much of the information in their book comes from sources channeled through a medium, with additional comments from a few professionals and parents.

Another person commenting on the new kids is Drunvalo Melchizedek, a self-realized mystic. In an interview with him conducted by Diane Cooper and later titled "Children of the New Dream" in an article she wrote, he explains that there are three different types of children now emerging: super psychics in China, indigo children, and kids born with AIDS.[2] He describes the Chinese youngsters as "psychic beyond belief." He says they have scored 100 percent on every test given to them, no matter what kind of test it was or how difficult. This has puzzled their parents, who often lament, "I have a kid who knows everything—what do I do about this?" He reports that such children are also showing up in Russia and the United States, and that these super psychics are similar to indigo children. (A man who writes at length about the Chinese children is Paul Dong in his book, *China's Super Psychics*.[3])

What excites Drunvalo the most, though, are the AIDS kids. He offers as an example:

> About 10 or 11 years ago in the U.S., there was a baby born with AIDS. They tested him at birth and at 6 months and he tested positive for AIDS. They tested him a year later and he still tested positive. Then they didn't test him again until he was 6, and what was amazing is that this test showed that he was completely AIDS free! In fact, there was no trace that he ever had AIDS or HIV whatsoever!

Drunvalo goes on to claim that, through close monitoring by medical researchers at the University of California, Los Angeles, researchers made the discovery that youngsters like this particular boy exhibit a unique DNA patterning no one else has: twenty-four active codons. (In human DNA the world over, twenty of the sixty-four possible different patterns of nucleic acids called "codons" are "turned on" and active, three operate like "stop-start" codes similar to those on a computer, while the rest remain inactive.) He claims that the children who have twenty-four active codons instead of the usual twenty have shown a resistance to disease that is quite remarkable. They seem to be immune to everything. Drunvalo believes this DNA advancement heralds the end of disease in that anyone, by choosing to align with unity and interconnectedness, as the kids do, can achieve the same result.

Dubbed "the peace troubadour," author/ singer James Twyman travels the world over giving musical concerts he calls "peace missions." In his book *Emissary of Love* he shares his own personal story of meeting an unusual child from Bulgaria and afterward discovering that he (Twyman) suddenly possessed psychic powers.[4] He found that he could alter the form of matter, read people's thoughts, and even transmit images to others via pure intent. Four months later he traveled to Bulgaria and, through interactions with the same boy and those like him, he learned that just by opening up to the consciousness of these children, he could hear them telepathically, no matter where he was, and he could manifest abilities they said were latent within him and in everyone else. His peace missions to Bulgaria as well as Bosnia and other war-torn areas have brought him face-to-face with many of what he calls "psychic children." His sensational claims about these children have spawned an explosion of books about Indigos, music just for Indigos, and Indigo camps, schools, literature, classes, toys, Web sites, and business logos.

This sampling of viewpoints about remarkable youngsters being born today necessitates that we ask another question: How much of what is being said about the new children actually holds up to scrutiny? Although there is no way to check every tidbit, I can comment on some of it.

Children who have indigo or purple auras, a predominant trend

The notion that children with indigo or purple auras are now commonplace is greatly exaggerated. Precursors to the sixth root race began arriving, as near as I can tell, in the late 1800s. More are coming in today, but in nowhere near the numbers currently being claimed. Although traits like higher intuition, mind-over-matter, various psychic abilities, and mental and technological expertise are the province of the fifth root race, and will be more so as it completes its evolutionary cycle, for the next 400 years or more it may be difficult to distinguish one root race from the other as characteristics will blend during the crossover from our present advancement in consciousness to the next. What is common, and will increase in the years to come, are sightings of a deepening in aura colors, particularly that of blue, around both young adults and children. This deepening is a sign of energy intensification. As the fifth world moves into ascension, so too does the fifth root race. The majority of "blues" already here and continuing to be born are really "ascended blues." Aside from aura colors, it's important to note body type, behavior characteristics, and mental and intuitive acuity to make legitimate distinctions.

True indigos, and so far I've only met a few of them, do not have the same physical stamina so prevalent with fifth and ascended fifth root races. What I mean by "true indigos" are those who bring in the more developed states of consciousness relative to the sixth root race. Seldom do you find developed individuals in the early waves of any evolutionary crossover. Each root race improves on the body type and consciousness of the one before it. The sixth will be much more refined than those currently manifesting, and well able to thrive in significantly higher states of mental and spiritual realities. Briefly, true indigos are challenged to appreciate sexual differences, seem to have "no skin" with regard to personal boundaries, and tend to ignore or detach from hygiene and health-care chores as if such things applied to others but not to them. Their grounding is not in the physical, but in the mental. It is the ascended blues who are made-to-order for tackling the immensity of today's problems. They are powerful fixers, broad-minded, and virtually unstoppable once they commit to a goal. They will never be satisfied with anything less than an overhaul of society itself, globally. To categorize our new children, as is being done in popular missives, with labels like indigo hero, crystalline, psychic, star seed, alien hybrid, blue ray, wonder kid, and other such names serves no one . . . and does more harm than good.

**Unusually psychic children now widespread,
some psychic even beyond belief**

Claims are being made of late about children who can move physical objects with their minds, levitate, foretell the future, heal people of illnesses, and other miraculous feats. Many of these claims are true. Hundreds of schools for psychic children have sprung up globally to work with children with such abilities, as have conferences, articles, and magazines on the subject. What is also true, but overlooked, is that all children, by right of birth, are psychic and display some or most of the same abilities now being credited to those who seem "special." I wonder if today's open climate for things "paranormal"—and parents being far more willing than in the past to allow their children to express themselves—is what really accounts for the unusual number of successful demonstrations of psychic ability with kids. Admittedly, as our environment continues to change (less oxygen, decreased magnetics, increased storms), we will see people of all ages become more psychically aware—as a form of self-protection, perhaps, and as a type of adaptation. Concerning the super-psychic children of China, researchers have noted that the majority lose their clairvoyant, telepathic, and mind-over-matter traits after puberty. This finding is consistent with what has been seen in other countries and established with reams of reports about parapsychological research conducted for over a century in England and Europe (and later in the United States). Psychic abilities are affected by states of mind, hormonal balances, and environmental influences. They are real, valid, and deserving of wider acceptance than being linked to superstition or subject to religious condemnation.

**Children born with AIDS
who recovered without a trace, even of HIV**

The original tests done on AIDS babies that made the news about a decade ago have since been discredited. In rechecking protocols, physicians discovered that none of the children ever had AIDS or HIV to begin with but, rather, other conditions that were misdiagnosed.[5] In the year 2000, the National Institutes of Health reported that in twenty years of tracking HIV cases worldwide, only five adults and twenty-seven kids mysteriously reverted to testing negative. Hardly a trend, by anyone's standards.

Children with DNA helix alterations, additional codons (nucleic acid patterns), mutations

Nothing in the medical literature backs up any discoveries or findings about the activation of additional codons in the human being, which is curious considering how important this news should be. What is gathering steam, however, at least in the alternative press, are stories about mutations in the helix spirals of DNA and of additional strands forming. A few of these claims have received a preliminary nod by medical researchers pursuant to rigorous study. Others are more questionable. One holistic practitioner by the name of Dr. Berrenda Fox (with doctorates in physiology and naturopathy) publicly stated that she already had solid evidence proving such mutations. A short time after her announcement, she closed her clinic, saying she was forced to "after a harrowing battle with the American Medical Association." Rumors are still circulating concerning her whereabouts and whether or not any of her claims were ever true. Most toss off the whole affair, and with reason, since Fox was once a writer for television shows such as *The X-Files* and *Sightings*.[6] But numerous psychics and channelers have said similar things. One in particular, Susanna Thorpe-Clark of Australia, states,

> We are being changed physically from carbon-based beings with two strands of DNA into crystalline beings with 1,024 strands of DNA (eventually), because only crystalline substances can exist on higher dimensional levels. We are in fact having our bodies merged with Sirian DNA strands, as this format is close enough to our own to be able to integrate with relatively little side effects.[7]

Susanna is well-known and well-regarded; so are others like her. Yet evidence to back up these revelations remains scarce—whether from channeled sources, medical physicians, or other health-care practitioners.

Children from war-torn countries
who exhibit unusual psychic abilities

It is well known in psychological and medical circles going back more than one hundred years that the majority of children who are abused, troubled, painfully shy, shell-shocked by wars and similar traumas, or suffering from neglect become quite psychic. Typical are reports of out-of-body experiences and telepathy, as well as the ability to affect physical matter with thoughts, know the future, and see and communicate with angels, disincarnates, and demons. A child's natural intuitive faculty tends to expand automatically into a survival mechanism during times of crisis.

Many of these children have been propelled into almost super-star status by well-known adults, including the aforementioned James Twyman. What he has accomplished by holding Peace Concerts around the world is incredible; his 2004 performance in Baghdad, Iraq, with mortars exploding only a few blocks away, is the stuff of legend, and a home for orphans established there by members of his "beloved community" has saved lives. Yet he has been heavily criticized of late for taking advantage of fears about war and the desire for peace to capitalize on his claims about psychic children. Twyman has admitted to exaggerating claims he made about these children in his book, *Emissary of Love*. He said he did it "for effect."[8]

Children who possess
a wisdom beyond their years

Adults are now turning to youngsters for advice on a multitude of issues, and receiving words of wisdom they say have changed their lives. When you examine what the children said, most of it is simple truth we all know but take for granted, like love one another, pretend and it is so, keep the faith, no one is ever alone, each person is precious, God is real, and God loves us. Keep in mind that modern kids, all of them, are able to communicate in multiple ways. Some have their own Web sites, publish books of inspiration, are featured on radio and television talk shows, even produce e-magazines and e-mailed newsletters. Or they have relatives who do it for them. It wasn't so long ago that people flocked to the beds of stricken or dying children to hear what they might say, believing that "out of the mouths of babes" came great truths. Of interest is that a number of the more exceptional youngsters are suffering from major illnesses or handicaps, are paralyzed (some use speaker boards, as their voice is gone), or are facing imminent death. What is different with these kids is their admission that "I chose to be born this way so you would listen to me" or "I'm here to spread love." Marshall Stewart Ball, a brilliant fifteen-year-old from Austin, Texas, is like this: seriously handicapped since birth, yet a constant source of inspiration and guidance for others. His Web site is well worth visiting, his books are treasures.[9] This is also true of Mattie J. T. Stepanek, age eleven, of Upper Marlboro, Maryland, who, despite a rare form of muscular dystrophy, triumphed in uplifting books of poetry before his death in 2004.[10]

The children seem unusually calm and loving regardless of circumstances

Many of today's junior citizens have a certain calmness about them that puts adults at ease and bespeaks a time when children were well-mannered and courteous. But this calm demeanor often hides confusion, indifference, and a restless impatience. Current newspapers shout out headlines like "Younger Students Getting Violent" ("I'm scared to even go to school," says a fifth grader), and talk about "rug rat rage" (detailing an epidemic of anger that seems to begin right after toddler-hood). In March of 2003, a reporter investigating the story about a father who killed his three sons and then himself, spoke with a child who knew the younger son. The boy asked rather matter-of-factly, "Do you think all dads should kill their children?" This indifference shocked the reporter. There is no doubt that the new children are loving and exceptionally generous, yet just below the surface can lurk a different face. These kids will talk back and question authority to a degree that is surprising *and* disconcerting.

Child geniuses, intelligence on the rise

Scores on standard IQ tests are soaring by leaps and bounds. We used to think that intelligence was inherited, that it was "in the genes," and that environment had little effect. Yet what is happening today defies nature *and* nurture. Psychologist Ulrich Neisser of Cornell University joins a growing chorus when he admits, "This shatters our belief about the rigidity of IQ. It's powerful evidence that you can indeed change it." *Psychological Review* carried a provocative article by William T. Dickens of Brookings Institution that at least addresses the IQ puzzle in a way that makes some degree of sense.[11] He advanced the idea of "the Flynn effect," building on an observation made by James Flynn in 1987 that "People's IQs are affected by both environment and genes, but their environments are matched to their IQs." (Flynn, by the way, co-authored Dickens's paper.) He continued, "Higher IQ leads one into better environments, causing still higher IQ."

The catch to Flynn's work, however, is that it addresses children in a group setting, and not as single individuals. What may be at work here is the multiplier effect, that when kids as a group are exposed to flash cards, "brain-twisters," and "brain-teasers," their IQ increases. Yet it doesn't seem to really matter whether individuals are motivated by others or if exposure is incidental—like playing games on the back of cereal boxes or doing crossword puzzles alone—intelligence still increases. Take a moment just to reflect on what the new kids are exposed to—then take a deep breath and realize that even those without this exposure are evidencing unusual jumps in IQ, too. (Caution: Some of the genius superstars are phony. They were caught being coached by their mothers. This doesn't change the intelligence phenomenon, but it does change how we regard the innocence of our children.)

Children who look different, like "aliens," with enlarged prefrontal lobes

Absolutely true. Tales are told of children with altered brain structures, nervous and digestive systems that seem to work differently, and unusually sensitive skin, ears, and eyes. Those I have researched in the general populace closely resemble children who have undergone a near-death episode. I have written extensively about physiological and psychological changes that can occur after such an episode, most recently in my book *The New Children and Near-Death Experiences*.[12] The pattern of aftereffects from a near-death experience closely resembles the traits children are now born with, such as increased intelligence, creativity, and psychic ability, awareness of things "future," healing abilities, inner knowing, and so forth.

This fact does *not* suggest that each child who displays these characteristics had a near-death episode, but it does confirm my notion that we can use the near-death phenomenon as a "model" to better understand what seems to be happening to the human family as a whole. What I recognize is the handiwork of evolution. Other researchers are coming to the same conclusion, among them Joseph Chilton Pearce. In his book, *The Biology of Transcendence: A Blueprint of the Human Spirit*, and specifically on page 251, are photographs of toddlers with protruding prefrontal cortices (lobes).[13] This protrusion curves outward from the top base of the nose to the hairline, creating a large and amply curved forehead. I have a granddaughter like this, and I have seen hundreds more. Pearce showed me some of his other pictures, of little ones who looked as if they were wearing helmets or had "football heads" (startling extensions of the prefrontal cortex as well as out from the back of the head).

During follow-ups, he obtained current photos illustrating how, as their hair lengthened, the anomaly was no longer visible, except for their unique foreheads. He found that these children were so advanced and so intelligent they appeared to be "otherworldly." He explained,

> The mothers of such children whom I have spoken with at any length have strikingly similar backgrounds. They are self-possessed women of strength and self-confidence and are deeply spiritual in a personal rather than formal sense. Many are in their late thirties or early forties.

As you can see from this brief exposé, some of the claims made about the new children have merit, some are hoaxes, some are visionary rev-elations, and some are currently outside of our ability to either verify or discredit. One thing's for certain, though. We are changing as a species, even on a cellular level. Our children are proof of this, and, oh, what amazing children they are!

7

A Hodgepodge of Voices

*God plays such an important role in my life. I wouldn't
have lasted five minutes on Earth. I was born and went into
arrest. I mean, I've already died twice and God really pulled
me through and I believe it's because I'm here for a reason.*

MATTIE J. T. STEPANEK

We can never comprehend the vast scope of new children and the range
of their abilities without listening to them, just hearing them talk. Sometimes they sound so wise, so spiritual and compassionate. Other times
they express themselves in the jumbled way kids always have—no different, no better. Still, we must listen, and that's exactly what we're about
to do thanks to the many parents, interested adults, and professionals
willing to share their stories about interactions with the young, and to
the various kids who wanted to chime in as well. This scattering of voices
sets the stage for a deeper look at the whole subject—our newest generations and the winds of change they ride as the world turns on itself and
shifts to a higher frequency of vibration.

We begin this chorus with Susan of Texas, a daycare provider, talking not just about her "odd" charges but about their equally "odd"
mothers.

"I ran a home daycare for newborns and infants. These babies were born between 1989 and 1992. I had the privilege of nurturing about 15 infants, some through toddlerhood. These babies were so unusual we still talk about them. They were without exception very intelligent, did not follow any by-the-book stages of development; and shared most of the same characteristics in two distinct groups:

> "Enchanted with what they saw above and around my head (mothers would explain their baby was looking at my bangs or hair); needed eye-to-eye contact; visually explored anything new; very, very calm and accepting; anchored to me and Mom; were not excited by changes in the environment like a doorbell or crying; enjoyed quiet nursery rhymes, nursery songs, and talking (one infant softly thumped out distinct music with his fingers); wanted to be held as infants, but often stiffened when touched as toddlers; not interested in crawling, late walkers; loved their veggies (one baby loved her strained peas so much I am still nauseated by the smell of peas).
>
> "Extreme curiosity; had to touch everything; early to crawl and walk; as toddlers starting their day with me, always circumnavigated the daycare area first; loved games and music, the louder the better; physically strong and active; vocal (one mother's 3-month-old was infamous for out-singing the church congregation); withdrew from most skin-to-skin touch; napped irregularly; bonded to anyone they liked; ate solid foods very early, fed by their parents solid foods they gummed like pizza, hamburgers, fries(!)."

Thirteen of the fifteen infants at Susan's daycare were stuck with indifferent parents.

"I specialized in newborn/infant care and was open 24 hours. Most of the mothers were shift workers in the medical, police, safety, and service industries. The mothers had circumstances and attitudes which ranged from the unwed or unhappy (he was an accident, if you like him so much, you take him), to the nervous (holding the baby so uncomfortably, my neighbor asked who she was), to New Age (I dressed him in purple, the healing color, because he has the sniffles; he doesn't like his car seat buckled so I put a golden glow around him). Only two mothers stood out as absolutely accepting their baby."

It is worth mentioning here that not all women are adept at mothering, sometimes men do it better; not all children are born with an even reasonable chance at what life could offer. Yet all children are gifts, ready and willing to unwrap themselves if given a chance.

As you listen to the chorus that follows, remember that both evolution and devolution are happening simultaneously now and in ways that amuse, horrify, and surprise. As the children must adjust to wide swings in that which is negative and positive, so must we.

Quotes from a few professionals get us started:

From Anna Quindlen, social commentator, New York:[1] "They are children, hundreds of thousands of them, twice as likely to repeat a grade or be hospitalized and four times as likely to go hungry as the kids with a roof over their heads. Twenty years ago New York City provided emergency shelter for just under a thousand families a day; last month [February 2001] it had to find spaces for 10,000 children on a given night. Not since the Great Depression have this many babies, toddlers, and kids had no place like home."

From Barrie Drazen, who runs a halfway house in Connecticut for males newly released from jail: "The younger age group [men in their late teens and twenty or so] seem to differ from their predecessors as follows: they don't seem to want to do any work, watch too much MTV, want everything done for them, and feel as if they've 'got it all coming' and therefore, generically speaking, 'society owes them.'"

From Mary L. Salomon, career coordinator, Washington: "I have had the privilege of meeting and interviewing a younger group of absolutely brilliant ones who are confident, well-adjusted, and defy description. They are eighth to twelfth graders, very high achievers, and full of light. I have never met young people with their capacity to love learning. They each take total initiative for their own learning, are open to all kinds of experiences, and have an infectious optimism!"

Now for some quotes from parents of preschoolers:

Lori Lite, Georgia:[2] Lori muses that one day her four-year-old said, "Mommy, do you remember before I was born when I was watching you?" Later, Lori recounts, "My husband and I sat out on the deck talking to my mother-in-law. My daughter was cuddled on my husband's lap. We were discussing some of the pain we still felt over my father-in-law's transition. During a moment of sadness, my daughter blurted out to my husband, "Your daddy is an angel! He's right up there." She was pointing to a spot above my mother-in-law's head. We looked at each other in disbelief. We had never taught her anything like that. It provided us with a feeling of peace.

Dora, Texas: "The most interesting part of raising Jacqueline has been guiding her spiritual and metaphysical growth. By her second birthday, she was routinely telling me things like 'I remember being born. It was like a big window opening' (with a big, opening-up-the-arms gesture). I had had an emergency C-section. She went on to say, 'I used to be an old lady' (while wearing an old necklace, her old Easter hat, and my old high heels)."

Tim, Illinois: "The other day as Sandy walked in the daycare room to pick up Erik everything was unusually quiet. She entered to see Erik sitting in the far corner on the reading mat with another little boy (both are three years old), and an open book about animals. All the other kids and teachers were on the other side of the room watching quietly. At first, most would think this is nothing to report. As Erik pointed out the words of the animals and said them out loud, the little playmate would repeat the word back to Erik. The little boy's name is Amika. His family is from Africa and he is autistic. Until that day, Amika had only said the word 'duck.' That's it! Never one single 'hi' and another kid's name.

Honestly, Erik was the only child to play with him at other activities, probably so he could have all the 'airtime' talking. Ha! Children are truly amazing and God has blessed us with a little boy with a tiny gift that will hopefully give forever."

Victoria, New Jersey: "My daughter cannot sleep in her room with the lights off. Sometimes, I find four lights on at the same time. She really has a thing about being in the dark. It seemed to have started when she was around five. She would scream and try to sleep with me, and my doctor told me to close my door and not let her in. It was one of those childhood phases. It killed me to hear her cry in such terror that finally I let her sleep with me. She would never talk about why she couldn't sleep in her room, until one day she told me that the people who visit her at night kept her up. I was so surprised at myself for not putting two and two together. I kept asking her about these people, and she said they talk to her all of the time and ask her questions. Sometimes I would pass her room at night and hear her answering questions. I consulted a local child psychologist and took her there under the pretense that this woman was my friend. Millie was wonderful with her, and was chatting about these people who visit her at night. I must admit, I thought there was something wrong with my daughter. So Millie talked to Jamie for about a half hour, until she finally said, 'Jamie, would you sleep in your room if mommy puts on a TV or radio?' She shook her head no. 'Mommy keeps the light on for you, but you can't sleep with the light on. What if Mommy locks the windows and the door so no one can visit you anymore? Would that make you feel more comfortable?' Here's a five-year-old little girl who then puts her hands on her hips and walked up to the therapist and said, 'What good would locking the windows and door be if they pop through the walls!'"

Lynn, Virginia: "One of the clearest examples of Sara as teacher for me occurred when she was about five years old. I had had a very frustrating day at work with a challenging employee. I had just about decided that it was time to fire her. That night, when I spoke sharply to Sara, I realized that I was taking out my frustrations from earlier in the day. So I took

Sara on my lap and apologized to her, explaining that I was frustrated by an employee who was not doing the things I wanted her to do. Sara then said, 'Did you ask her nicely to do it?' When I nodded my head, she said, 'Well, did you tell her firmly to do it?' I said that I thought I had. There was a very brief pause before Sara tried again: 'Have you tried sending her love?' That question certainly brought me up short. No, I had not tried sending love toward that employee. Rather the opposite, in fact. So that night, before going to sleep, I consciously found the loving space in my heart and let that love radiate to the troublesome employee. Sure enough, the next morning when I arrived at work, my relationship with her had taken a great leap forward, and that employee was not fired."

Now we'll hear voices from grade school children:

Trish Alley, President of the Board at Greensboro Wonder & Wisdom School in Vermont, told me about a little girl named Alice and what she had to say in class about arguing:[3]

"Arguing is like being on an escalator. If you are fighting or arguing with a friend, you are each saying things that take you up the escalator. Fighting keeps you going up, and the energy of the argument goes up and up. The situation gets worse and worse because you are breaking, and losing, friendship. To keep arguing, and not solve the problem, you'll just keep going up that escalator. And lose. You want to go back down the escalator by saying nice, kind, helpful things to create friendship again, but it's hard to bring hurt feelings back down to be able to solve the problem. When you are on that escalator you go up and down, up and down. To avoid going up that escalator, you are better off not getting on that escalator in the first place. To stay off the escalator, you need to keep working on friendship and how to solve problems. But, not really. When you have to earn friendships back, it's having friendships in a cheating way. Once people know that you will take them up the escalator, it's hard to ever have real trust again. A real friend will keep from going up that escalator in the first place."

Lori Lito of Georgia relates this story: "I put my six year-old son to bed. My husband and I finished up the kitchen and started to discuss the status of my son's health. He had been on an antifungal for one year. We had seen huge improvements in his health and hyperactivity had decreased. Our doctor wanted to keep him on the medication. My husband and I were not sure if that was the right decision. We went to bed still wondering what to do. At breakfast the next morning, my son came into the kitchen and informed me that there was an angel in his room last night and she said that he was healed. Needless to say, we immediately discontinued his medication with no regrets. I was thankful for this message."

Some comments from and about teenagers:

Gary W. Hardin, an author, met Joey Klein, a new kind of teen:[4] "Joey means to change the world, pure and simple. He spoke with me in front of The Society of Psi Research in Fort Collins [Colorado]. They had the largest crowd in their history show up for the presentation. I was my naturally wonderful self, but Joey completely caught me off guard with the amazing energy and comfort he has with the audience. He decided to do a healing session right in front of the audience. There wasn't a dry eye in the place. One of the leaders of the Sai Ma folks (akin to Sai Baba) met Joey in New York and told him he thought Joey had the power to call dolphins. Okay. So what does he do but fly out to San Diego to visit Sea World and plan a boat ride out into San Diego Bay. While at Sea World two dolphins swim up to him and put their heads on his lap. He later visited one of the below-level viewing tanks and put his hand up on the glass. One of the manatees who had been hiding in the back swam up to his hand, bumping the tank and muzzling his hand until he took it down, several minutes later. Weird stuff. Then he goes to the marina to get a boat and the boat people tell him there are no dolphins out in the bay, that he is wasting his time and his money. He takes the boat anyhow, with a few friends in tow. They get out into the bay and twenty dolphins start swimming around the boat. Joey puts on his wet suit and jumps into the water. They start swimming around him and coming up to him. Then this white dolphin shows up and swims to Joey and dives under him. Joey can hear the 'voice' of the dolphin telling him things. He gets fried by the energy of the white dolphin and his friends have to take him out of the water."

From Tori, age sixteen, Virginia: "Days come and go and only memories are left behind. Try to make those memories positive, try to not let the little things get to you. Chances are you won't remember what upset you tomorrow. Take all advice with a grain of salt, and remember no one's opinion is as good as your own if its your own life in consideration. Go with your gut, do what feels right. Establish your own morals and figure out what is important to you, and stick by it. If you can't stick by yourself, you can't stick by anyone. I don't want to know what they are teaching us in school, all the useless information that is drilled endlessly at us, all the information that we regurgitate on tests. I don't want to know that! I want to know why we can't go inside a black hole, and do other life-forms exist? I want to know if there is a God and what created stuff in the very beginning? What made it all start? Where the hell did matter come from? Questions are the main thing in my mind lately, and I can't get them answered."

From Jennifer, Texas: "I made a conscious choice when I was fifteen that has shaped my life in the most incredible ways. I decided that I wanted to become a United States Marine. I had always wanted to be a Marine, but I didn't verbalize that thought until I was 15. At the time I'm sure the idea seemed a little crazy. I was heavily overweight and extremely inactive. And, as most of my friends pointed out, I was a girl. Still, I was convinced I was meant to be a soldier. I knew that in my last lifetime, I died a violent death as a common foot soldier in WWI. Ask my mother, and she'll tell you that I came into this life still marching, and looking very, very surprised! Starting around 14, I had vivid dreams of being a war leader, dressed in leather, carrying a heavy weapon, consorting with many and various women, and pillaging villages. What mystifies me to this day is that I was born into this lifetime a woman. Actually, it usually makes me extremely upset that I was born a woman. In addition to a sense of always being very uncomfortable in my skin, how scary is a five-foot-two Marine? And God made sure that I could never be mistaken for anything but a woman; I'm built like a frickin' Barbie doll. How am I supposed to fight, and blow things up, and win battles, and lead men, if I'm a woman who (1) is prohibited to be engaged in combat, and (2) couldn't drag her wounded buddy out of harm's way even if she was allowed to fight. All right, God, what do I do now?" [Update: Jennifer lost her extra weight, toughened up, and joined the Marines. She's now in the corps, a proud and happy Marine serving her country.]

And listen to these eighth-graders, sounding off at a school in Berkeley, California:

Alexandria (Hispanic): "I am willing to make a special and kinder world. I think the world around me is a terrible place where everyone tries to wreak havoc and there are only so many good people left. I would change things by helping as many people as possible—if you can help three you can made a difference. I don't feel as though I fit in this world. It's hectic and cruel and I'm neither. My purpose and reason for being here is to help change the world. I feel I do have the power to do or be whatever I want to."

Anne (Japanese-American): "I think of myself as a lot of different things, and in different ways. I can be patient and kind, and very quiet. But I can also be rude and 'shine on' and ignore people I'm angry with. Still, I'm very proud of all my accomplishments, including my grades, my ice skating, and my acting. I believe I am pretty honest. Of course, like most people, I do lie occasionally. No offense to all my teachers, but I think it is easier to lie to them than my parents. When I lie to my parents I feel really guilty, and it haunts me for the rest of my life. I feel everyone was created for a reason, and we are all part of the fate of the earth. One person's choices affect the whole world, which is why we must consider others before we decide. I believe all the people on this earth today will somehow affect the years to come, and the lives of all people to come."

Kyerra (African-American): "I'm honest to a limit. Sometimes I get afraid of telling the truth so I lie. Honesty means being faithful. Honesty means a lot to me because it says about 90 percent of who you are. God spoke me into the world, so I am here. Religion is a wonderful thing to me because it has a lot of meaning to do with commitment and honesty. Marriage is the same reason. Abortion is depending on religion. Personally I think it's cruel. Suicide is senseless, careless, and cruel, too. Family death is just something that has to happen."

Shehzad (Pakistani): "I came from Pakistan, a little town called Tano where I helped my grandfather in the fields, smelling the dark-rich soil where plant life begins. I am willing to risk my life to help advance the farmers in my country. My religion is Muslim. I pray five times a day. I like my religion. It helps keep me in control. I will fall in love one time, marry one time, because you only get life one time. After I die, I will go to heaven, a beautiful land created by Allah for his followers. Only time will tell if I go there."

Grace (Caucasian American): "I often think of myself as a walking contradiction. I feel like an outcast and one of the popular kids at the same time. On the surface level, I get along with just about every person in my school. I like to keep tabs on everyone and know a little of everyone's interests and backgrounds. Because of this attribute, I am welcome in almost every group of friends. However, I have this general feeling that I have absolutely no friends. I feel like I don't connect with anyone my age. I have tried to become more connected in a deeper way to the girls in my class, but before each attempt I get this feeling that I am lying. I feel like I'm joining the conformity when I try to connect with these girls. Ever since I was very young, I have never questioned that I will be an environmental scientist. Never mind the fact that I hate science and the environment depresses me horribly. I have always just known that the Earth is in sad condition and needs as much help as possible. Obviously, not many people share this view and this is the reason that the Earth continues to be trashed. Religion is a bad idea. Huge groups of clashing believers that are willing to kill to get their point across is just illogical. I think that having spirituality with the Earth is fine."

Ellen, a mom in New York, talks about her college-age son. "There were times in college when forty people per night would show up in his dorm or frat room looking for him to see either: (a) Where's the party/fun (obviously with Micah), or (b) the person needed help or advice. He never cried as a baby, merely cleared his throat when he was in need of attention or a diaper change. He is a very old, very aware soul. His dynamic, charismatic energy is amazing (and he is humble and helpful, not full of ego). One thing which has always disturbed me, though, is that this kid has absolutely no fear and can tend to be something of a daredevil! His loving girlfriend of three years keeps him anchored there. He used to pull a few risky stunts (on his rollerblades, hitching rides on the backs of trucks when he was younger, and zooming between cars on the rollerblades in front of my eyes when he was 16, almost gave me heart failure, etc.). His brother is a much more cautious type. Micah hit the ground running, skating, flying, taking chances. He's been that way all along.

"Interestingly, he told me, out of the blue, as a child, 'I know you worry about me, Mom, but you shouldn't. I know I never met your grandfather (he died years before Micah was born), but I feel him around me, protecting me all the time.' I have always had a feeling that this son was my beloved grandfather's direct incarnation, that he came back in this life to be with me and my family once again, and I recognized this the first time I saw my son (I thought 'he's my grandfather'). I never mentioned this to Micah. He has his energy, and there's definitely something about him. H-m-m-m-m."

The new children have been entering our world for some time. The childhood memories of Cynthia Sue Larson of California, an adult "new kid," will strike a chord with a lot of people:[5]

"I feel that people around me did the best they could to treat me with dignity when I was growing up, yet they did not seem to understand that much of what they said and did looked outrageously primitive to me. It was strange to be told how to do things 'right' by people who clearly were still working on some pretty big issues. I could tell how people around me were thinking and feeling, and was really confused that adults seemed incapable of doing so. This knowingness of what was really true for others and the ability to pretend to ignore that knowledge appeared to me to be the root of most of what we call 'evil' in our world.

"When I was very young, I remembered what it was like before I was born. When I was about five years old, I felt like I'd made some kind of mistake being here on Earth. I felt like I wanted to say, 'Whoops! Wrong planet,' to whoever was responsible for sending me here. I longed to once again be surrounded by conscious sentient beings who KNEW they could read others' minds and feelings, and also knew everyone else could read them. What a compassionate place that is, the one I so clearly recalled! I longed for it so much that I had an ache in my heart from it. Then I noticed that cars sped by very fast on my suburban street, and realized that if I were to jump in front of a fast one, I'd be back where I was before I was born. I made up my mind that I would soon leave this world. The simple act of making this decision soothed me, as I savored what I felt to be my last few days with my family and friends.

"On one of these days, I was surprised to walk into my bedroom and feel time slow down to a stop as a number of brightly glowing humanoid forms gathered around me. They showed me my possible life paths, and told me that I had a choice to make. I could choose to live my life fast, or choose to live it slow. To my five-year-old mind, the question of whether I wished to live fast or slow was a good way to pose the question, 'Do you really want to end this life so fast, or would you rather live it more slowly?' I chose slow after seeing everything they showed me. As soon as I made the decision to live a longer life, I came back into real time and ordinary reality feeling refreshed and invigorated. I wanted to enthusiastically tell the world, 'I CHOSE SLOW,' but was certain that nobody would understand."

Joanne Ambrus of Wisconsin, another adult new kid, adds, "I don't think it's odd that these children are surfacing now. I think it's odd that no one noticed we surfaced much earlier." She explains:

"We have been having children who are like us and now researchers are realizing there is something different going on in the world. Take a look at all the people who are going 'back to nature.' It's a longing to go back to the world of feeling. To feel yourself part of a cosmic whole. To step outside of today's world and into the world these children are showing you. We, who live in both worlds, can tell you how difficult it can be and how frustrating it often seems. The material world has little attraction while something else keeps calling to us. I think there was something with World War II that produced children like me. Once we began, we have been passing our inheritance along to our children and grandchildren. Since our numbers are increasing, we are finally being noticed. So, you see, this is not a new finding at all. Rather, it is more of an awareness that has been missing for the last fifty years."

8

The Lure of the Astral

It takes courage to grow up and turn out to be who you
really are.

E. E. CUMMINGS

All the people we have just heard, voicing their stories in a chorus of amazement and discontent, bring us to the point where we can focus more on the new children themselves and how they differ from any other generation—certainly in modern history, and in all probability going back at least several thousand years. It's not that any one cluster of traits define them; rather, as you have already seen, a larger pattern of enhanced characteristics sets them apart as being forerunners of a new genetics. They truly are unique. To help you grasp the import of what I just said, I'll spend the next seven chapters sharing what I and numerous other professionals and visionaries have discovered about the new wave of children rapidly spreading across our planet.

Joanne Ambrus, whom we heard from in the previous chapter, has more to tell us about what it is like to be "different" in the sense of being exceptionally psychic and sensitive and tuned into realms other than this one *as a natural part of everyday life.* An interesting aspect of her comments that follow is that both she and her son are "new children." His traits are the same as hers. Learning how to parent him enabled her to better understand her own childhood and why she reacted in the manner she did to the way she was treated.

"The one thing I discovered in raising an exceptional child was don't treat him like a child. His favorite comment was 'I may be just a kid, but I'm not stupid!' You treat them like intelligent creatures in little bodies.

"My son was doing rolling falls off the hassock when he was two. It drove my mother crazy, but we left him alone. He knew what he was doing and did it very well. He was dexterous at an early age, potty trained overnight—said he wouldn't wet again and he didn't. He is very athletic and very curious (or nosy, depending on your definition). But the worst part is, he's very easily bored. He would play with the same item for hours, but repetitive schoolwork bored him to tears. He had a long attention span when playing but once he learned something, he wanted to go on to something new.

"We're very independent. We like to strike out on our own and try new things. My job bores me silly, always the same thing over and over. I enjoy new challenges. I'm ready to retire and try new things. Life is an adventure!

"I always feel as if I'm out of sync with the rest of the world, though. Like they all read the instruction manual and I didn't. My son and I are very practical with inordinate amounts of common sense which makes living in the world a challenge. I've come to the conclusion that people are basically insane! Irrationality seems to be the norm, not the exception.

"We 'know' things before they happen sometimes and have a wonderful rapport with animals. Dogs come up to us that won't go to anyone else. Cats too. Ferrets come and hit the deck running. They just move in! It seems as if my son and I operate on a different wavelength and pick up distinctly different information.

"Take the sense of smell. I could never figure out how someone could get twins mixed up. There's a different smell. People all smell different. I'm very nearsighted. Without glasses, I'm legally blind; yet, living on a farm, I've never needed a flashlight to see my way. For some reason, there's a light. I don't know what kind of light or how I see it, but there's this light. My son is the same way.

"Then there's the sense of touch. I took a Reiki [healing energy] class and freaked everyone, including the teacher, by not only feeling energy but manipulating it. I told a healer once who was working on my knee exactly where the energy he was using came from. It stunned him. This hypersensitivity we have, it's like we live and work in another dimension and only spend part of our time in this one.

"Another thing. My son and I treasure peace. The idea of war is revolting. I'm not really a pacifist. Sometimes wars need to be fought. But I don't understand the current mind-set wanting to go back to imperialism, run the world."

Are the characteristics Ambrus described familiar to you?

In a nutshell, the new kids (some of their parents and possibly you, as well) think differently, have a certain "charm" about them that attracts animals (even in the wild), are hypersensitive to field effects (whether out in nature or around equipment), have an insatiable curiosity and hunger to learn, see, feel, hear, sense things at levels that are uncanny, must be cautious of overexposure to light, sound, and chemicals, can be "displaced" by crowds or the energy at school, are natural healers with an intelligence level that seems somehow more mature, display a comfortable ease with things mystical and spiritual, and—are you ready for this?—they "know" things. They are exceptionally psychic, or, if you prefer the other term, intuitive.

That's why they amaze us—they do things that seem spooky. For instance, *the majority* can remember their birth (as if they were an observer), and their previous lives (some in detail). Most know they are here for a reason, a purpose, and many know what that is. They readily converse with angels and aliens and light beings and otherworldly guides and guardians, as well as demons and devils and other "mixed-up folk." They see the dead as if alive and consider Holy Ones (like Jesus) to be their best friend; God, too. And they tend to recognize each other instantly *even though their only previous meeting was in "the invisible,"* at what they call "grids" (those already in existence and other grids they are actively building together as if they were of one mind, a "group mind" tackling a "group project"). We know this from their own self-reports and those of their parents, and from researchers such as myself actively studying the phenomenon. Their claims check out again and again.

Let me be more specific about what's showing up in research: A large number of today's children do indeed appear to meet with each other in consciousness at night, play, and attend school, without ever leaving their beds or waking up.* They take on assignments or special missions for the forces of light (that which empowers) or for the dark (that which disempowers). Some of the schools the kids say they attend are based on magic (a Dungeons & Dragons kind of thing), and some cover in-depth instruction about developing and strengthening grids. Their goal, at least what they share with folks like me, is to create a heart-based communication system between people worldwide so the damage done by war and the rage unleashed by war can be repaired.

In case you are unfamiliar with the term *grid*, it refers to a lattice-like netting or "fabric" formed of pure intelligence. These grids are said to cradle or hold together the varied matrixes or planes of consciousness. Grids fill the ethers and surround the planet, and have existed for as long as consciousness itself. Their threading increases in complexity as the human family advances in its ability to develop and express its own potential. The integrity of mass mind or collective consciousness depends on the strength of grids. A popular term referring to this threaded fabric is "the web of life."

There is precedent for such a thing in quantum physics and the new sciences—that on some level all minds are connected, that there is indeed a fabric to consciousness, a web of life. The new children are born already informed: *They know how to create more grids to hold more*

---

* We know this is so not only because kids report doing it, but more importantly from third-party testimonies from people who are present when children who are unknown to each other meet in chance encounters. Recognition between them is instantaneous if they have shared nightly adventures together; their chatter about the grid where they meet and what they do there, the same. Such youngsters rarely live in the same area. Often they live hundreds, if not thousands, of miles apart; their chance encounters usually occur at parks or in restaurants, sometimes at airports.

consciousness to do more things, using the formula of thought plus feelings, directed by intent, affirmed by knowingness.

Wake up, parents. Your children are very busy at night and occasionally during the day. Is it any wonder that so many of them show signs of being tired and fatigued when there seems no logical reason for either? True, having a television set in the bedroom or late night reading or computer use can explain some of this. But what about kids who don't do any of that yet still wake up exhausted? I'm not exaggerating. And don't confuse what I'm saying with dreams or pretend, although children will often say such things to alleviate parental concern.

Bobbie Sandoz, a therapist and award-winning columnist with a decades-long friendship with dolphins and whales throughout the world, wrote several books, among them *Parachutes for Parents: 10 New Keys to Raising Children for a Better World*.[1] Some pertinent comments:

> In my 1997 release of my book, I point out that in many indigenous cultures, the period from six to twelve years of age is considered the best time to teach children the powers of their psychic experiences, such as fire-walking, spoon-bending, cooperative fishing with dolphins, remote viewing, and telepathically communicating with animals, nature, each other, and angels, in addition to other such skills. In our country we have disdainfully labeled this a period of "magical thinking" in which the child "erroneously" believes that his thoughts have the power to actually influence the results of his world. Instead of honoring the power and value of this very real magic and its scientific basis, we have viewed it as an age-related phenomenon in need of being suppressed.

Face it. The new children are "groupies" who love the invisible. They walk between worlds as if an interplanetary collective of kindred souls. To them, "night school" is where they can augment what they miss during the day. What do they miss? Any curriculum that has to do with the astral. Ah, "spooky" has a definition.

In esoteric teachings, it is understood that there are three basic dimensions to consciousness, and each one corresponds to a particular brain or mind function:

> *Physical Dimension:* All that is visible, tangible, and measur-
> able; the realm of the conscious (left-brain hemisphere)
> *Astral Dimension:* The invisible reality that supports manifesta-
> tion; the realm of the subconscious (right-brain hemisphere)
> *Spiritual Dimension:* The interconnecting foundation and
> source of all existence; the realm of the super-conscious
> (limbic system and prefrontal lobes)

The astral can be fun, especially for children, and contains therein Middle Earth, the muses, fairy folk and wee people, energy beings, ghosts, disincarnates, demons and devils, the hag, emotional and psychic residue and leftovers, passion forms, imprints, futuristic manifestations, aliens or greys, intentional creations, jinn, enchantments, tricksters, animal and nature spirits, guides and guardians, shape shifters, phantoms, lost souls, watchers—*the lower kingdoms of ensoulment.* (The higher kingdoms of ensoulment are said to be found in the inner planes: heavenly beings, ascended masters, spiritual hierarchies, angels, the elders, spirit keepers, matrix stewards, the untarnished soul, access to the great plan of creation.)

It's no mystery that kids love the astral and go there as often as possible. But the astral is a tricky place, its lure hard to resist. There's ready access through the subconscious function of our mind to its limitless terrain—termed "the realm of the imagination" or "the dreamland of the soul." Still, there is more to the astral than that. What is created or met there can *physically manifest* on the earthplane and cause problems later on or lead to mental instability. The protection afforded innocents doesn't always apply; instruction does.

Since adults pay little attention to how states of consciousness can vary, few children ever receive a meaningful education in how to control and direct intuitive skills, handle psychic phenomena, or discern the difference between that which glorifies the ego versus that which feeds the soul. Today's children say, pretend that what you want to be true is true, then fill yourself with God's breath as you link back to Source. By pretending that you are enlightened, you are. By affirming something as so, it is. To them, their intuitive abilities are an open door to the treasure trove that is the imaginal realm (which is true). They dive in en masse, flocking to the astral without a hint of hesitation, but with mixed results. Their "magic" isn't always that magical.

Headlines in magazines and newspapers blare: ten-year-old girl has x-ray vision; autistic boy heals hundreds, five-year-old can diagnosis illness; young girl, nine years old, can see auras around people and knows what each color means; youngster moves small objects around with his mind; boy of four knows who's going to die and when; and so forth.

What these children are doing is breathtaking, yet their lack of instruction shows in how confused they can get, how frightened they can become of performances, how tired or fatigued they can seem, how selfish or egotistical their "stardom" can make them, how controlling and obnoxious they can become (as if they are the parent bossing around adults), how devoid of morals they can be once they discover that others virtually worship them.

Are the new ones the answer to our prayers, what society needs? Well, that depends on the guidance we give them and the examples we set. So far, the jury is still out. These kids need responsible parenting no matter how mature they may appear. Too bad so few get it. What is happening in the "indigo" or "crystal" movement is a case in point. Labeling children in this manner promotes elitism and exclusivity. The results of such miscasting are now apparent: the teenage indigos who use the term as a credential on their resumes and who practice indiscriminate sex with those in awe of their charisma; the youngsters featured at indigo conferences to wow the crowds who become selfish braggarts once off-stage. Indigo Web sites, Internet tests to see if you are one, books and tapes for indigo and crystal children, indigo schools, indigo summer camps, indigo fashions and jewelry, astrology for indigos, classes on how to raise indigos . . . sensationalizing our precious young.

Adults are doing this, cashing in on the label without regard for how it affects the child over time or even how accurate or valid it is. The vast majority of these children reject such labels; it is the parents who aren't listening, who aren't challenging sources. (Channeled information, as an example, is not necessarily spiritual; it can be astral based). A wonderful Russian Proverb says, "Trust, but verify." We must ask questions, do our research, balance the head with the heart. How can we teach discernment to our children if we fail to practice the attribute ourselves?

We see to it that our children are educated in public or private schools on how to be productive and intelligent citizens. The material they study prepares them for life in the world external to their senses and sense of self. If we want healthy, sane adults, however, we must also educate them about the inner worlds—the other half of their existence, the core reality of self-hood. Additionally, if we teach children (or adults) that the imaginal realms are little more than a diversion, then we are teaching them that the creative urge and the ability to vision and find meaning are false.

Be honest now. What is the real difference between an artist and a shaman, a witch and a healer, a child's imagination and an architect's vision? Intent. The skill is the same, anchored in the same realm of thought, feeling, emotional vibration. What determines result, how the skill is used, is always . . . intent.

Take a good look at the *Harry Potter* series written by J. K. Rowling.[2] Sure, tales of an orphaned boy who attends a school in witchcraft while being stalked by his parents' murderer (the one who also tried to kill him) stuff each page of each hefty book, along with a language of curious phrases, magic spells, monsters and wizards and flying things (replete with broomsticks). All of it, pure astral.

Look again. These books are about the type of hero every kid can admire—one who is disheveled, wears glasses, is unpopular, gets picked on by bullies, and is persecuted by his adoptive family—a nerd. Harry gets into trouble for making strange things happen that he has no control over until he finally makes friends, receives instruction in addition to regular school, and learns how to use his wits to triumph over everyday adversities. The series has rekindled the desire in millions to not only read, but also to rediscover the exquisiteness and beauty of language. The tales wrap around the power of love and the eternality of the soul while illustrating that service to others is more important than self-centered desires.

Thank heaven for Harry Potter. He's reaching a generation of children few others can touch. Even so, a few words of wisdom on the topic might be helpful.

The word *magic* simply means "receptive." Our forebears knew that when someone was receptive, or displayed receptivity (a willingness to receive), that person could then draw to him or her all manner of unique or desirable happenings with little or no effort, almost as if charmed (possessed of magic). In modern parlance, the word magic is an indicator of influential powers that are recognizable by the "color" of how they're used:

White magic: Spirit-based, for the purpose of healing one's self and others; emphasizes growth and guardianship; enhances, charms, protects

Black magic: Ego-based, for the purpose of adding to one's self-importance; emphasizes possessions and status; indulges, exploits, enslaves

Grey magic: Belief-based, for the purpose of acquiring attention or imposing a point of view; emphasizes wishful thinking and cultural fixations; entices, coerces, programs

Real magic (transparent): Feeling-based, for the purpose of establishing an open and accepting mood; emphasizes receptivity and sensitivity; enables, readies, resonates

Soul magic (luminous): Source-based, for the purpose of learning through experience so the soul can evolve; emphasizes self-empowerment and personal responsibility; uplifts, frees, brings together in wholeness

There are now a myriad of excellent books, tapes, teachers, and opportunities to develop and explore one's intuitive and psychic abilities and become more knowledgeable about the positive and negative aspects of the astral realms. Here are a few suggestions to get you started:

For kids: *Mountains, Meadows, and Moonbeams: A Child's Spiritual Reader,* by Mary Summer Rain. *A Boy and a Turtle, The Goodnight Caterpillar, The Affirmation Web,* and *A Boy and a Bear,* all by Lori Lite. *Freddie Brenner's Mystical Adventure* series by Kathy Forti, Ph.D.[3]

For teens and adults: *Karen Kimball & the Dream Weaver's Web,* by Cynthia Sue Larson. *Second Sight,* by Judith Orloff, M.D. *The Intuitive Heart: How to Trust Your Intuition for Guidance and Healing,* by Henry Reed, Ph.D. and Brenda English. *Diary of a Psychic: Shattering the Myths,* by Sonia Choquette. (Each one of these people is a teacher of considerable experience in the psi field.)[4]

Summer camps for children: A.R.E. Camp (in operation for more than forty years), Rowe Camp (long-standing reputation), and Enchanted Forest Intuitive Camp (new).[5]

What excites me the most about working in this area with children are the programs developed by psychic crime investigator Pam Coronado. Under the title "Smart Hearts," she teaches practical self-defense skills to children that blend intuition with common sense. "After experiencing so much heartbreak and frustration in trying to locate missing children," explains Coronado, "I developed my own prevention program called Smart Hearts. This differs from other 'stranger danger' programs in a few significant ways." Coronado defines these as giving children permission to trust their instincts, teaching them to listen to their intuition or "hearts," showing them safe ways to contact strangers should they ever need to, and helping them gain practical self-defense skills and knowledge. She emphasizes, "Children don't have to be victims. They may be small, but they are by no means powerless." Her teaching program is available on video; she has also authored an important book, *Kid Safe! How to Protect Your Family from Molesters & Kidnappers.*[6]

The imaginal realms of the astral are totally real, vibrant, and alive to those who visit them. And we all visit them. Not to do so means to cease being human. All the more reason, parents, to dive in and help your kids learn how to harness the magic of this powerful and important aspect of the subconscious mind.

Embracing Spirituality

I long for the day when the statement, "Our God is love,
our race is human, and our religion is oneness," is more
than the musings of my mind, but is the creed of the heart of
the human family.

REV. JIM ROSEMERGY

Knowledge of the spiritual—that deeper awareness and understanding of the inner planes and our connection to Source, to the God of our being—although more of a possibility than a reality for most of us, is front row, in-your-lap truth for the new children. Because kids such as these are mushrooming in numbers, and because we all hunger to know more about the spiritual side of our nature, religious themes and spiritual imagery have suddenly burst upon the scene.

The sacred has popped into pop culture.

Example: In April 2004, *The Passion of the Christ* (Mel Gibson), was number one at the box office; *Hellboy* (Guillermo del Toro), number two. Believe it or not, the Son of God and the son of Satan shared in top popularity billing with moviegoers. Both movies focused on the negative and positive aspects of the astral (excessive violence, horror, the force of evil versus supportive uplift, unselfish desire, the force of good).

It was only during the last two minutes of *The Passion of the Christ* that the full power of what Jesus did was revealed. *The Gospel of John* (Philip Saville), a truly remarkable film, was a much better version of the story of Jesus and his Ascension into Christhood than Gibson's. Why then did people flock in record-breaking numbers to the Gibson movie and not Saville's? Why did its impact seem almost as powerful as the Messiah's Second Coming in how it changed lives? Those last two minutes. Gibson understands the art of manipulation. Rapid action, few words, stunning effects, a shocking contrast of cruelty with the miraculous . . . sensationalism. Where Saville's movie illumines the teachings of Jesus, Gibson's pounds us for "our guilt" in the death of Jesus.

If there were ever a metaphor for the difference between spirituality and religion, it is illustrated by these two movie depictions of the Messiah's message. (Gibson's reflects the religious tradition of overemphasizing suffering and guilt, and our powerlessness in life without seeking God's forgiveness for our sins; Saville's portrays the spiritual tradition of overcoming adversity by right thinking, and demonstrating our powerfulness and our worth as children of the living God.)

All races, all cultures, embrace some form of religious order that sprang from an awe-inspiring experience someone had of omnipresence. To preserve this revelation of Deity, dogmas developed—doctrines, creeds, and laws that enabled the few to direct the many. Religion itself serves the function of mutual guidance and protection, as necessary to a healthy life as water, air, and sun. Problems arise when people fixate on dogmas to the degree that they forget that wellspring of wisdom at the core of what guides them, and when they insist that what they believe is better or best. Since "no tree would be so foolish as to fight among its branches," the belief in exclusivity, of being chosen, negates entirely any such claim.

Spirituality, on the other hand, is a personal, intimate experience of omnipresence that returns the province of Deity to the individual. I love the way Reverend Don Welsh puts it: "Spiritual growth is really a process of pushing back the boundaries of our ignorance of God and our own nature, so that we grow into who we already are."[1] We engage the spiritual directly by doing this. The heart and core of true religion is based on experience, not belief. It is the ultimate human journey beyond the self to the ecstasy and bliss of oneness with the One.

Yet the revelators of religious orders, be they shamans, wise ones, ministers of great calling, or spiritual adepts, developed a relationship with God as children that later led to a personal commitment. If truth be known, just about everyone does that, makes a covenant with God as a child. This promise or agreement informs our behavior throughout our growing years and our expectations as adults. Some people deny this or simply don't recall ever having done it. The bet's still on that they did. Why would I say such a thing? Watch the young.

Children have rich and sometimes complex spiritual experiences, almost from birth, and they talk about them once they are verbal. They talk about the angels that take care of babies who are ill and the "red man" (fever) who comes to make them sick. They dialogue with animals and see rivers (wind currents) in the air. They pray ceaselessly and naturally, sometimes in gibberish yet always in praise, dancing and singing in the joy of being alive as the children of God they know they are. Many remember life in the womb and can describe what they heard and saw while there, much to the embarrassment of their parents. And they often remember past lives as if a soul glancing back on the skeins of time ("records" in the ethers of our comings and goings as souls in a process of growth and learning throughout Creation's spiral).

Melissa Martin had this to share about her son Todd.

"When he was four years old, he told me that he used to live in a place called Australia. At that time I don't think he had ever heard of Australia. He related a brief story about being a single father of a boy and girl who sounded like teenagers. They apparently lived in the outback and the mother had died. He died when his children were in their late teens or early twenties. Todd sounded sad and far away while talking about it. I asked him if he missed them. He said, 'No, because I'll see them again.'"

I've been witness to such recollections with the new children. Not only do a remarkable number describe their birth and "womb with a view" (memories usually begin at around seven months in utero), some also speak of existences in other worlds and on other planets, as if there were a universal life continuum, an unending stream of consciousness that we exit at birth and reenter at death.

Certainly, from time immemorial children have had experiences of the spiritual realms and higher aspects of living. We're hearing more of this now partly because we're finally paying attention; we're learning how to listen to small voices, giggles, and whispers. Of all the books ever written about this, *The Secret Spiritual World of Children* by Tobin Hart, Ph.D. is by far the best, and the ChildSpirit Institute founded by him and his wife Mary Mance Hart is the most active in conducting research and educational projects, including their annual Conference on Children's Spirituality.[2] Every parent and every teacher on Earth should have a copy of this book. It is that important.

The first half of the book is chock full of stories that will amuse you and grab at your heart, like that of the three-year-old who said, "Mommy, I know everything you know." The mother admitted the child was right. The second half focuses on parental guidance, dos and don'ts, techniques, exercises, meditations—a skillful weave of tested and proven insights that, although simply stated, are as helpful to parents facing their own spiritual issues as to the children. Spirituality, after all, is often a mixed blessing. An open door to the secrets of the universe can be both a burden and an excuse to feel special, better than anyone else. Finding one's balance between heaven and Earth is a challenge at any age. "We know the world differently when we serve it," Hart offers.

Let me repeat that: "We know the world differently when we serve it."

The powerful truth of that one statement takes us to the edge of what is happening in our world . . . as a cry from frustrated adults, as a demand from the largest "youthquake" in recorded history, as a mission for the closing days of the world we have known and for the new world being born in our midst. A new spirituality is rising: a new worship, a new church, a new sense of "worthship," a new revelation of God and of our charge as children of God. This movement, this urge, takes its root from the new sciences and the outreach made possible through the global frontier of Internet communications . . . the heart seeks to be unified with the head.

What is the yeast raising this new "loaf?"

A yearning for a greater realization of God.

A personal realization.

Neale Donald Walsch has been talking to God for years. Considering how many people have bought his books, the insights he pens from what he considers to be Source seem to strike a very large chord in the hearts of many. About his latest, *Tomorrow's God: Our Greatest Spiritual Challenge,* he says,

> Every aspect of human endeavor has made stunning advances over the past two thousand years, with one single, sad exception—humanity's theology. This causes a large number of human beings to walk into the twenty-first century with first century or pre-first century moral, ethical, and theological constructions. The ethical and moral dilemmas with which we will be confronted in the twenty-first century cannot be successfully negotiated using old ideas . . . .

He predicts: "Humanity is going to create a whole new theology and a whole new God in the next two to three decades."[3]

Walsch is thinking like the kids are. The young and the young at heart look at history's messiahs and note this repetitive pattern—prayer, preaching, teaching, healing, fellowship—and say to themselves, hey, that's us, we can do that: *We are the church!* It's not God *and* us, it's God *in, through, and as* us.

Most of the kids born since 1982 love science and reason as follows: Since science has shown that the particle and the wave are the same, that means that God is both immanent and transcendent, internal and external, composed and compassionate, the One while also the many in the One. Their logic is a major challenge to religious theology. So are the rediscovery of the Book of Thomas and The Lost Gospels; the reinterpretation of the Bible's Mary Magdalene as a Disciple of Jesus and not a prostitute; the revelation that the sexual abuse of boys by the priesthood is a long-standing practice in most religions, including Buddhism; the realization that fundamentalist clerics the world over control the faithful by refusing to acknowledge the excesses and misinterpretations they commit in God's name.

Already major changes are occurring in the human family's hunger to connect with God. Our instinct, our health, our very souls push us in that direction. The new children will push even harder as the years pass. For a sampler of the latest trends, exercises, and aids, read on. (Although I'm reporting here on what's happening in the United States, the same pattern can be found globally, even in countries where forbidden by law.)

Mysticism is making a comeback. Defined as the art of union
    with reality, through mysticism one seeks to know a thing by
    uniting with it, by assimilating it into life in a practical way
    . . . living what is true.

Soul awareness exercises. There are many. One, called "soul
    prints," asks you to name your soul, then remind yourself
    every morning that you have a spiritual identity that comprises
    a distinct essence that is yours alone. By watching how you
    respond to what happens in your life, you begin to recognize
    the belief patterns you have incorporated and may want to
    change. Another is "soul letters." For ten days, each night
    before you go to bed, write a letter to God. Pour out your
    heart, speak as you normally would, then put the letter in a
    box or drawer marked "night letters." Every morning when
    you wake up, become God writing you a letter. Just start writ-
    ing, writing as fast as you can; do not read what you write. Put
    your letter in another box or drawer, this one marked "morn-
    ing letters." After the full ten days are up, read all your letters.
    Maybe God will speak to you from those letters, but it's certain

your soul will. Compare nightly musings or complaints with the offerings of morning. The soul is wise and it will convey needed truths if we give it a "voice."

Spiritual mentorship as service. People unconnected to church or religion are now getting personally involved in helping others with their spiritual growth—perhaps through a spoken word, praying or meditating together, or just by caring enough to listen. Classes are taught in how to do this. One I know of is offered through Atlantic University in Virginia Beach, Virginia.[4]

Emergent churches. Cutting across denominational lines, these mostly small churches seek to reclaim a sense of mystery and awe found in the rituals and symbols of the ancient past. Sometimes called "seeker churches," they are headed by young evangelicals, often meet in people's homes, and design their devotionals in a manner that initiates and honors an "ancient future faith."[5]

Booze-free nightclubs for worship. "Get your praise on" is the chant of young people who gather at nightclubs to party, praise, and pray. Considered to be an act of religious desegregation, adherents are not afraid to try new things in their desire for a form of worship that speaks to them in their own language.[6]

Meditation and study groups. Truly the people's choice, there are hundreds of thousands of these; in a few more years they may number in the millions. Most meet in people's homes or in library rooms to discuss spiritual books, listen to uplifting tapes, and practice various forms of meditation and healing prayer. Through the fellowship of like-minds, they center themselves in the power of silence with the God Within. Although some New Thought churches like Unity and Religious Science sponsor groups such as these, the majority are unaligned and owe their existence to the willingness of individuals to "step out and start up."

The return of labyrinths and medicine wheels. Churches, hospitals, clinics, senior citizen centers, city parks, people's gardens . . . the rush is on to build these ancient structures everywhere possible. And it's not difficult to understand why. Shapes such as these are designed to enable an individual to enter a prayerful or healing state of mind more quickly than any other posture, setting, or environment. Labyrinths are especially effective in this regard. The rediscovery of their significance has returned sacred ritual to the individual.[7]

Creating sacred spaces and altars. There is a large movement afoot to build meditation gardens, preserve wild spaces on one's property, plant butterfly bushes, create a place inside or out that is calming and special. Having an altar in your home is becoming almost as important as having a television set or a sofa. Check inside your children's bedroom. They may already have one. Look for items arranged together as if to create a small scene, or clusters of objects that seem somehow sacred as symbolized by their shape or color. Their idea of an altar may not be the same as yours.

Feng shui and sacred geometry. Feng shui, the art of right placement, is based on the flow of energy currents and the effect they have on home construction, landscaping, and furniture or objects. *Sacred geometry* details the spiritual realities present or absent in architectural designs, land use, relationships, and behaviors. Both are now being used to spiritualize and revitalize where and how we live.[8]

New seminaries for training and ordaining a new type of minister. These are springing up everywhere. Look for names like New Being Seminary, Interfaith Seminary, One Spirit Seminary, The Religion of the Heart. You guessed it—the direction the new spirituality is taking us is toward honoring the underlying truth found in all religions, fusing feminine and masculine polarities, and making plain that *a religion that cannot be questioned is a religion of man, not of God.*[9]

Spiritual divination. Our newer generations readily blend
the intuitive arts with spiritual realities through the use of
divinatory practices, objects, and skills. They recognize the
meaningfulness that can occur when disconnected thoughts,
feelings, and events suddenly converge to support and clarify
a greater issue. This experience of synchronicity can make
quite an impact. Some aids to support this endeavor are *Soul
Cards* by Deborah Koff-Chapin, *Wisdom Cards* by Paul
Ferrini, *Vibrational Medicine Cards: A Sacred Geometry
of the Self* by Rowena Pattee Kryder, and *Goddess Runes*
by yours truly.[10]

The new children know that "Christ" is a state of consciousness anyone can attain, not a man's last name. They see right through you; they
see your soul. Belief systems that inspired previous generations do not
interest most of them. They prefer, instead, fluid-flowing worship and
systems of thought that include, not exclude, that embrace, not deny.
Because of this, learning spiritual discernment is a necessity. Elizabeth
Lesser, author of *The Seeker's Guide: Making Your Life a Spiritual
Adventure,* cautions:

> Many modern seekers skim off the ritual trappings of a tradition with
> little respect for the depth behind it. In democratizing spirituality and
> bringing it to the daily life of each person, each one of us risks becom-
> ing a messianic little pope, or a humorless saint, or just an unbearable
> profound person, grander or better than others.[11]

Never were truer words spoken. The new spirituality, created from
the longing of our hearts and from the inspiration of our children, does
indeed give us a greater realization of God—*at the same time challenging us to recognize the difference between that which nurtures the soul
and that which entraps it.*

Always at question is "worthship." The aftereffects, the consequences,
of whatever we do determine the worth of what we do. What I have

repeatedly seen is that if we choose to live a life of forgiveness and faith, ever mindful that behind every visible thing is an invisible pattern of the divine, then automatically, by the simple act of our presence, we tend to heal and uplift broadly—the air we breathe, the ground we walk on, plants and growing things around us, the animals, birds, and crawlers, people's attitudes and feelings (even passersby whom we've never met), weather patterns and rainfall.

See how valuable each person is? See how important it is that we become or at least relate to our true self? Just ask a kid. Any kid. They'll set you straight. Or read their poetry. They worship through what they create, you know. God to them is a presence, not a person.

Edie Jurmain, a woman who fled Austria during the Holocaust, is one of the new ones, creators of our new world. She is lovingkindness personified who carries within her heart of hearts the perennial wisdom our children are born knowing. She explores this wisdom in a conversational piece between her and God, entitled "Searching:"[12]

Who are you, anyhow?	*I Am that I Am.*
What is your name?	*I have many names: Father–Mother–Source–Allah–Divine Presence–Creative Energy–Supreme Being–God.*
Do you have a body?	*I am not a physical being. I am Spiritual Energy.*
How can I find you?	*You can feel my presence, if you become conscious of it.*
Where can I find you?	*In the pure eyes of a newborn; the voice of the singer; the hand of the surgeon, pilot, or artist; the roar of the ocean; the fragrance of a flower.*
What holds me back from experiencing life more fully?	*False beliefs. Stop identifying with your past. Forgive anyone who may have disappointed you.*

| What is my purpose in life? | *To reach for greater understanding of your spiritual heritage—to view the world as your playground—to live life fully enjoying each day.* |
| Will you always be there? Even when I die? | *Of course, my beloved child. There is no beginning, and there is no end— I will never forsake you. Life is Eternal.* |

A Peculiar Anger

*This is a time for a loud voice, open speech, and fearless
thinking. I rejoice that I live in such a splendidly
disturbing time.*

HELEN KELLER

Excerpts from children's dream journals, especially in the northeastern
United States, show that kids were picking up on the 9/11 attack in New
York City before it occurred. Some entries I have seen date back two
years before. To say that our children know things, that they are attuned
to the future and the underlying energies of causation and collective consciousness, is an understatement. Our new kids are almost frightening in
their ability to see right through you or know your thoughts or foretell
your actions or challenge what they're being taught. They're also a pain
in the ass. Have you ever tried to raise one? Their mothers and fathers
have my sympathy. I'm a grandmother. I can walk away. Parents can't.

As they say in the popular vernacular, "This is where the rubber meets
the road." The new kids are angry. That signature for a peculiar kind
of anger, appearing in children born since around 1982, exists as an
undercurrent just below the surface, and it can be found in even the
most loving. Anything that doesn't fit—that is phony, hype, double-
speak, exaggerated, dishonest, or not genuine—can trigger an anger

response in these kids that is unlike patterning from previous generations. And because of that undercurrent, the new children can easily be
manipulated or used. What is theirs by nature gives them the ability to
be detached observers divorced from the normal processes of decision
making—made-to-order revolutionaries or rebels or activists or change
agents or . . . killers.

Consider the social climate in which they are growing up. Bill Clinton
lied about having sex with "that woman"; Enron executives lied about
"cooking the books" leading to heartbreaking losses for trusting share-
holders; top leadership at the United Nations lied about the corruption
that spread from misusing the millions paid for Iraqi oil. George Bush
lied about no new taxes; George W. Bush lied about the Iraq war and
what it would cost us. Those men were our presidents and most admired
advisors. The trickle-down effect shows up in several recent surveys.
Three-quarters of high school students polled said they had cheated on
exams; 43 percent of the population as a whole said it was okay to lie or
cheat to get ahead. Our willingness as a society to condone untruths has
earned for us the title of the "Pinocchio culture."[1]

Have you heard of "rug rat rage?" There is an epidemic of anger
in youngsters, kids hardly more than toddlers, who want somehow to
strike back at anyone around. Television shows, video games, and rap
music exploit this. Games like "Grand Theft Auto" go beyond violence
to reward children and teens for engaging in organized crime, murder,
and other forms of perverse behavior. In some countries, children vio-
lently slap each other around while filming what they do, in a game
called "happy slapping." Serious injuries have resulted. Affirmed in
far too many board rooms is the credo "Who cares what the product
teaches—how much money will it make?" One Mexican lawmaker was
quoted as saying, "Public morals? What are those?"

There are many causative factors, of course. Psychologist Ron Taffel,
author of *Parenting by Heart*, puts it this way:[2]

> Today's children are angry because they feel invisible and ignored by
> parents who do not hear or see them. They are desperate to be seen

and known, rather than scheduled or psychologized. They are craving one-on-one time.

He cautions that kids turn to junk culture, what he calls the "second family," to fill the void created by parents too busy to spend time with them. Taffel's point is undeniable. Still, there are other aspects to the peculiar anger of the young than what psychology can clarify for us. Most of these aspects center around three things: the natural tendencies found in fifth root race advancements, the twin urges of evolution and devolution, and revolutionary cycles triggered by youth-bulges.

NATURAL TENDENCIES

According to traditions of Chinese prophesy, we are entering the "fifth turn of the great wheel" when the force of fury will challenge all peoples and children will be born with anger in them; things that happen will be intense and intensely felt. What I have recognized in the young with this anger is an unusual impatience that comes from a strong sense of entitlement; others name it "affluenza." It is true that many modern parents seem to believe that buying their kid something equates to good parenting, creating spoiled children in a self-indulgent, increasingly co-dependent society.

The result? Powerful children who lack direction, a substitution of consumerism and pleasure for compassion and caring. Kids are being stuffed with the very things that satisfy them least, which leads to temper tantrums, frustrated speech, and a bland indifference. These reactions are a natural response to energy that is "spiking," meaning the frequencies are rising faster than most people can cope with. Change comes so rapidly now that it is a challenge for anyone, at any age, to keep up. Without patience and tolerance, it is difficult to value ideas and opinions different from your own or to respect people foreign to you. The touted "children of light" are as sorely pressed as any other children in learning how to handle anger successfully and in dealing with the excesses of privilege or poverty.

THE TWIN URGES OF EVOLUTION AND DEVOLUTION

As the aura of a person deepens in color, the energy he or she possesses becomes more extreme in how it manifests and in what is necessary to maintain control. Deeper colors signal intensity and the possibility of behavior anomalies. The higher frequencies of color (blues, indigos, purples, violets), more so than other colors, carry with them the twin urges of evolution and devolution once they deepen. Simply put: The more one's energy intensifies, the more powerful one becomes and the more one is capable of doing—for good or ill.

On the positive side, the higher, deeper colors of the aura are indicative of individuals who are loving and calm, unusually compassionate and understanding, even empathic, in their concern for the welfare of others. On the negative side, that same aura arrangement expresses in the opposite manner: cold, cruel, insensitive, aloof, aggressive, dangerous. A positive focus uplifts the soul and aids in the evolution of the human family as it progresses into even higher states of consciousness. A negative focus negates the soul and devolves potential steadily into lower states of consciousness that impede any gains the human family might make.

What determines the direction this powerful energy takes? For children, it is supportive families and folks who care. For adults, it is intention—to improve the self and the conditions of others. The millennial generation that began in 1982 is the first truly global generation in the history of the United States, and, in fact, the world. Thanks to technology, the media, the Internet, cell phones, and the like, they can connect with virtually anyone, anywhere—personally and in real time—even without wires or cables. Because of this, they have been swamped by more diversity, demands, opportunities—more of everything—than *any* child has ever had to face. As energy continues to intensify, as we move further into ascension, the twin urges of evolution and devolution will become even more extreme and divisive.

THE YOUTH-BULGE

Throughout Africa and the Middle East (mostly in the Muslim countries of the world), there is a youth-bulge. More than half of their populations are younger than twenty-five. History shows that in societies in which this has happened in the past, the people have fallen prey to widespread revolutions. Examples: There was a youth-bulge in France just before the French Revolution, the youth-bulge in Iran was used to topple the Shah in the 1979 revolution, and the resurgence in medieval fundamentalism now occurring in the Islamic nations mimics the rise of Nazism during World War II. Of these, the resurgence of Islamic fundamentalism with the young is the biggest and most dangerous of situations, precisely because of its timing.

With more than half the populations of these countries under the age of twenty-five, that means the current youth-bulge consists entirely of millennials and 9/11s—fifth root race types born with an undercurrent of anger already instilled, and in the youngest, fear. And indeed, these children are impatient, restless, frustrated, confused. Raised in cultures of great disparity where questioning and critical thinking are either frowned upon or disallowed, they are exposed constantly to expressions of rage and scenes of violence, which significantly decrease the intelligence of the young. This condition is as applicable to the ghettos of Chicago as the shambles of Palestine. Because children once frustrated or angered are easy to manipulate, there is a rash worldwide of using children as soldiers and drug runners and thieves. We are talking here of children in massive numbers and of a situation that has grown explosive. The real heart of this anger, though, is a rebellion against that which is not genuine, honest, or real. Children everywhere either feel this kind of anger or have had to deal with it in some major way.

So what can we do about this? Let's begin where we can, with small steps, the way the kids do:

- Teach anger management and mediation skills beginning in grade school. From the fourth or fifth grade on up, enact honesty codes and class courts in which the children themselves learn how to investigate, listen to all sides, discern motives, vote, and carry out decisions in a fair and equitable manner.
- Have special sessions that deal with the problem of class bullies

and the best manner of defense to use. Follow-up sessions may be necessary.

- Instigate time-out periods or discussion times when things get heated.
- To retrain behaviors, insist on the use of respectful language—even when arguing.
- Honor the absolutes: good nutrition, exercise, and creative play.
- Support activities like sports, music, marching, and dance.
- Encourage kids to volunteer, especially at animal shelters or senior citizen centers.
- Teach kids to regain self-control through massage, yoga, meditation, prayer, creativity.
- Be sure kids have a responsible job of some kind, for which they earn money (and teach them to save half of it).

It would be helpful about now to hear how one set of parents managed to raise their raging rug rat. (Names have been altered; Mom is the narrator.)

"Sadly, I can best describe Joanne as being uncomfortable in her own skin. She has been dominated by an anger that still simmers lava-like just below her surface. As early as age two, she was receiving gifts of records and books with titles like *I'm So Mad*. She specialized in what we coined 'slam hugs.' The hallmark of raising her has been to support and try to work within her emotional confines. The qualities we have had to cultivate in ourselves as parents have been patience, persistence, and more patience.

"Discipline at first was actually easy. Most of the time I did what was natural for us. I taught Joanne the golden rule. The television stayed off 99 percent of her waking hours. I moved to the rhythm of her day and did not, when possible, force her to move to a schedule of my own making.

"I also gave her control of events by outlining step-by-step exactly what we'd be doing outside home. For example, I'd explain: We're going to put on your coat, open the door of the apartment, go down the steps, open the car door, get in the car seat, etc. As Joanne got older, I worked four or five hours a day, one to two days a week. I sang her the same 'day care song' I had made up over and over to her in the car, and then she knew what to expect. We also said 'bye-bye, see you again' to places she loathed to leave, like the playground. I made longer tasks shorter and did them more often, like grocery shopping. When Joanne became frustrated or misbehaved I did what I termed 'abandon ship.' That meant leave immediately and without anger the grocery cart, the swimming pool, the library, the restaurant, or the park. Joanne rarely made a repeat performance in the same place.

"I also allowed Joanne to do things I still wonder why other mothers of young children called 'crazy.' Joanne finger-painted, made glitter pictures, dug in mud, played in my lower kitchen cabinets, dressed herself in stylish color combinations, used blunt scissors and markers, cooked with me, played endless dress-up, and took a lot of baths in water I'll admit I dyed Easter-egg colors. I pretty much figured I could hose her down or change her clothes after any activity.

"Over time, Joanne's anger had dominated her considerable intellectual and physical abilities. Much to our sorrow, her anger thwarted involvement in activities that could have given her a measure of happiness, contentment, and accomplishment. Joanne's life lessons came hard and fast, repeating until she got it.

"I know Joanne has often felt ostracized, unsupported, unloved, and misunderstood. We realized early on that no amount of love and understanding from us could change her perceptions. We found out down the road that no matter what we did, we could not make our child cooperate, fit in, feel understood, or feel loved. She was alone and she simply had no peers.

"This was a child who, at age ten and under my tutelage, read books like *Black Like Me, Around the World in Eighty Days, Princess Sultana's Daughters,* and Lincoln's Emancipation Proclamation. This is a child who I taught religious tolerance to by teaching her the fundamentals of the world's major religions. This is a child who is color- and race-blind.

"Joanne did battle with an internal 'push me–pull you.' There was no middle ground. She was emotionally fragile or powerful, indecisive or self-directed, unaware or insightful, inert or energetic. She would bounce from one mode to the next over a brief time period. She would revert to behavior modes from years past but talk intellectually about current events.

"One of the things I instituted in early childhood, mainly so I wouldn't go mad, was quiet time. This was a period of time of my choice, which varied in duration and scheduling over the years. Joanne could do any safe activity in her room as long as it was quiet. For years we had a kiddie gate at our bedroom cum office door. That little fence stopped everything from a toddler to a charging teen from entering my kingdom of serene sanity. Another time that helped us as she got older was to make an 'are you on fire?' time. During that time, if the child was not physically on fire (which we later changed to include extreme bleeding), Joanne could not interrupt that parent at all. That rule works to this day."

Joanne was also unbelievably psychic. This could have been a nightmare for her and her parents, except that they never made a big deal of it (so Joanne wouldn't), and from the start they emphasized ethical behavior—for example, you must respect the privacy of others; you don't "enter" another person's mind without his or her permission.

Anger is both the Achilles' heel (the weakest characteristic) and God's gift (the strongest trait) of the new children.

True anger simply powers up our energy, motivates us to set things straight and get things done. Rage is not the same as anger. Rage is suppressed or repressed emotional baggage (unfinished business) that can surface if anger overheats. From rage comes the greatest threat of violence. The peculiarities of anger, the different ways it can be expressed, offer fifth root race types abundant opportunities to be of service. Because the energy current it rides is hot and spicy, these people will tend to be exceptionally motivated and empowered in whatever they do. They are natural leaders, movers and shakers. Light their fire and they'll reshape the world.

Not all children express anger as anger, though. Many are afraid to, or don't know how to do so in constructive ways, like cleaning up the house, weeding a garden, participating in community projects and litter patrols, making pottery on a potter's wheel—anything that is physical and, to a point, physically demanding. Anger with no place to go can sink into depression. Medical news circa April 2004 reports that more than ten million children in the United States are on drugs to treat their depression.[3] (The number of kids who actually suffer from depression is thought to be much higher, as most cases go unrecognized.) Yet the very antidepressants supposed to lift youngsters out of emotional danger are suspected of causing some of them to worsen, even turn suicidal. We must, all of us, kids and adults, learn how to work positively with anger, as suggested by Neil C. Warren in his important book, *Make Anger Your Ally: Harnessing Our Most Baffling Emotion.*[4] The wonderful qualities of courage, determination, and strength of will are positive extensions of the anger signature . . . and so is the ability to heal.

Curiously, there is a link between anger and healing. Get angry enough, really motivated, even to the point of becoming a fighter, and you can lick most illnesses and repair the damage caused by most injuries. Use this energy with care, and you can set the stage for miracles. Anger is power, and that power either pushes or inspires you to move. You get things done in jig time and usually with less effort. But commit that energy to the greater good, offer it in service to help another, and, presto, the power of anger transmutes into healing energy that warms and uplifts and makes whole.

The signature marker for the new children is anger, and these kids are natural healers. Get it? This is no coincidence. *From babyhood on, the new children seem to know what that power current within them is for.* Call it instinct. So we have these stories, amazing stories, of children who walk up to people out of the clear blue and offer a hand or a smile or a pat on the cheek, and suddenly the individual feels better. Seldom do the kids display any conscious understanding of their actions. They just do what they do because it feels right. Many see or sense energy coming out of them—sometimes in bright colors, sometimes gold or sparkling white, sometimes with an accompaniment of special imagery or sounds or angels.

Headlines blare: "Girl turns illness into inspiration," "Student with Down syndrome beats the odds," or "Five-year-old saves man from heart attack." Frank DeMarco of Hampton Roads Publishing Company dealt with the subject in a most personal way after two children, ages seven and five, healed him of a serious health condition by "psychically applying colored [energy] bands" around the affected areas of his body.[5] Because of what happened to him, DeMarco started investigating similar stories. His book, *DreamHealer: His Name is Adam,* is about a boy of sixteen who is credited with healing hundreds of people, often remotely. Included on Adam's list of miracle cures is Ronnie Hawkins, a Canadian rock star who was diagnosed with terminal pancreatic cancer and given three months to live. An article about Hawkins's recovery appeared in the November 27, 2003 issue of *Rolling Stone* magazine. Yes, Hawkins is back to work making a new CD, thanks to Adam.

Miracle stories like this will become quite numerous. These youngsters know how to use the energetic intensity of color and sound to alter genetic codes. That's how many of them heal. A particular energetic healing system that covers this very thing is called reiki, and it can be taught to children as well as adults as an aid for self and others.[6] Once a child learns about reiki techniques and how to apply them in an appropriate manner, he or she is able to handle stressful and trying situations much more easily and knowledgeably. This is empowering for the child and a blessing to all else.

Anger as a primal energy is a challenge to civilized society. We can't think it away or intellectualize about its various facets or use it to excuse violent or unhealthy behavior. You must face anger head-on, with techniques and training that enable you to diffuse, redirect, or calm its power. Forgiveness and reconciliation are the counterpoints to anger . . . again, the fifth chakra issues of "power over" or "power to."

Because of this signature marker in the new children, they will have the energy and the drive to accomplish whatever they need to do. Truly, this is no coincidence. It is a blessing in disguise.

11

Quirky Kids
and Jumping Genes

I Love You, You're Perfect, Now Change!

TITLE OF CONTEMPORARY MUSICAL
BY JOE DiPIETRO AND JIMMY ROBERTS

Did you know that in sports contracts between universities and media sponsors, there is an incentive for a sizable bonus *if* players behave and stay out of jail?

Unbelievable as this seems, the fact that schools of higher learning need to use such persuasion techniques to rein in their athletes opens up another aspect to the new children that we would be wise to explore, along with other perplexing situations many of them confront in society. Let's set the stage with a quick review of the idea of generational signatures, which I examined in detail in chapter 5. Remember, each generation is born with and imprinted by particular traits or characteristics (energy patterns) that undergird its cycle. These can be identified and studied as a way of preparing society for its next batch of citizens. Signatures refer to those energy patterns that are most prominent, like an overall theme or strong urge that motivates and propels action or response. So far, we've focused mainly on one of these signatures, a peculiar anger found in millennials. Although they are a tolerant bunch, that impatient streak of theirs can override even their best intentions. Allow me to reemphasize that as the great wheel turns to the fifth world and its ascension, fury becomes the *atmosphere* of our passage—not as a generational signature, but as a "climate" that colors what our various societies must face. Since millennials supply most of the muscle that takes us to and through the Mayan gateway, it is crucial that we understand their signature: tolerance on the positive side, an impatient frustration on the negative.

But what really constitutes positive or negative here? That anger of theirs that seems so counterproductive can actually be a godsend because of the energy and drive with which it blesses them, more than enough for them to succeed as the change-agents and activists they feel pressed to become. Tolerance? Certainly the willingness to consider or at least invite different or foreign viewpoints is desirable, yet that wonderful quality can just as easily foster a do-nothing, lackadaisical attitude that undermines what it was meant to uplift.

So how do we call it: positive or negative? Keep that question in mind throughout this chapter, as we tackle some hefty issues, like learning disorders, jumping genes, and television gone mad.

Today we don't say kids are cute or active or daydreamers or inventive so much as we classify them in accordance with their disorders: ADD (attention-deficit disorder), ADHD (attention-deficit-hyperactivity disorder), ODD (oppositional-defiance disorder), PDD (pervasive developmental disorder—somewhat like autism), AS (Asperger's syndrome), SID (sensory-integration dysfunction), and ASD (autistic-spectrum disorder).

Current statistics show that two out of every five children in our country have some type of learning disorder, one out of ten is mentally ill, and more than seven million have ADD; cases of ADHD are up 600 percent since 1990 and autism is now so pervasive it is considered an epidemic. Should we accept as causal charges of poor parenting, little or no discipline, complaints from over-stressed teachers? Maybe, but this recent finding may cause you to wonder about other causative factors, in addition to what seems so obvious: *ADD and ADHD show up as anomalies in brain scans of affected children.*[1] Sorry to burst your bubble, but the disorders are real.

Because the ever-evolving vocabulary of childhood dysfunction is so complex, some professionals are worried about how the many labels will affect the children as they grow. Dr. Mel Levine, a pediatrician who opposes diagnostic labels, notes: "Let's identify what someone needs and help them, rather than branding them." Thus, from the community of experts has arisen a term to cover them all: "quirky." The kids aren't eccentric or odd or disordered or dysfunctional, they're quirky. And that fun, affectionate term is now used so routinely it has caught on with youngsters.

But how are the quirks in quirkiness treated? With drugs. Powerful drugs. Children have surpassed seniors and all other age groups as the fastest growing segment of the prescription drug market. Ritalin, Prozac, and Risperdal are the most commonly prescribed; the replacement for them is Concerta. *There have been no long-term studies on how these drugs affect children.*

What science *has* learned is that Ritalin can shrink a child's size and weight, and may cause permanent changes in the brain; Prozac can cause violent and bizarre behavior; children treated for ADHD have unusually high incidents of depression and suicide regardless of what drug is used; the most helpful medication yet found with the least harmful side effects is illegal—marijuana.[2] Drugs of choice used in treatment remain "iffy" with kids. No one really knows what drug is best, its long-term effect, or if something besides the use of drugs is the better way to go.

I've already pointed out some of the similarities I've observed between near-death experiencers and the new kids. Another discovery I made researching near-death states that applies here is that *anyone, child or adult, becomes more sensitive to pharmaceuticals after a near-death experience.* This is part of the aftereffects. Typically, experiencers become almost hypersensitive to taste, touch, texture, smell, sound, pressure, pulsations, rhythm, sensation. So much has been written about how their energy interferes afterward with electrical fields and high-tech equipment that it has become the stuff of legend. (I still cannot wear a wristwatch, for instance, and I am careful of equipment that is not used to my energy surges.) This sensitivity also applies to a decrease or loss of tolerance to chemicals like pollutants, additives, and pharmaceuticals. Allergies become commonplace.

Child experiencers have always been of special concern to me because they cannot articulate what is going on with them or why they feel the way they do. Few ever connect the dots to link their "differences" to what happened that fateful day they nearly died or really did die. The pattern of physiological and psychological aftereffects are more pronounced in children than with adults, and it is these children—child experiencers of near-death states—who are the most like ascended fifth root race types.

This quotation from my book, *The New Children and Near-Death Experiences,* warns of this increased sensitivity to drugs:[3]

> When a child is ill, he or she is rushed to a doctor or maybe the emergency room in a nearby hospital, where a shot is administered or pills are prescribed. This is standard procedure. But if the little one is a near-death survivor and suddenly more sensitive, possibly even allergic, to the type of pharmaceuticals normally administered to a child of his or her weight and age, the treatment can be more dangerous than the illness [or injury]. Alert the physician.

Children who experience the near-death phenomenon come back unusually sensitive, as if rewired, reordered, and reconfigured somehow. The majority of the children entering the earthplane since around 1982 are born with that same sensitivity and evidence many of the same changes to the brain, nervous and digestive systems, and skin. (The key link I have found concerns energy acceleration—what existed before, even as potential, expands afterward. This models what I believe is happening globally as ascension energies alter life processes.)

Note: *These children, who can least handle drugs, are given the most powerful, and medicated at the same rate as adults. The insurance* *industry gives incentives for medication and disincentives for therapy or more natural substances that could be used in treatment, such as herbs and homeopathic remedies.*

Add these to the sensitivities near-death kids have—soft drinks, junk food, alcohol and tobacco, toxic metals, air pollutants, chemically treated clothing and bed sheets, food additives. And care must be taken in their exposure to television and computers electrical fields and high-tension power lines. There are antidotes, adjustments that can be made to help them not only handle but thrive in today's world, but it takes adults willing to recognize the situation for what it is before anything gets done.

But guess what scientists, doctors, and determined parents are now finding with those different since birth? Somewhere around 80 percent of their childhood disorders can be connected either directly or indirectly to food allergies, poor nutrition, and improper digestion. Other problems commonly found were conditions such as thyroid disorders, amino acid deficiencies, essential fatty acid deficiencies, inflamed intestines, ingestion of pesticides, growth hormones and irradiated food, immune system disturbances, a build-up of toxic metals, being too close to high tension power lines, as well as overexposure to high-tech equipment. The number one culprit, though, is suspected to be mercury, perhaps inhaled from toxic emissions in the air, but more specifically from childhood vaccinations in which mercury is used as a preservative and multiple serums are combined (for example, MMR, the three-in-one vaccine for measles, mumps, and rubella).

Note: The link between the advent of MMR and the skyrocketing number of autism cases in the United States, Canada, and Britain was discredited by medical researchers in spring 2004. Even though no link ever existed between autism and single doses of each serum, the three-in-one, now officially considered safe, is still subject to question. The reason? *A combination of factors as being the culprit was never investigated by the medical community.*[4]

Note: *Many of the directors of our nation's largest fast-food and junk-food corporations also sit on the board of directors of our largest media* *corporations and drug companies.* Thus, while stories about very profitable drugs make the news, stories about the benefits of an "eat healthy and take a few vitamins" lifestyle rarely are covered.[5]

I have been brought up short by a cost analysis done by researchers I know who check out profitability factors among drug companies. What they found backs up what concerned parents have been telling me right along, that *the most profitable industry in the United States is children's drugs.* This suggests, at least to me, why drugless measures—things like good nutrition, a healthy lifestyle with a focus on spirituality, and limited or adjusted exposure to electromagnetic fields—are seldom, if ever, mentioned in the mainstream medical community as recommended treatments for childhood disorders.

What I discovered with near-death kids mirrors what I and others are finding with the new kids. These sensitive youngsters have a tough time dealing with the excesses of society; their challenge begins in the womb with the excesses of their mother. Like "canaries in the coal mine," how they are affected is a warning signal to the rest of us about what can happen to the human race as a whole if we don't start correcting those excesses.

A growing alternative treatment movement seeks to do just that. Quirky kids so treated are becoming much less so; some of their disorders are straightening out completely.[6] A few examples of these alternative treatments: Professionals are using chelation therapy with autistic kids to remove toxic metals, and cranial-sacral therapy (a technique to balance the cranial membranes in the head) has proven helpful with some who have ADD or ADHD. Special diets have resulted in the dramatic cessation of many childhood disorders, especially autism (the number of children allergic to wheat, oats, barley, rye, and eggs is surprising). Limiting computer use and exposure to television with the very young (making adjustments as they grow) accounts for a significant increase in their ability to hold a focus, concentrate, be creative and imaginative, and act in a more respectful and calm manner.

One more tidbit. According to a report published in the April 2004 issue of *American Journal of Clinical Nutrition*, "The current epidemic of obesity is linked to the use of high-fructose corn sweeteners in food and soft drinks." Need I say it? Soft drinks are sugar water. Corn is what farmers use to fatten cattle. There's nothing wrong with sugar or corn. The problem is one of excess; overconsumption and overuse turns what was once good for us into that which harms.

The more we return to the natural order, the healthier and happier we will be. True, yet is that realistic? Take television, for instance. How can we live without it? The tube has enriched our lives beyond measure, placing us front row and center for late-breaking news, tours through cultures we could never hope to visit, educational opportunities of unprecedented value and significance, and entertainments of our choice. Yet that which enriches us has a shadow side: content and startle.

Concerning content, we finally have meaningful numbers: Children under the age of four who watch television are 20 percent more likely to develop ADD by the age of seven than young ones who don't.[7] Children of any age who watch three hours or more of television programming per day are twice as likely to become violent than other kids. Prolonged viewing of media violence can lead to emotional desensitization toward violence in real life; in the long-term study that correlated Chicago children's viewing habits in youth with what they were like twenty years later, *a direct link was found between exposure to television violence and becoming violent.*

People in other countries object to our movies, music, and television shows—too much violence, too many drugs. Our media wizards are giving out the wrong message and selling our country short—not to mention the effect their products have on growing hearts and minds. Television executives admit that their goal for a half-hour show is to eventually have fifteen minutes of commercials and fifteen minutes for the program. They hope to accomplish this feat by teaching actors and actresses to speak faster (which is already being done). Television executives don't care if older viewers miss dialogue; they are after the young, who, with their short attention spans and quick minds, can easily keep up—further interfering with brain development and increasing the risk for ADD.

Reality shows like *Fear Factor* now involve whole families: mom, dad, and the kids. The kids are subjected to incredible stress. "I love it," laughs a little boy as he bats away huge insects. Study what the child is subjected to, however, and the stress it creates, then imagine how that might affect other children who watch the show. Stress is the problem, not bugs, and that stress creates "startles" (sudden, unexpected sounds or scenes designed to keep the brain awake and involved). The most insidious, most damaging aspect of television to the development of a child's brain, which affects not only the child but the future of how the human race might evolve, is the startle effect in television programming and its excessive use.

Many voices are warning us about this. Two in particular are Marie Winn, author of *The Plug-In Drug*, and Keith Buzzell, M.D., author of *The Children of Cyclops: The Influence of Television Viewing on the Developing Human Brain*.[8] The upshot is that a steady flow of startle flickers must be programmed into a television show in order to keep the brain alert. Quick changes of camera angle, unexpected or surprising sounds, sudden actions, rapid-fire scenes—all of this startles the brain enough to hold its attention and creates just enough stress to activate body preparedness for defensive action . . . thanks to a continuous, low-level stream of cortisol entering the viewer's bloodstream.

Cortisol is part of our body's "flight-or-fight" response, released by the pituitary if adrenaline from the adrenal glands is not enough to help us deal with prolonged or long-term stress. It takes from eight to twenty-four hours for cortisol to clear the bloodstream after entry. Advertisers often insist that a certain number of startles appear in each show segment. It's part of their contract with the television producer. Startles ensure that viewers see commercials (which are wild with startles). The neurological impact this has on kids is akin to child abuse. It impedes normal brain development, decreases intelligence, and interferes with the nervous system and emotional response patterning. The impact on pre-borns is even greater, because of the blood-tie between the mother and her fetus. The tadpole can be flooded by mom's cortisol again and again. This is why it is so important for pregnant women to live in as stress-free an environment as possible. (One case of damage done by cortisol to a late-term fetus is addressed in my book *The New Children and Near-Death Experiences.*[9])

So content, as problematic as it can be, is not the only problem with television. Thank goodness for the magic of competition and the fact that there are over 400 channels to choose from. Yup, because of the intense rivalry between Disney and Nickelodeon, safe, wonderful programming now exists for preschoolers. In fact, excellent offerings with minimum startles are once again popular.

We human beings learn best through interpersonal relationships and hands-on activity, not television. The bodies we have are adjustable, though, because of how our genes can jump around. We are not stuck with the genetic patterns we were born with, nor are our children stuck with what they inherit from us. Genes change, especially in response to environmental pressures and stress. Barbara McClintock, the Nobel Prize-winning geneticist, proved this. Our chromosomes have *transposable* elements in them, meaning that the genes we possess have the ability, as a part of their basic makeup, to alter, even quickly.[10]

Ah, maybe you've guessed where I'm going with this stuff about genes, and you're right. Some of the disorders our children are manifesting, specifically ADHD, arising as it does from excessive stress, tension, and the pressures created when society turns a blind eye to how far away from the natural order we have strayed . . . actually portend evolution at its best. What happened about forty thousand years ago to save the human race is happening once more and right now—with the return of the "hunter's gene."

Scientists tell us that because of massive volcanic eruptions on at least three continents during that time frame, not to mention little sun because of all the ash in the air and the release of harmful gases, the die-off rate of the living was beyond belief. It is estimated that no more than fifteen thousand to forty thousand people survived worldwide. The population crash produced a bottleneck—a situation so severe and so intense that genetic mutations occurred rapidly—producing "the dawn of human civilization." You can credit ADHD, which most often stems from several genes in combination, or more specifically, DRD4 /R allele (the main or most prominent gene in cases of ADHD). If you haven't read this book, please do: *The Edison Gene: ADHD and the Gift of the Hunter Child* by Thom Hartmann.[11]

Hartmann, an authority on childhood disorders, maps out (and brilliantly) how the rise of what we today call ADHD saved humankind. Novelty-seeking, attention-getting distractibility, constant scanning, curiosity, cleverness, impatience, being quick to change—these were the traits that guaranteed survival in the past. Today, the instinct of the hunter (or inventor, or initiator) enables individuals to thrive on the knife's edge of risk and challenge, to be creative intuitives who "think outside the box." Although the "hunter gene" has remained in the human gene pool since its sudden appearance eons ago, rising and falling in accordance with society's needs, its extraordinary and spectacular reemergence in global populations since the middle eighties, specifically in the last five years, may indeed signal . . . that we are on the brink of a major evolutionary turnover in the population . . . perhaps even another crash. (Many of the same traits are also evident in near-death kids—further evidence of the transposable element in gene makeup.)

Childhood disorders, media ploys, modern excesses, jumping genes . . . who can call it: Positive? Negative? What do you think?

12

Soaring Intelligence, Lost Potential

Mind mirrors a universe that mirrors man's mind. Creator
and Created give rise to each other.

JOSEPH CHILTON PEARCE

Teachers near retirement complain that the majority of the new children are the dumbest, laziest, rudest, most disinterested kids they've ever encountered. Huh? That's not what William Strauss and Neil Howe tell us in their latest study, *Millennials Rising: The Next Great Generation,*[1] a very upbeat and heartening study of today's teens. Yet the duo only investigated two fairly mainstream high schools. That's not a broad enough base, in my opinion, to give a real picture of the status of the millennial wave of citizenry, yet they did confirm a suspicion of mine; that is, this particular generation has the drive, energy, and know-how to match the G.I. Joes, or better. These kids really could save the world. So why the shaking of heads and gnashing of teeth from so many teachers?

The answer may lie in the study of yet another phenomenon, the sudden rise of dyslexia in today's children. Christine Gorman, who wrote the article "The New Science of Dyslexia" for *Time* magazine, offers an insightful comment:[2]

Perhaps because their brains are wired differently, dyslexics are often skilled problem solvers, coming at solutions from novel or surprising angles and making conceptual leaps that leave tunnel-visioned, step-by-step sequential thinkers in the dust. They talk about being able to see things in 3-D Technicolor or as a multidimensional chess game. It may also be that their early struggle with reading better prepared them for dealing with adversity in a volatile, fast-changing world.

Dyslexics are over-represented in the top ranks of society's achievers and in the bottom ranks of the prison population. What makes the difference between top and bottom? Opportunities during their early years that supported and encouraged their unique ability to "think outside the box" . . . to abstract.

Does this ring a bell? Whether or not a child is dyslexic, the new children, at least the majority of them, start abstracting at early ages. They talk early, walk fast, learn quickly, are extremely sensitive and intuitive, highly intelligent, natural healers and fixers, *but they do not think sequentially, nor are they interested in the process of learning how.* They fight, ignore, shun, or stick up their nose at the current system of education. A quarter of them never finish high school.

The new kids are not disordered so much as they are ordered differently.

They possess brains that structure and process information in unusual ways. Neither their parents nor our educational system is prepared to handle the challenges they bring. That goes double for medical, therapeutic, and law enforcement professionals, not to mention would-be employers.

I discovered a similar situation with child experiencers of near-death states. After their near-death experiences, 48 percent of those in my research whose episode occurred between birth and the age of fifteen tested out on standard IQ tests with scores between 150 to 160 (132 to 140 is the generally accepted cut-off for genius). If I focused only on those under the age of six, the number scoring in that same range was 81 percent. If I separated out cases involving infants and newborns (especially those who experienced a "dark light" during their episode instead of a bright one*), the percentage of genius was in the middle nineties and their scores began at 182.

This may seem unrelated, but bear with me. Some of my other findings with children who experienced near-death states: half remembered their birth (most were correct); one-third had prebirth memory, and that memory began at around seven months in utero (when the fetus responds to pain). Most of their memories centered around the emotional thoughts and words of their parents; some could "see" outside the womb (and with amazing accuracy). Ninety-three percent had enhanced ability in math; of those, the majority had equal enhancements in music. The regions for math and music are located next to each other in the brain. Both seem to accelerate together during childhood near-death episodes as if the same unit (which speaks volumes to school systems that budget math departments over music). Males and females exhibited equal talents with spatial reasoning and visuals.

Now let's see how this relates to the intelligence of the new kids.

The light effects and the physiological aftereffects tell me that a powerful intensity is at the core of near-death states. I call it a "power punch," and it most affects the brain, nervous and digestive systems, and the skin. What I keep seeing with children who underwent this phenomenon mimics what is being reported globally about the new children—one models the other. Genetic alterations are obvious, at least to me. We're talking here about millions upon millions of children.

And here's another comparison. Once recovered from their episode, the majority of near-death kids appeared to be rewired, reordered, and reconfigured in such a manner that they were better able to cope and thrive in a world of technology and optics. *Yet only a third of them did anything with these abilities.* This loss of potential is happening with the millennials, too.

---

*The kinds of light encountered in near-death states are reported as being a raw, piercing radiance or primary light, a warm protective dark or black light with purple tinges to it, or a brilliant white or gold light of unconditional love. Child experiencers name the primary light "God's Light," the dark "Mother Light," and the bright "Father Light." They are adamant in stating that both Mother and Father Light come from God's Light.

By the way, each country that administers standard IQ tests reports the same jump we are seeing in the United States and in my near-death research. The rise is truly global. Sharon Begley, author of a *Newsweek* magazine article entitled "The IQ Puzzle," notes, "The rise is so sharp that it implies that the average school child today is as bright as the near-geniuses of yesteryear."[3] The Flynn effect helps us to better understand this phenomenon by showing how intelligence can be affected by groups of children being in a stimulating environment together: improve the environment and the interactions between the children and the IQ improves, a higher IQ leads to better surroundings and more stimulating interactions, which again improves intellect, which leads to even more stimulation, and so forth.[4] Still, the Flynn effect does not adequately address what is really happening with our newer generations. Most of these children are born this way, irrespective of heredity; many are stuck in surroundings that seldom change in any meaningful manner, especially in countries with little industry and greater economic challenges.

To find a theory that explains this phenomenon we must look elsewhere—to evolution. There is a "genius code" in the human family that is now being activated. What was once dormant within us is awakening.

So what is this soaring intelligence that drives teachers nuts?

It takes someone like Soleira Green, a global visionary, consultant, writer, and trainer, to put things in perspective. She identifies five forms of intelligence (don't you love that number *five*), in her article, "Quantum Intelligence, Beyond IQ, EQ and SQ . . . .The Evolution of Intelligence."[5] As she explains, IQ (the intelligence quotient) is just the beginning:

Once you open your heart, you gain access to intuition and a more balanced approach to emotion . . . *Emotional Intelligence (EQ)*. If you integrate your spirit (that greater external you), you gain access to wisdom, as well as an openness to spirituality (a quest for deeper meaning and greater understanding), and all that that journey entails . . . *Spiritual Intelligence (SQ)*. If you open up your soul (that inner essential you) to life, you discover your access to innate sensing, knowing, and telepathy . . . *Wholistic Intelligence (WQ)*. With an expansion beyond yourself to consciousness and creation (Allness), you discover hyper-speed thinking and processing, super-creativity and vibrant multiplicity . . . *Quantum Intelligence (QQ)*.

The chart presented here, reprinted with permission from Soleira Green, clarifies what she wrote.

INTELLIGENCE EQUALS EXPANDED CONSCIOUS AWARENESS

LOCATION	CONNECTION	INTELLIGENCE	OUTPUT
Mind	Individual	Intelligence (IQ)	Thought
Heart understanding	Beginning to open to others	Emotional Intelligence (EQ)	Emotional Intuition
Spirit	Connecting with higher self and higher purpose	Spiritual Intelligence (SQ)	Wisdom
Soul/Whole sensing	Connecting profoundly with others and with potential	Wholistic Intelligence (WQ)	Knowing, Innate telepathy
Creation (Processing and consciousness opening)	Connecting with Allness	Quantum Intelligence (QQ)	Hyper-speed, Bandwidth, Super-creativity

A significant number of the new children fit the characteristics of SQ through QQ. This is why parents and teachers are in such a quandary. Intelligence beyond what can be measured with the standard IQ rating system is considered to be mere fiction.

No one understands this situation better than Joseph Chilton Pearce.[6] He talks about the prefrontal lobes of the brain (which develop after birth) as the seat of judgment, morals, empathy and compassion, a sense of well-being that gives rise to the highest and best the human family can attain. He believes that the transcendence of the ego leads to a more spirit-filled life of peace, tolerance, and reason, and that well-developed prefrontal lobes are essential to this attainment.

But get this: *The mother's state while carrying a child determines the kind of brain her child will have.* A supported pregnancy with a minimum of stress and upset tends to reduce the size of the hind brain (the instinctual, survival oriented part of the brain) while enlarging what will be the prefrontal lobes. A distressing pregnancy with many hardships and worries tends to reduce the potential for prefrontal development as the hind brain is enlarged. On a cellular level, there is constant communication between child, mother, and environment. Everything hinges on the perception of safety. The brain of the fetus will develop according to that perception. A safe environment signals that it's okay for the brain to develop higher modes of functioning. An angry or fearful environment means the brain needs to switch to baser modes that will ensure survival. What happens to the mother during pregnancy creates the child that will recreate the world in the image of his or her brain.

What about these smart kids? Even from infancy they are aware and often passionate about social justice, human rights, civil rights, peace movements. You got it. Prefrontal stuff triggering our latent genius code. But remember that underlying signature for anger. These children, who possess so much potential, can easily be misled and manipulated . . . that precious potential lost to impatience and frustration.

In prefrontal lobe formation, the first three years of life are the most important; the next crucial period is puberty. The developing brain doesn't mature until the individual is around age twenty-five, which runs counter to age-of-consent laws and explains why advertisers target ever-younger audiences and why feudal societies still flourish (heavy programming before judgment faculties have fully formed). Children are particularly vulnerable to post-traumatic stress disorder because *violence virtually destroys the prefrontals.*

To understand the intelligence factor, though, we need to recognize that the major source of intelligence in the body is actually the heart, our fifth brain. The heart broadcasts throughout the entire spectrum and connects and interacts with other hearts. If within three feet, hearts will entrain and create a "heart field" or single wave form. That's why hugs are so important.

There are three phases to the heart's beat. The first gives us the courage to live (faith), the second gives us the desire to relate to others (hope and love), the third keeps us connected to Spirit (Source). It's no wonder that the new children talk so much about love and compassion and caring for each other. Their consciousness tends to remain centered in heart space longer than most. When they move on, it's usually into higher modes of intelligence and knowing, rather than the conventional route of first stabilizing the consciousness in the brain. Thus, their IQ scores do not reflect the intelligence potential they possess or the way their minds work.

Because the variance between how they perceive reality and how others do can be confusing to them (and to others), it would be wise to include in the youngsters' regimen extra opportunities to physically "pull things together." A few techniques and sources of instruction that are helpful in this regard include:

Brain Gym: Physical touch and exercises based on muscle testing and how the brain interacts with the nervous system. Contact Educational Kinesiology Foundation in Ventura, California, for information about trained practitioners in your area.[7]

Pegasus Group: A single facility specializing in how children learn; offering up to seventeen different teaching modalities to select from, plus nonpharmaceutical vibrational medicines if needed. Operates out of The Movement Centre in Winnipeg, Canada.[8]

Collot Painting Therapy: An expansion of the teachings of Rudolph Steiner (founder of Waldorf Schools), further developed by Liane Collot d'Herbois. Contrasts light, color, and darkness to interpret brain-body processing. Contact Martha Loving, the first to specialize in using the Collot method with children.[9]

Itsy Bitsy Yoga: Beneficial with toddlers in coordinating brain-
body processing. Also see the Web site and book by the same
name.[10]

Other Activities: Dance, playing a musical instrument, swimming,
gymnastics, and pottery making are also excellent activities for
brain-body coordination.

Meditation: Meditation nurtures and enhances the prefrontal
lobes (at any age); it is effective even in brief sessions of a
minute or two with children. Meditation brings more oxygen
to the brain, cleans out body toxins, and aids in concentration
and calming. Books and teachers are widespread.

Prayer: Imbues the importance of faith, gratitude, and the discipline of daily devotionals; deeply affects brain patterning,
initiating coherent wave forms that can produce physical
effects. Turn the power of prayer to praise, and one's mood
and attitude expand. There are many methods and teachers;
affirmative prayer is the most effective.

Lots of kids can see prayer. I mean literally, as an airborne substance
that moves rapidly. A number of child experiencers of near-death states
also report this, describing the prayer they saw as a beam or ray of light
that arcs from the one saying the prayer to where it is intended. The
youngsters called them "prayer beams;" some said they were brilliant
white or gold, others spoke of them being rainbow colors, not in layers
like a rainbow bridge, but rather in vertical bands. I asked one little boy
what it felt like to be on the receiving end of a prayer beam. "Oh," he
giggled, "when it hits you, you feel warm and tingly all over." His was
a typical response.

Paranormal is normal for the new children: Vivid dreams, real-life
mind projections, creative imaging, telepathic communication, and clear
or clair seeing, hearing, sensing, knowing, and smelling are common.
The prefrontal lobes are active in higher states of intuitive knowing.
They operate like the "wings" of the brain—opening our minds to richer
experiences of ourselves, our relationships with others, and our world.

Your kids probably already know and identify with this greater aspect of intelligence. Let me give you a taste of it too, so you'll have some idea what they're talking about.

All living organisms, even bacteria, demonstrate real-time reactions to their environment, basic intelligence, memory, intuition, and a feeling sense. Children pick right up on this, but only in the last decade has the work of Cleve Backster, the leading researcher in this field, been verified by experiments conducted by other researchers worldwide. His latest book, *Primary Perception,* will make you think twice about the consciousness of the food you eat and the plants in your house.[11]

To quote biologist Marc Bekoff, a preeminent researcher in the field of animal emotions: "Five years ago my colleagues would have thought I was off my rocker, but now scientists are finally starting to talk about animal emotions in public. It's like they're coming out of the closet." And what our scientists are finding is that animals experience surges of deep fear, jealousy, grief, and love, and that some can understand the words we speak—even deduce the meaning of a word they've never heard before. And if taught sign language (what deaf people use), certain animals can reply in knowledgeable, appropriate sentences. Scientific demonstrations show that intelligence and emotionality are widespread across the many kingdoms of life on earth, and that what links all aspects together is a field of conscious awareness.

Cellular receptors in our body store memories everywhere, even in such unlikely areas as our skin and spine. This memory network represents the physical link between matter and spirit and the state of our health—all of it based on molecules of emotion. Neuroscientist Candace B. Pert, Ph.D. proved this, that our internal chemicals, the neuropeptides and their receptors, are the biological underpinnings of awareness. "There's a higher intelligence, one that comes to us via our very molecules and results from our participation in a system far greater than the small, circumscribed one . . . we receive from our five senses alone."[12] So many of our youngsters are natural healers for this simple reason: Their sensitivity enables them to feel what cells remember, allowing *that* intelligence to direct the healing.

Continuing along this line of thought, we know scientifically that all living things spontaneously emit photons, which are light, and that light stores, carries, and communicates information. We also know, thanks to thousands of years of mystical tradition, that when in a relaxed, meditative state one can see these lights, and they appear as if bubbly threads in a light-filled web or fabric, with individual lights winking on or off with each birth or death. This web or field of light reflects the intelligence of its members and responds to an even greater intelligence beyond yet still present within the field. The field itself is conscious. I have seen and experienced this myself and can attest to it.

Scientists have gradually become aware that what modern folks like you and me and the wise ones of yore describe has merit, that there really does appear to be a unifying energy structure to our universe, a field of intelligence permeating all things. Lynne McTaggart documents the growing evidence for this theory in *The Field: The Quest for the Secret Force of the Universe*.[13] In a nutshell, science is saying that *everything that vibrates possess intelligence, and everything vibrates, and there is a central intelligence everything vibrates to.*

That was a mouthful! But there's an easier way to say it:

Global Consciousness: The great knowledge, existent and
   available
Global Mind: Individuals awakening and responding to this
   knowledge
Global Heart: Emotional sensitivity to this knowledge on a
   molecular level that encodes and directs heart function from
   individuals out through all of creation

One more thing. Human DNA is a biological Internet that is superior to the artificial one, and 90 percent of it is considered to be "junk" by scientific researchers. The newest cutting edge in science, wouldn't you know, is the exploration of this so-called useless DNA. Russian scientists are the leaders in the field thus far, and they have found that "junk" DNA is actively engaged during psychic activities and with intuition. They have advanced the theory that this 90 percent may directly or indirectly explain such phenomena as psychic ability, spontaneous and remote acts of healing, self healing, unusual light or auras around people, the mind's ability to affect weather, and the power of one's spoken word on the condition of the body. They have also found evidence for a new type of medicine in which DNA can be influenced and reprogrammed by words and energy frequencies, rather than resorting to surgical procedures. Junk DNA seems linked to group consciousness, group endeavors, and group memory.[14]

Their discoveries suggest that the 90 percent of our DNA that has previously appeared useless is exactly what our new children are activating, and supposedly with new strands of DNA. Hey, maybe that junky stuff has been recorded snapping into action simply because we finally have large enough segments of our population willing to shine their light on greater aspects of what they're capable of. Maybe it's not so much new DNA, but rather "junk" DNA that's finally being recognized for what it really is and the use it was intended to have.

Here's a testimonial for you that puts true intelligence into perspective. Sara Lyara Estes writes:[15]

"I was on a business trip from Santa Fe, New Mexico to San Francisco in the fall of 1993. As the plane went over the Rockies en route to Salt Lake City, we encountered some turbulence and the plane began bouncing around. I was unafraid, but many of my fellow passengers did not share my calm. The fear levels rose palpably. All of a sudden, an 18-month-old boy stood up in his seat near the front of the plane and began making eye contact with each person on the plane. He just looked them steadily in the eyes and you could just feel the tension subside. When he had completed his task of calming everyone down, he turned around and sat down again. He had not done anything but look each person in the eyes. He had not smiled or made a sound, and his parents made no move to prevent him from standing there in his seat, despite the motion of the plane. I just 'knew' he was a little 'master,' and because he had very little hair on his head, I associated him with the Buddha."

New Ways to Educate

*The whole purpose of education is to turn
mirrors into windows.*

SYDNEY J. HARRIS

First the bad news.

Ten years ago, the average American fourteen-year-old had a vocabulary of 40,000 words; today it's 10,000 and dropping. The percentage of students entering college today who need extra help with basic logic is greater than 29 percent, forcing institutions of higher learning to teach grade school material before advanced curriculums can be tackled. Parents lament that they have to medicate their kids, then stand beside them day in and day out to make certain they even read their assignments—yet 53 percent of these same adults avoid reading anything more stimulating than an office memo or cookbook.

What happened to the desire for literature, for discovery, for learning? In her book, *The Language Police: How Pressure Groups Restrict What Children Learn,* Diane Ravitch attempts an answer by pointing out that years of well-meant efforts to remove overt or implicit bias from educational materials has led to the unintended consequence of stripping away everything that is thought-provoking and colorful from the texts children encounter . . . thus *changing and revising historical accuracy*![1]

Here is a startling comparison that may seem unnecessarily "off-the-wall."

From a report given about *madrasas* (Islamic schools) in Pakistan, it is noted that boys as young as five become live-in students studying the Quran and teachings of the prophet Muhammad with the hope of becoming mullahs or spiritual leaders. Most of these students are never exposed to critical thinking; their curriculum is based on a design created by a Mogul emperor who died in 1707. What few science books they have date from the 1920s. According to Thomas L. Friedman of the *New York Times*, "In 1978 there were 3,000 madrasas in Pakistan, today there are 39,000. The real war for peace in this region is in the schools."[2]

From Joan Brannigan, a junior high school teacher: "As I look at my students today, I see many of them who lie on their desk during class, who don't have a clue that it is their "job," their responsibility, their opportunity, to get an education. And this, unlike 25–30 years ago, cuts across socio/economic/racial/cultural lines. When I ask them who their heroes are, they are invariably and almost exclusively sports stars, rapsters, or other entertainment celebrities. Adults would be aghast at the names they do not know—basically anybody from history. They are *children of the media*—and have absorbed all the celebrities but very few of those in other areas of human endeavor who have achieved great things or contributed to humanity. When I say Michelangelo, Donatello—they think, Ninja Turtles. They are children of the moment—they know about what has happened in their lifetimes and not a great deal more."

Don't think me daft for comparing a school system in a third-world country with one in the United States. They actually do share a commonality that truly is startling: Both have failed utterly in adapting to the changing needs of their populations. Aside from basic intent and teacher dedication (which is laudable), the governing body of these school systems has ignored or miscalculated the escalation of human knowledge and the power of the quest to know and interact. Holding to the traditions that spawned them was appropriate for the initial generations they served, but conditions have changed, and so fast, that even the finest schools are hard pressed to keep pace.

You think I'm stretching things here, being unfair?

Consider this. Few freedom-loving Americans realize that the basis of our modern educational system—the "five-core curriculum" of social studies, English, mathematics, science, and foreign languages—was adopted in 1899 from a structure developed by Catherine the Great of Russia to produce good soldiers who would follow orders, good factory workers who would perform assembly-line tasks, and good tax-paying citizens who would not question authority.[3] By sticking with this curriculum, or modifications of it, we have slowly reverted to the "one size fits all" mentality that is perpetuated in madrasas and many other of the world's schools. Standards are essential, but those standards must allow for creative innovation. If they don't, educational systems will emphasize instead rote memorization and the passing of tests over encouraging the development of a student's innate intelligence and critical thinking skills.

Now the good news.

The new kids won't stand for this. Either educational systems the world over change, and radically, or these youngsters will opt out. The smartest already have.

Surprising as it may be to some, there are *seven types* of intelligence and learning styles teachers must account for in planning lessons.[4] These are:

1. *Linguistic intelligence:* Highly developed auditory skills
2. *Logical-mathematical intelligence:* Conceptual reasoning
3. *Spatial intelligence:* Thinks in images and pictures
4. *Musical intelligence:* Sensitive and responsive to musical sounds
5. *Bodily-kinesthetic intelligence:* Fine motor skills, body oriented
6. *Interpersonal intelligence:* Understands and enjoys people, intuitive
7. *Intrapersonal intelligence:* Deep awareness of inner world, reflective

How the actuality of what they do stacks up is another matter. Here's what the pollsters tell us: 40 percent of the students in attendance at most American schools are predominately visual, 40 percent are predominately kinesthetic (feelers), and 20 percent are predominately auditory. *Yet the average educational system is based entirely on auditory learning, which bypasses 80 percent of its students.*

We've managed for generations to get by with this lopsided formula—but no longer. The ascension that is currently underway within the fifth root race is mutating DNA as brain structure, chemistry, and function alter and the nervous system, digestive system, and skin change (modeled by what happens with near-death kids). In her important book, *Endangered Minds*, Jane Healy, Ph.D. shows why even some of the newest educational formulas still won't work . . . *the brains of today's children are literally shaped differently!*[5] Changes in head shape have been recorded, and in many cases internal brain structures and processing modes have altered.

A new type of intelligence is emerging. Grab the book *Upside-Down Brilliance: The Visual-Spatial Learner* by Linda Kreger Silverman, Ph.D.,[6] then insist that all the school teachers and educational authorities you know read it, not to mention parents. We begin necessary changes with the material in this book.

Dr. Silverman coined the term "visual-spatial learner" in 1981 to describe the unique gifts of people who think in images (note the year, just as fifth root race energy began to accelerate). She explains:

> They get the big picture because they see the world through artists' eyes. They remember what they see, but forget what they hear. They're disorganized, can't spell, and have no sense of time; *but* they have an infectious sense of humor, wild imaginations, and can lose themselves completely in the joy of the moment. Visual-spatial brilliance created the computer and the Internet, the vivid displays at the Olympics, and the International Space Station.

Too many of the initial wave of these kids either flunked out of school

or were so bored they refused continuing education once they gradu-
ated. The present bunch is luckier; greater numbers of parents are home
schooling or enrolling their youngsters in e-schools and e-learning via
the Internet. Don't confuse today's e-schools with the televised classrooms of the past. No way! E-schools are fast becoming wrap-around
opportunities for multiple-intelligence learning at any speed, anywhere,
anytime, complete with teacher guidance, social interaction, 3-D effects,
and global participation—much of it live.

One of the leaders in this new field is Benay Dara-Abrams, Ph.D.
CEO and Chair of BrainJolt. Dr. Dara-Abrams jets around the world
advising, teaching, and leading in "Futures of Learning" conferences.[7]
When I spoke with her, I was surprised to discover that science-fiction-
type educational programs are already on the drawing boards. She's passionate about finding ways to reduce "status stress," what youngsters go
through in traditional schools to keep up their grades, look good, and
be popular. This kind of stress pushes many into depression and suicide.
She is convinced that e-schools would change this, and very much for
the better.

Jay Munro, a senior project leader for the *PC Magazine* testing lab,
was quoted in a special issue of *Newsweek* magazine, cautioning the
public about the technological expertise of today's youngsters "far out-
stripping teachers."[8] In the same issue of *Newsweek*, Bronwyn Fryer
emphasized that kids think anything in print is truth. "Kids need to learn
to sort the wheat from the chaff, fact from opinion." The danger of using
computers too much or in isolation was offered as an additional caution,
since a lack of adult oversight can lead to unexpected problems.

I want to make certain you understand the gravity of what is happening in the human family, cross-culturally, before we go much further.
Dr. Silverman, in addition to being an author and clinical researcher, is
a recognized authority on giftedness.[9] "I have been studying gifted children since 1958," she notes. "One would think that I had seen it all, and
yet, I have been astonished by the children who have come into my life
in recent years. It feels like they are a new breed." She continues:

I have been asked by dozens of reporters if the remarkable abilities of some of the children I work with are due to heredity or environment. Lately, I've had to respond, "Neither." Neither heredity nor environment can explain the awareness, the consciousness of this new group of children. Their heredity and environment are not fundamentally different from all the children we've encountered in the past. Yet, there is a remarkable difference in these children from the children we've known in the past. The only explanation I can think of is evolution. I believe we are witnessing the evolution of the human species, and that this evolution is becoming apparent first among the gifted.

So where does this leave us? Toss high schools. You heard me. Most youngsters by the age of fourteen can use computers like a pro and build one from scratch. Once they've completed the tenth grade, students should be routed into two years of community college before full-time employment or choosing among a career track at a university, the military, vocational school, or a service-oriented program like Head Start, Doctors Without Borders, Habitat for Humanity, or the Peace Corps. They'll be exposed that way to social interactions free of excessive status stress, and to real world relationships that are more apt to be positive or at least meaningful.

As resourceful and clever as today's young people are, high school social scenes are still iffy, emotions immature. The generations coming after the millennials will possess increasingly higher states of brain-mind development, enabling them to make mature decisions at younger and younger ages, but we're not there yet. In the meantime, we can and we must transform the process of education itself.

Allow me to offer my ideas and suggestions, starting with the fetus:

Be sure to establish a safe environment for pregnant mothers.
　　The forming brain in the fetus begins its search for a sense of safety during the latter part of the first trimester, continuing into the third. What it perceives determines whether the hind brain or the prefrontal lobes will predominate. Thus, the

state of the mother's pregnancy is quite literally the child's first school.

Communicate with the newborn. Once born, baby talk and scribbles enable the child to relate sounds with words. Engage all five senses during read-aloud times, and read to the child often.

Encourage exercise. Exercise is of paramount importance, even for babies. A wonderful guide to use is *Smart Moves: Why Learning is Not All in Your Head* by Carla Hannaford.[10]

Provide unstructured time. We are hardwired to connect. Play is essential in this regard, interacting with others, give and take. Boredom is just as important, occasionally doing nothing but letting imagination fly with birds and clouds. Youngsters need such blank spaces in which to zone out, so brainwave frequencies can shift.

Be certain kids get enough sleep. Today's kids aren't getting enough sleep; much of the problem lies with anxiety and stress. Of the many ways to deal with this, my favorite is the sleep kit designed by medical intuitive Caroline Sutherland. It consists of a stuffed angel pillow, a cassette tape, and small booklet entitled "My Little Angel Helps Me Go To Sleep."[11] Surprisingly effective.

Rethink the traditional school setting. Smaller schools sharing facilities with other groups and organizations to cut costs are better than what we have now. A given building then can be divided into several sections to accommodate the needs of each group, or it can be used on an off-hours or round-the-clock schedule. Classroom redesigns using the ancient art of feng shui (right placement) would uplift both students and teachers.[12] In South Dakota, all schools in the state—public, private, tribal— are connected in the Digital Dakota Network, so that people three hundred miles apart can talk to each other face-to-face at any time, transcending the need for classrooms to have walls.

Enrich the curriculum with meaningful "extras." Fifth through twelfth graders at Ross School in East Hampton, New York start their day by going to a Center for Well Being, where they eat a breakfast of locally farmed, organic foods and then join in meditation sessions, practice yoga, study t'ai chi, or learn Native American chants and dances. These practices complement an already effective and successful curriculum.[13] One of the best enrichment programs for early grades is the Adawee Teachings (*Adawee* is Cherokee for "guardians of wisdom"). Developed by Linda Redford and her daughter Anne Vorburger, the course consists of text, self-discovery book, and a T-shirt each student receives that says, "*I am important to the world. The world is important to me.*" Classroom tested, the Adawee Teachings are powerful in how they inspire behavior improvements.[14] Other ideas that can enrich the school experience:

- Place interesting adults in the classroom for volunteer stints as teachers
- Use freeze-frame focusing and relaxing techniques (a type of positive visualization) to improve performance[15]
- Access Edutopia from time to time (the educational Web site created by George Lucas) for creative assignments aimed at both students and teachers[16]

Make philosophy classes standard by the third grade. This gives children a forum in which to explore the deeper aspects of life while learning question-and-answer techniques. There is no realistic way to shield children from violence, loss, confusion, and grief. They need tools early-on to help them cope.

There are schools operating today that, by design, prepare fifth root race types for the emerging, new cultures of the ascended fifth world. Some examples:

Waldorf Schools: Created by Rudolf Steiner, one of the greatest thinkers of the twentieth century, a clairvoyant and mystic, with an unusual way of understanding how individual consciousness unfolds during the wonder years of childhood. Schools, colleges, and centers exist worldwide.[17]

Montessori Schools: Created by Maria Montessori, M.D., the first woman physician to graduate from the University of Rome, Italy, and based on her scientific observations of children's behavior. Her methods center on the "whole child approach" and self-directed learning. Schools worldwide.[18]

The Mead School: Created by Dr. Elaine de Beauport, an example of a local educational system in a large area that focuses on a student-centered, two-teacher system throughout the grades and with active parental involvement. "Thinking outside the box" in creatively different ways is encouraged.[19]

Greensboro Wonder & Wisdom School: Created by Trish Alley as a multigenerational, community organization dedicated to life-long learning, with Beyond School Enrichment programs. An example of what caring, dedicated people in a small area can do to provide innovative, whole-person learning.[20]

iEARN: Created by Peter Copen as an international education and resource network that reaches thousands of schools in more than 51 countries. iEARN empowers teachers and students to work together to make a meaningful contribution to the health and welfare of the people on this planet.[21]

Schumacher College: An international center for ecological studies with an emphasis on sustainability and holistic science, based in England; also includes St. James schools for children, juniors, and seniors. Learning centers have now spread to many cities in the United States and elsewhere.[22]

Union Institute & University: A design-your-own Ph.D. program outside the classroom is offered through their schools of Interdisciplinary Arts & Sciences and Professional Psychology. Offering fully accredited, innovative learning opportunities and programs, they encourage students to combine spirituality with science and feature transformative learning as a specialty.[23]

Half of all new teachers quit within five years. Low pay is part of the problem, yes, but the main reason voiced for leaving is the lack of an educational culture that supports excellence in learning and unstinting professionalism. Teaching the teachers will not suffice, until the system in which they perform is transformed as well. Laura L. Sawyer, a graduate of Union Institute & University, makes a point: "Of particular value in today's world, I believe, would be a model which tempers the current emphasis on increasing complexity with a greater emphasis on the development of compassion, empathy, spontaneity, and inner grounding."[24]

Bobbie Sandoz, author of *Parachutes for Parents*, goes a step further:[25]

Thirty years ago I was one of the co-founders of a preschool. We decided to allow children more real experiences, and the morning healing circle was one of their favorite parts of the day. It proffered miraculous healings as well as the loss of friends who didn't make it. We then dealt with the reality of these varied results, and faced the hard questions of why, what death really is, and learning how to continue to feel the essence and energies as well as communicate with these friends on the other side of the veil. At first we were viewed with suspicion, but when 100 percent of our applicants scored off the charts on IQ tests and were admitted to elite private schools almost impossible to gain entrance to, our waiting list grew quickly into the hundreds—and teachers and administrators from the elite private schools, as well as all public and private schools throughout the islands, came to study with us to better understand how we had achieved these kinds of qualities and skills in the children under our care. [Sandoz was living at the time in Hawaii.]

What Bobbie Sandoz and her associates did and what Laura Sawyer foresees is crucially important for our current crop of youngsters and for the millions yet to come. Educational systems now and in the future must include in their *basic curriculum* classes in intuitive or psychic perception (beginning with kindergarten), the body-mind connection (how belief as well as life choices affect health and healing), environmental and economic sustainability, and the keys to success—creativity, spirituality, meditation, yoga.

That which defines the cultures of fifth world ascension, where we are headed as a people, is revealed in the eight intuitive principles developed by Jeffrey Mishlove, Ph.D.[26] These principles undergird the very concept of education.

EIGHT INTUITION PRINCIPLES
as developed by Jeffrey Mishlove

Inner Essence. The source of being within each of us and within the universe itself is also the origin of intuitive guidance and of self-esteem.

Complex Wholeness. As we accept the fullness of our being, we achieve higher levels of inner refinement and integration.

Unique Integrity. While all beings are one at the level of essence and wholeness, each person represents a unique integration of human possibilities.

Autonomous Purpose. We are grateful for the autonomy to discover and be guided by our own intuitive sense of purpose. We support others exercising this right.

Paradoxical Authenticity. While we seek inner peace and serenity, we also seek to dissolve the walls of numbness that separate us from the pain of others.

Conscious Evolution. By consciously refining and healing our inner being, we are refining and healing the world.

Living Community. We support and nurture intuitive communion with all beings.

Conscious Value. That which enhances and refines consciousness is intrinsically of greater value.

As we advance toward a Renaissance-style smorgasbord of educational opportunities, the biggest challenge will be slide rules, mechanical drafting, square roots, and equations. What will we do with them? Who will practice the old-fashioned way of step-by-step processing, calculation, documentation from premise to conclusion? What about mathematical and scientific verification, testing, cross-checking, and lab work? What about the fine points of communication and discovery?

We are faced with the necessity of adjusting and remolding our conceptual understanding of learning. To the ancient Greeks, all learning was considered *remembering*. To them, life was but the act of recollecting knowledge the soul forgot at the moment of birth into a physical body. Reincarnation and the idea of past lives were integral to their worldview. Perhaps this explains why the word *education* originally meant "to draw from that which was already known."

I've noticed in my research with the near-death kids that after their episodes, they suddenly know things unknown to them previously—even complex scientific and mathematical epistemologies. They solve engineering problems without the slightest notion of how they did it. Yet they fail in mathematics, physics, and engineering classes, not because they can't get the right answers . . . *but because they can't delineate how they arrived at those answers!*

Innate knowing from deep memory is surfacing with the new children, too. Processes are being discarded in favor of creative innovation and intuitive perception. And the kids are accurate! Fonts of information are opening up for them so easily that they have no appreciation for what's happening, no way to respect and honor either their abilities or what they find. They walk away from detail work because it's too tedious and too boring. They walk out on significant breakthroughs because it's more fun to hang loose as a computer nerd. They prefer to avoid hassles and stress . . . *because they don't want to wind up like their parents.*

The puzzle they present us with is a strange one.

Intelligence is leapfrogging past boundaries and borders and beliefs. However, without some sense of limitation, the mutual agreements that enable societies to exist and cultures to flourish dissolve into chaos.

That's scary, until you realize that chaos always leads to new beginnings and better environments.

Eventually, schools as they commonly exist will be a thing of the past. People will be inspired to create uniquely different ways of learning, living, working. Our memories, what surfaces from the depths of the soul's wisdom, will replace the fear that currently drives behavior. Until that future time, let's pick up the pieces of what we have now, roll up our sleeves, and get busy. We've got some changes to enact—whether through the process of petitioning school boards, lobbying state legislatures or congress, or via the wonderworks of imagination and "sweat capital."

Zippies, Tweens, and Mini-Me's

We have, we are, a mosaic of gifts.
To nurture, to offer, to accept.
We need to be.

MATTIE J. T. STEPANEK

Why don't the new kids want to be like their parents? Make no mistake, these youngsters are natural born entrepreneurs. They love money and they love to spend money, and they have no fear of working hard or long hours. The rub comes when they see their parents chained to their jobs with no time for family, friends, or fun. To them, this type of success sucks and they aren't interested. Employers take note: Our new citizens are group-oriented and think and move like a collective—even when alone, and even at night in the etheric grids they oft-times visit.

Welcome to the world of nerds, geeks, goths, freaks, punks, preps, born frees, zippies, tweens, and mini-me's. It's tribalism manifesting as culturalism. To understand this worldview, rent the video for the Jon Amiel movie *The Core* and notice how Rat, the computer nerd, along with the young scientists in the film, outsmarts and outmaneuvers the know-it-alls to save the world. Or read "Non Sequitur," the syndicated cartoon strip by Wiley that features smart mouthed Danae trying to out wit her broadcaster father in a battle between values and convenience.

With apologies to native peoples, identifying with a "tribe" has become the modern equivalent of finding your true self—of dodging the cultural taboos of the day by creating new ones. For example, in case you missed the headlines, "tweens" is now the official name of the puberty crowd (mostly ages ten through twelve, although many nine-year-olds claim to be tweens, too). Not kids. Not teenagers. These fresh-skinned body morphs have cast aside any association with quirkiness. They have come of age . . . they're tweens!

The phenomenon of expressing self within a tribal context is global. Take the "born frees" of South Africa. These fifteen- to twenty-five-year-olds are convinced there's nothing they can't do. They are racially color-blind, self-confident, opinionated, apolitical, and devoted to brand-name consumerism and techno-gizmos. They don't give a hoot about the past or the so-called wisdom of elders. Theirs is the struggle for authenticity, realness. "Be true to who you are" is their credo.

Then there are the "zippies" of India, the bright-eyed wonders who have a zip to their step and an endless ooze of attitude, ambition, aspiration, and self-confidence. This crowd, numbering about three-fourths of India's young, are destination driven, not destiny driven; outward looking, not inward looking; upwardly mobile, not held back by tradition, religion, or family. They are "liberalization's children," the first in India to shift away from socialism to global trade, entrepreneurialism, and technology.

In our own country, sociologist Murray Milner, Jr., author of *Freaks, Geeks, and Cool Kids—American Teenagers, Schools and the Culture of Consumption*, discovered a direct link between unique fashions and status seeking and the evolution of a caste system in our schools, complete with pecking order.[1] He describes the hierarchy as follows: "nerds" (those only interested in academics) are on the bottom rung; "geeks" (the socially inept) come next; followed by "goths," "freaks," or "punks" (depending on which tribal allegiance the student professes); and "preps" (those who dress well and act mature as a cover for deviant behavior). Milner found little envy among the new children for those "on top;" rather, they displayed a dismissive attitude about popularity while insisting upon group loyalty. Of secondary education, he had this to say: "The status systems of high schools were and are an important contributing factor to the creation and maintenance of consumer capitalism." (Another reason to toss them.)

So we have "gamma girls," the self-possessed femmes more interested in sports than cheerleading and in writing an opinion column in the school newspaper than going out on a date. Not your typical mother's daughter, these girls are aggressive, have strong values, and display "in-your-face" attitudes. Teen "zines" (that's kid-talk for magazines) appeal to them because of ads that hawk provocative clothes for daring risk-takers willing to experiment with who they are.

Oops, let's not forget the "mini-me's" or "adultolescents." These young people, usually those still living at home with their parents, are in no hurry to reach for the traditional benchmarks of adulthood, such as marriage, having kids, owning a home, financial independence. Too stressful and anxiety-producing. They opt instead for negotiated living spaces and routines so they can save money. Hardly slackers, they're simply in no hurry to chain themselves to indebtedness.

Do the new children have too much power and too much freedom? Are they spoiled? Perhaps.

Keep in mind, though, that theirs is a cyberworld of "toys" that redefine the very essence of life and living. They're the quick-click kids awash in an energy pressure cooker of television sets, microwave ovens, cell phones, computers, picture messaging, iPods (that play back digital files as music), and Wi-Fi—wireless Internet connections that enable unplugged chunks of civilization via "mesh networks" set up on buses, in cars, or virtually anywhere, to connect the unimaginable with the unfathomable.

Wi-Fi changes everything. Teamed with digital geography, it is that first step toward a future in which no one can hide, where privacy becomes a privilege of the past. Secret knowledge will surface too, once all the books in the world are scanned into databases (Amazon.com has already scanned the table of contents and a few pages of more than 120,000 for their "Search Inside the Book" service). Quotations, obscure facts, the ability to cross-reference—the sum of recorded human thought instantly available—is just around the corner. No place to hide. No privacy. Knowledge *sans* secrets. Can we handle that? Not even the new kids can. Generations will come and go before humankind can make the leap. Issues like this, of deeper import and complexity, are for the sixth and seventh root races, not the ascended fifth. As a people, we must learn the difference between "power over" and "power to" and apply what we have learned before we can develop such an elevated consciousness.

The best of the best and the worst of the worst comprise the energy pressure cooker our new kids reside in and the toys they play with. Crime on a massive scale accompanies the miracles of the World Wide Web and the wonders that lie at our fingertips. Just for starters, we have things like identity theft, hacker attacks, fraud, and online stalkers of both children and adults. Entire economies and governments can be overturned or brought down (and have) by "smart mobs"—people who e-mail each other to appear at certain places at certain times to accomplish specific goals.[2] People by the hundreds of thousands answer the call by actually showing up. "Flash mobs"—in which folks text-message others to invite participation in simple pranks or a little camaraderie—are more benign. Still, whether through smart mobs or flash mobs, the new power we have to connect carries with it a heavy burden of responsibility and ethical behavior—*a major challenge for fifth root race types.*

To appreciate the enormity of that challenge, consider that kids today mature physically at younger ages than did their parents or grandparents . . . yet the prefrontal lobes lag far behind, tricking kids into thinking they're smarter and more in control than they really are, especially during the teen years and early twenties, when they have nearly the same access to power as adults but are less able to make sound judgments. During puberty, when the brain consolidates its circuits, pruning back those no longer needed, the choices young people make determine how their brains continue to form. Whether they choose art to occupy their time and talent, or music, sports, video games, volunteerism, outdoor activities, literature, or criminal behavior, *that choice reshapes the structure of their brain*, its chemistry, and its function (expanding or shrinking the prefrontal lobes).

Noteworthy is the link that can be made between the initial perception of safety that the fetus has while still in the womb and the increased number of births of advanced fifth root race types. Safe and supportive environments are more the norm now. As democratic movements spread, opportunities for the young greatly expand, heightening overall consciousness. The born frees and the zippies are examples of this, living proof that a freer society produces better people who improve society even more. 'Tis the ripple effect.

The reverse is also true. Along this line, did you know that lying causes changes in the brain that are cumulative and can be seen and mapped? Brain scans are more accurate in this regard than lie detectors. Plainly visible on such scans are the ways in which lies limit a person's potential for higher states of creativity and consciousness. With almost 90 percent of our population now more tolerant of lying, and with our leaders lying on a regular basis, we are steadily fashioning a culture of deceit that ignores long-term consequences. And nothing is more indicative of this than what is currently happening in the fields of marketing, advertising, and promotion.

Marketing specialists, armed with the latest in brain research, are targeting younger and younger customers to implant brand name imagery and slogans in their minds before the prefrontals strengthen. Lifelong brand loyalty is their goal, along with "affluenza" (a craving for stuff). Schools starving for funds are all too happy to cooperate by allowing businesses to furnish supplies (with logos and Web site addresses splashed across each item) or by renting out space for product sales, such as soft drinks.[3] Stores like K-Mart have recently begun to sell items with tracking devices on them that continue to emit information to the item's manufacturer long after a purchase. A host of pharmacies and grocery stores are following suit, allowing minuscule transmitters to replace bar codes. Lower income minorities are targeted directly, solely because they are less likely to notice or fuss. The public is being spied on with chips smaller than the smallest ant and it isn't funny. Neither is mass manipulation of our youth's brain development masquerading as truth in advertising.

One of the consequences of consumerism and technology devoid of ethics is that children grow up without the satisfaction of *earning* things, money or respect. They turn instead to violent movies and video games or to local gangs for the satisfaction they seek. The downside of advanced fifth root race types, even those with well-developed prefrontal lobes, shows up starkly in their relish of rewards, whether from self-serving or antisocial behavior or the murder of innocents. Kid gangs, thanks to the greater intelligence the new children possess, have evolved to the point at which dues are charged, mission statements followed, pecking orders defined, compliance and intimidation enforced. These kids are better organizers and enforcers than adults, and more reckless with the rewards of sex, drugs, power, and money.

An epidemic of depression is another consequence of the challenges that threaten to consume our children. Since the early days of the twentieth century, each generation has doubled in its susceptibility to this waster of health and happiness. Because of how their brains develop, kids are especially vulnerable to stressful emotional experiences that can trigger suicidal tendencies. Social pain—the power of words to hurt—affects the brain much like a physical injury. What no one wants to admit is that the positive, can do, cooperative, and generous millennials are the worst in history for committing self-mutilation. Far too often, cutting their own flesh becomes a substitute for expressing emotions. When I asked a number of them why, they each gave me the same answer: "*I just wanted to feel something real.*"

What can we do about the downside of our spunky new kids, who must somehow thrive in a pressure-cooker world? Ah, I thought you'd never ask. Begin with parenting. "What reflects favorably on us as parents is seldom in the best interest of our children," say Hugh and Gayle Prather. I recommend their book, *Spiritual Parenting*, as well as *A Parent's Toolbox for Spiritual Growth* by Johanna van Zwet. Joan

Bramsch, host of the Web site www.EmpoweredParent.com, offers a host of great ideas and good suggestions as well.[4] The key here is a spiritual approach, one that honors creative intuition while instilling the need for self-discipline and accountability. You don't lecture the new children, you show them by getting involved one-on-one in a consistent, loving way.

Have an astrological reading done while the child is still a babe—the psychological kind, *not* predictive. Basic leanings, strengths and weaknesses of the personality, and the best way to apply discipline can be recognized early on by a competent astrologer. This type of information is invaluable to parents. Stay away from anything predictive, as this style of interpretation programs people and denies free will. You might go to several astrologers to compare their techniques.

Counterbalance computer use with active time spent outdoors or with a pet. Stretching exercises are super important. So is putting hands and feet to work in soil (gardening), with clay (making pottery), or molding cookie shapes or veggie sculptures by hand; so are dancing, climbing, jumping, family field trips, chores, and learning to play a musical instrument.

Once the child is of school age, a slice of lemon or lime (or a squirt of either from juice concentrate) in a daily glass of water will help to alleviate most mood swings and perk up the brain. Drink right down, as the fruit is acidic.

Teach kids about the wise use of money—how to earn, save, and spend it. Half of all money received or earned should go into a savings account or be invested. As soon as practical, explain what a credit rating score is and why it's important, and teach about credit and debit cards and banks. It is essential that the new children understand the *concept* of money, as societies around the world are going digital, then will switch to optics. If the concept behind money is not understood, these conversions could be disastrous to individuals.

Parents, relearn the simple basics of food and drink. Fats and sweets are addictive, leading in excess to obesity and chronic health problems. Soft drinks are sugar water; junk food is junk. I've already discussed the latest findings on conditions such as autism and a host of learning disorders, indicating that nutrition and food allergies, as well as the chemicals applied to food as it grows, may be culprits. But plastics and microwave ovens may be problems too. This means thumbs down on prepackaged, instant meals. The more natural the diet, the better. While relearning things, include medicine. Alternative and complementary measures are often much more effective than conventional medicines, cost less, and have fewer side effects. Include water, light, prayer, and vibrational and affirmation therapies in your exploration, as they constitute the medicine of the future.

Necessity is bringing back the tradition of multiple generations living together for mutual support. The financial and emotional advantages for each age group (not just the mini-me's) far outweigh the disadvantages. This time, though, multiplex housing not only accommodates privacy concerns, but clever designs make it a desirable choice, not just a necessary one. Generational mixing (and not just with blood kin) encourages rather than squelches the growth of higher consciousness, as long as the ground rules of patience, respect, and forgiveness are observed and the common courtesies of praise and gratitude thrive. Caution: Make room for anger. It's natural and it's okay. That quick surge of hot, spicy energy serves to cleanse (get honest) and motivate (get moving). Anything else that busts loose is not anger, it's rage (repressed emotions). Find a safe place or a safe venue to express and release anger energy (house cleaning and exercising are two healthy choices).

Native American teaching stories (and those from other native peoples) are wonderful for giving children and their families positive guidelines that are simple yet effective in imparting ethical behaviors. Paula Underwood, an oral historian of the Walking People, has produced exceptional materials in this regard. Her video, *Learning Your Way Through Chaos,* and her book, *The Great Hoop of Life,* clarify the decision-making process and how to set goals and values.[5]

For those who missed teachings like this during their early years and wound up in prison, moral reconation therapy (or MRT) fills the gap.[6] This program, taught in a group setting, is a runaway success at every prison where it has been used. In a nutshell, prisoners learn that a moral code exists within them if they but attune to it, and that it will prevent them from acting out negative thoughts, dreams, and fantasies. Some time-honored moral codes are the Ten Commandments of Christianity and the Four Agreements of Mexico's Toltec Indians.[7] The "golden rule" (do unto others as ye would have done unto you) exists in some form in every culture ever known, as does the knowledge that if you give a child a model of love before the age of seven that he or she can respond to and understand, that child will adjust to life's challenges with a built-in sense of fair play and honesty.

I have emphasized teaching the basics of moral and ethical behavior, good decision-making skills, and a healthy sense of self, because the new children will turn social taboos upside down during the course of their lifetimes. As long as they have learned the basics, they will be capable of participating in civil discourse and solution finding.

Our first test with this as a society concerns the subject of sex. And of all the social taboos, this one is the most sensitive, volatile, and immediate.

Earlier I mentioned that the fusion of polarities will commence during fifth world ascension. To the average person, this translates into the alteration or balancing of gender differences. Does it strike you as odd that there is so much ruckus lately about homosexual and lesbian coupling, with the Vatican decrying the social swing toward gender ambiguity this represents? The issue has been around for thousands of years; suddenly, it's a big deal. And it's going to get bigger. Don't blame television and media alone for what's happening. We are presently in that preparatory state the world must pass through before we reach the Mayan portal and the beginnings of an entirely new and different energy matrix—the intensification of fifth world ascension. In other words, it's time. Already, in the United States, we are experiencing role reversals of every stripe: house husbands, female ministers, daddy daycare, mommy managers, women fighting alongside men in battle conditions and with security details. Male and female roles have ceased to have clear divisions.

That's on the surface. Wait 'til you see what else is happening.

Because of the twin urges of evolution and devolution, we are witness to the fusion of polarities playing out in simultaneous trends toward risqué and modest behavior. Here's how that is shaking out at present.

The birth of hermaphrodites is on the rise. These are children with the reproductive organs of both sexes inborn (leaving parents with the agonizing decision of which way to go with surgery: Should the child be male or female or left as is?). Seemingly regular kids are convinced today and at younger ages that they were born of the wrong sex to begin with. Prostitutes are steadily getting younger. The average student is bisexual; 2004 statistics show that 47 percent of our nation's high schoolers have sex with four or more partners, sometimes simultaneously (which stretches the imagination)—and many consider oral sex as casual as a handshake. Some youngsters are involved in sex clubs and sex rings and think nothing of nudity. The question is not "Where is your child tonight?" but "Who or what are they sleeping with?"[8]

When I say that many children today are into sex, sexy clothes, near-nudity, and nakedness in a big way, I am not exaggerating. They also enjoy tattooing, body piercing, and body modification (like having their tongue split or Teflon inserts surgically implanted under the skin in various places for various reasons). Have you seen some of these kids? I have. The first few times I almost puked. Since then I've learned to be more tolerant. They're good kids. A little weird, but then, that's my age showing. I'm not tribal. They are.

And the way the sexes mingle and socialize is equally far out:

NetGen: This software is the online equivalent of a pajama party for those who want to play or experiment with creating different environments and situations that encourage varied types of relationships, referred to by users as an "anti-productivity tool." This technology connects peer-to-peer (person to person) with direct links that avoid servers. It offers the ultimate in social groupings via a computer. Each "posse" or clutch consists of up to ten people for real world interactions and the sharing of music.[9]

Skateboarding: The constant motion, perceived risk, airborne suspension, and heavy beat music appeals to skinny kids with high IQs who can turn professional and make millions. The sport matches the fast action of video games, which match the way the young people's brains work.

Raves: Gatherings function as "church services" by uniting the many tribal allegiances into a philosophical oneness. Involve constant motion, flashing lights, as few clothes as possible, risky dance moves, loud music, and lots of drugs, especially ecstasy (which is linked to cognitive and psychiatric problems; the drug makes a person feel sad and sluggish afterward).

New Age Raves: An underground movement that blends electronic music and dance marathons with spiritual and religious rituals. No alcohol or drugs are allowed. Gatherings start with chanting and yoga, body rubs to loosen muscles, trance dancing, lights, tantric circles (redirecting sexual energies into "mind highs"), a smorgasbord of raw foods and herbal drinks.

NetGen, skateboarding, and raves (both types) have in essence become opportunities for spirited gatherings where the young "worship" the sensations of intimacy—feeling their own bodies interact with others as they experience the freedom of enhancing every feeling, making it larger and more sensuous (hey, even NetGen can be racy and risky). They are driven to see how far they can go and what else they can feel.

The ritualistic aspect of the new kids' social events mimics brain wave activity, which mimics the new technologies, which mimic the overstimulation caused by the startle effect from television, all of this demanding that stimulation increases even more, even if it means periodic violence or pain, just so they can *feel* the next level, the next high, the next pulse beat.

Changes of every ilk are occurring too fast for the human family to absorb. It's no wonder the young are hurting themselves. Still, they're clever rebounders. Take the fact that nearly three-fourths of American teenagers have tried illegal drugs by the time they graduate (if they do), yet significant numbers are now turning away from drugs entirely. Younger ones see how rampant sex orgies lead to premature aging and sexually transmitted diseases; growing numbers are choosing virginity. The connection between high schools, consumerism, and porno-fashion is losing its grip. Large numbers are instigating a backlash—modesty is "in."

The children of our future will continue to break apart the taboos that once held society together. Don't breathe a sigh of relief that virginity and modest dress are at last preferred. Sexual mores have only begun to shift as the desire to free ourselves from the limitations of gender identification and gender roles accelerates. The day is coming when the sexes will intertwine and children will be born self-aware. Until that day is here (and it's quite a ways off yet), I highly recommend that all of us, kids too, rediscover the simple pleasures of sensuality.

Let's face it, we're social, sexual beings who thrive on touch and need to feel. And sensuality is not just swaying hips, lowered eyelids, tongue licks on the skin. It's that vast realm of sensation reawakened from the numbness of our pressure-cooker world. What senses do you favor? What wakes you up? What delights you? *Feelingsense* is what makes the world come alive; it's what colors experience.

Sensuality occurs when we allow our senses to open up to the sensations around us. It enhances our faculties so that we can taste the wind and hear the water, smell happiness, see the inner voice as it speaks, feel light. We do this by deciding to, then, with intent, slowly, easily, reaching out with body and mind to caress what's there, to feel in a new way, awake to each minute sense report. With the smooth gestures of an inwardly aware mind, we can better feel the motion of body organs and genitals, breath as it flows in and out, heart thump, as we respond to others, our lives, our world.

Here's an exercise for you. Read the following story carefully and slowly.

Eight-year-old Amanda was eating and talking with members of her family.

"I'm sick of being called the miracle child." (It took her mother fifteen years and two miscarriages to have Amanda.) *"And, besides, I picked them."* When asked what she meant by that, she replied, *"Well, I looked down and I picked you and you [pointing to each person], and I picked my parents because they needed me."*

"Where were you?" her aunt Annette asked.

"I was up there, well, you know, up there."

"What was it like up there?" Annette probed further.

Amanda smiled. *"It's really, really bright. And all the colors are really, really bright, and you can see everything!"*

Now *be* Amanda for a moment. *Feel* what she just said. *Engage* every sensation. The story means more now, doesn't it? It has dimension because you gave it life with your feelings about it.

Trust your body. Trust your heart. Encourage your children to do the same. For generations to come, being able to feel the sensations of life will be more valuable than wealth.

Their Charge to Change

JOB OPENING: Young visionaries needed immediately in every field at all locations throughout world. Rewarding work; flexible thinking; no previous experience necessary. Get in on the ground floor of this growing, high-potential field. Apply in person at a problem near you.

WILLIAM UPSKI WIMSATT

To our newest citizens and those yet to come: Turn off the television set. There's a world out there and you have a job to do. It's your turn to clean up messes while redesigning infrastructure and policy. Issues of the extreme left or the extreme right promote "We Are Right" thinking (WAR), which negates the creative process that leads to progressive and positive solutions.

Register to vote. The minute you turn eighteen, register to vote, and vote in every election, local, state, and national—every year. If you're traveling or slated for surgery, vote absentee. Don't believe the naysayers. Your vote really does count.

Be an educated voter. Know your candidates and their platforms. If you don't like what you hear, do something about it. Become an activist or run for office yourself. Being a Republican or a Democrat used to mean something. It doesn't anymore. Either help to reform these parties or start a new one. Forget the Greens and the Libertarians, at least as they are currently structured. You are part of a new group of voices tagged by poll takers as "cultural creatives" (Renaissance people) and you are already the largest, fastest-growing political entity in the United States.[1] Your basic agenda is spelled out in the book *Radical Middle* by Mark Satin;[2] the how-tos you need to know in *The Future 500: Youth Organizing and Activism in the U.S.* (multiple authors, among them William Upski Wimsatt, who was quoted at the start of this chapter).[3]

Keep capitalism, but merge it with social responsibility so it's more humane. Today's change incubators are professional groups, so join one. Plan on using your job, your profession, as a political vehicle. Recent shifts in university curriculums are a direct result of such activism. Examples: Many medical schools now offer courses in alternative medicine, most business schools now feature training in environmental issues and entrepreneurship, nearly every law school today emphasizes dispute resolution techniques (skills in mediation, arbitration, and restorative justice and reconciliation).

Work for a true global village. You can't stop globalization from happening, so don't try. The ideal is to establish free markets, democracy, and progressive social and economic developments. What gets in the way is twofold: a lack of corporate integrity and corporate citizenship, and a hodgepodge of differing ethical standards within countries themselves. Both issues are tied to the question of values. Governments, businesses, and individuals alike are using the value differences among them as a wedge in trade negotiations, worsening the very problems globalization was meant to correct and resulting in gargantuan disparities.

Let's take a brief look at how this is currently playing out in the United States.

Knowledge-based jobs like computer programming and customer service are being outsourced to countries like India (where people speak English). Assembly-line manufacturing is getting shipped to places like China and Malaysia (where language doesn't matter). Things like chemicals and computer chips, which require advanced expertise, are "insourced" to the United States. This is far from an even exchange on the job front, but at least employment opportunities are spreading out as never before, which helps debtor nations pay down interest on their loans (pleasing bankers).

However, because of broad variances in the understanding of ethics, there is no regulation with teeth in it to ensure that benefiting nations pass along those benefits to their workers. That means American labor must now compete with fourteen year old girls in Indonesia, eight-year-old boys in Pakistan, and virtual slave labor in China. Just when the middle class is shouldering more of our nation's tax burden, they have less income to use. Interestingly, giants like Wal-Mart, Costco, and Best Buy purchase most of their inventory from outsourced locations, enabling them to sell at prices so low American dealers can't compete. At the same time, they are paying employees lower wages for longer hours, so their workers can only afford to buy at the giants the very products they were once paid good wages to produce. This encourages local governments to abuse eminent domain laws by condemning personal property so it can be sold to the giants to increase the tax base, displacing healthy competition and versatility in the marketplace, which weakens the middle class to the point that politicians can easily control them by preaching fear (pleasing corporations).

Adding insult to injury, laid-off workers must train their replacements, and most workers over the age of fifty must prepare for job reduction—less hours, less money, less opportunity. The zippies of India are required by *our own business leadership* to take "transformation classes" in how *not* to be friendly and how *not* to provide good service (based on the false premise that getting rid of customers is more cost effective than finding new ones).

Now do you get it? Without some form of shared values, the ascended fifth world could stall at the gate, ushering in little more than mean-spirited, dehumanized mediocrity, or benevolent dictatorships that guarantee life necessities as a way to undermine or control creative innovation and independent thought (pleasing governments).

Once you've finished screaming about the inequities of the global village, I want to acquaint you with holons. Ready? A *holon* is a whole made up of its own parts that is still part of a larger whole. Holons consist of opposing forces working together for mutual benefit: for example, an assertive drive to preserve individual identity in competition with others joining with an integrative desire to cooperate in league with larger wholes for the greater good. A holon, then, is like the particle and the wave of physics—complete opposites in complete accord. This push-pull action between balanced polarities unleashes variety and free will *in concert* with cooperative relationships and broad-scale planning.

And this is the energy pattern of fifth world ascension, dominated neither by left nor right brain hemispheres. It is the energy of a holon—whole-brain thinking.

The Syracuse Cultural Workers of Syracuse, New York, a group of young activists, gave me permission to share this with you from a poster they created.[4] The sentiment expressed in their poster is based on the premise of a holon.

HOW TO BUILD GLOBAL COMMUNITY
as put forth by the Syracuse Cultural Workers

Think of no one as "them"

Don't confuse your comfort with your safety

Talk to strangers

Imagine other cultures through their poetry and novels

Listen to music you don't understand

Dance to it

Act locally

Notice the workings of power and privilege in your culture

Question consumption

Know how your lettuce and coffee are grown: Wake up and
    smell the exploitation

Look for fair trade and union labels

Help build economies from the bottom up

Acquire few needs

Learn a second (or third) language

Visit people, places and cultures—not tourist attractions

Learn people's history

Redefine progress

Know physical and political geography

Play games from other cultures

Watch films with subtitles

Know your heritage

Honor everyone's holidays

Look at the moon and imagine someone else, somewhere else, looking at it too

Read the UN's Universal Declaration of Human Rights

Understand the global economy in terms of people, land, and water

Know where your bank banks

Never believe you have a right to anyone else's resources

Refuse to wear corporate logos: Defy corporate domination

Question military/corporate connections

Don't confuse money with wealth, or time with money

Have a pen/e-mail pal

Honor indigenous cultures

Judge governance by how well it meets all people's needs

Be skeptical about what you read

Eat adventurously

Enjoy vegetables, beans, and grains in your diet

Choose curiosity over certainty

Know where your water comes from and where your wastes go

Pledge allegiance to the Earth: Question nationalism

Think South, Central, North—there are many Americans

Assume that many others share your dreams

Know that no one is silent though many are not heard—work to change this

The days of spirituality and religion existing in opposition are starting to dwindle, as is the need to divide and conquer or have greed determine profit margins. We need a new model for ascension's children. Think of Benjamin Franklin, one of the most delightful characters imaginable. According to Thom Hartmann, this founding father was possessed of all the known traits of the hunter's gene, DRD4 7R allele—the gene mutation that once saved the human race and reoccurs in the population whenever a crisis is afoot. Surely, his place in history affirms the gene match, as does his personality and habits. You fixers, movers and shakers, stuffed full of new energy and new visions, fifth world types of every persuasion, are Benjamin Franklin clones to my way of thinking. He lived his life in accordance with seven great virtues: an aversion to tyranny, a free press, humor, humility, idealism in foreign policy, compromise, and tolerance.[5] Learn from his model.

Your charge to change also includes setting up the mechanisms, measures, and processes necessary for those who will follow you. Your generation, the millennials, is the first massive, worldwide entry of ascended blues into the earthplane. Because of this, you must establish the growth pattern for this phase of higher consciousness development, which, according to prophecy, will last a thousand years or so.

To help you aim your focus, I've arranged a collection of issues made to order for your mind and muscles. We begin with first things first.

- *Return to civil speech and civil behavior.* "Hate speech," on the level it now exists, began with the rise of conservative radio talk shows, later followed by the liberal side. This daily flood of loud diatribes and demonizing has silenced meaningful debates and disagreements, resulting in short-term "Band-Aids" rather than long-term solutions. Years of such pounding has affected everyone, vulgarizing how we speak to and treat each other. Civil speech is not just courteous, it's respectful, at least to the point that cuss words and sexual innuendos are avoided and time is taken to listen. President Ronald Reagan is not remembered as much for his policies as for his friendliness, and his willingness to extend the kind of touch that says "I care about you." The global village makes civil speech and civil behavior a necessity. Change must begin here. The time is coming when anything less will bind the world to a baseless, self-generating hostility.

- *Return to a common language.* "Tribalism manifesting as culturalism" has split the common tongue, challenging how we communicate in the United States. Words alter to fit the symbols of whatever is popular, which is how language evolves. But what has happened today is beyond the typical. Thanks to starkly different symbols presented via television, movies, video games, music, and fashion, values as well as language have splintered. Different groups literally cannot understand each other. Add to that the U.S. immigrant population and you have a situation in which we either agree to use English as the shared language held in common, or we lose our effectiveness as individuals and as citizens. This issue directly affects national sovereignty and safety.

- *Learn from history.* Harry Truman was the only modern president without a college degree. He was an expert historian, however, and because of that he was able to make the difficult decisions others couldn't. History repeats itself if we don't learn from it. Depend on that. Never be satisfied with what appears to be true on the surface. Dig for what is hidden. The truth can be painful, but it can be dealt with. A lie corrupts and enslaves over time. Intuition, knowing things, is no substitute for the scope of what history can teach. And help to protect that history. Digital data, photographs, keepsakes on magnetic tape are wearing out or being destroyed by the chemicals meant to preserve them. The more technologically advanced we are as a society, the more fragile that which defines us becomes. Find ways to counter this. Use backups and multiple means of storage. Laminate if possible.

- *Don't give your brain away to drugs.* You're going to need that incredible brain of yours. Chemical highs are not worth the risk of lessening or ruining your brain's ability to function. You can get better, longer, higher highs, and often, via spiritual pursuits or when engaged in compassionate service to others who are in need. Some do benefit from taking certain drugs at certain times, but not without observing rules of preparation, quality ingredients, time-honored ritual, elder supervision, and counseling when finished. Using drugs for entertainment or escapism accomplishes neither. You won't know until later on, even years later, if your brain and nervous system have been damaged, your reproductive capacities affected. As fifth world types become more sensitive, the ability to tolerate addictive substances will fade. And a further caution: Follow the money. What happens to the funds you pay for the drugs? Who profits? What country supplied the core ingredients? Is your money contributing to that country's welfare or impoverishment? You cannot divorce yourself from the impact of the choices you make.

- *Protect yourself from policy changes in the television industry.* It's going to take a groundswell from youth to stop current television programming that aims to fill every half-hour with fifteen minutes of commercials and fifteen minutes of content. To accomplish this feat, actors and actresses are taught to speak extra fast so what we watch appears as quick action when it is really squeezed material. Using discoveries from neuro-economics (bio-economics—how the latest research on the brain can be used in business to affect the bottom line), advertisers can now entrain the brain of viewers with the exact combination of startles and symbolic imagery necessary to impact individual reasoning. This policy reshapes brain structure to some degree, numbs the nervous system, interferes with the prefrontal lobes, and becomes, in many cases, a causative factor with ADD. The television industry will not listen to adult complaints about this, so it's up to you to seek a solution or compromise. I cannot begin to emphasize how important it is for you to have optimal brain function as we move from terrestrial to extraterrestrial environments and beyond.

- *Read more literature.* What you read on the Internet and in the newspapers isn't enough. Put a book in your hand and read it.

Readers are smarter than nonreaders, and are more inclined to imagine, visualize, dream, emphasize, do volunteer and charity work, visit museums and cultural performances, and avoid the trap of narcissistic behavior. To dumb down a society, discourage reading. To enslave a society, destroy the books. Eventually, the shape of what we read will change as the classic "book" evolves in its material make-up and design.

- *Connect with the spiritual.* Start each day in meditative silence. Bless the day. Affirm the healing of self and others in accordance with divine order, and ask that you be used for a purpose greater than yourself. Isolation, feeling separate from God, is at the core of all depression and all violence. We kill our own spirit by this belief in separation. There is no separation. We are, have always been, and will always be part of the larger family of created souls. Knowing this, feeling its truth each day, opens your awareness to divine guidance, otherworldly helpers, and the comfort of sacred fellowship. Thanks to the rise of spiritual cinema, even movies meet this need, this desire to connect with greater truth.[6] Spiritually aware people are happier and healthier, live longer, and are more generous than those who aren't. Each succeeding generation of new children will be more spiritual than the last and more intuitive; the actual extent depends on the flowering of prefrontal lobes.

- *Improve relationships.* No relationship can fulfill all your needs, nor should it. Realize that 10 percent of the people in your life love you no matter what, another 10 percent can't stand you, and relationships with the remaining 80 percent depend on how you treat them. That's why humor, patience, respect, and forgiveness are so important. Communication is the key to success, which means listening as well as speaking, giving as well as receiving. Riane Eisler, author of *The Power of Partnerships,* shows us how a "dominator model" of relationship evolved during the historical shift from matriarchal to patriarchal societies, from female to male leadership.[7] Fear and violence became the acceptable downside of

the powerful dominating the weak. In the much older "partnership model," relationships had more to do with mutual trust
between peoples, with males and females valued equally. Domination is not now and never was normal. Ascension frees the inher-
ent spirituality within all of us. Greater meaning, purpose, and
pleasure will define the relationships of the future.

- *Enter into committed partnerships.* Your life will be lived in
  chunks of time, about twenty years apiece. Reinventing yourself,
  transforming yourself during each segment will become the norm.
  Some of you may opt for different partners and different professions as you go along. Medical advances will make it possible to
  live past the age of 150 and extend reproduction into the senior
  years. The communities of the future will feature child centers for
  the care, training, and entertainment of youth. The family unit,
  though, will remain the central core of loving support and bond-
  ing for its members. Committed and loyal partnerships will grow
  in importance, but not to the point of replacing marriage. Wed-
  ding rituals will eventually merge ceremony with activism. Suggestions: Guests join the happy couple to help out at a farm that
  feeds the needy, or participate in a bone marrow or blood drive,
  or send donations to favorite charities in addition to or in place
  of gifts. With the freezing and adopting of embryos, use of surro-
  gate mothers, and having test-tube babies, the gene selection that
  occurs will redefine parenthood while advancing the body type of
  ascended blues. The unborn will take on new value and respect.

- *Harmonize with the environment.* Seriously consider living in an
  earth ship, even if you have to build your own. Earth ships are
  self-sufficient homes that are off the electrical grid.[8] Be certain
  to have a dowser or feng shui practitioner check out your land
  before you build, and again afterward to make certain landscaping and home decorations are in accordance with the natural flow
  of chi (earth energy or "breath").[9] To make certain you understand the importance of natural systems and how to harmonize
  with them, learn all you can about permaculture and ecological

design.[10] While you're at it, explore natural systems agriculture, where farmers mix different grains together rather than segregating them. The goal is to mimic the way nature does things. Results are stunning—richer harvests, better soil control, fewer weeds and pests.[11] How to think and act in ways that emphasize the wise use of resources is now known internationally as the sustainability movement. Spin-offs include a preference for old-fashioned neighborhoods, intersections, community gardens and markets, and the recognition that even cities are ensouled with their own unique character and heritage. The success of the sustainability movement will determine how well we live in the future. Proof that we can build what we can dream can be found in and around the large bio-domes of the Eden Project in Cornwall, England.[12] Eventually, we will grow our homes from plant membranes that are shaped and tended by bio-builders, and we will garden in league with angels and fairies.[13]

- *Go deeper into the environment.* You will encounter a powerful symbiotic relationship between humankind and nature that is staggering to behold when you investigate the new sciences of eco-psychology and deep ecology. Earth-systems science recognizes Earth as having a *biosphere* (living organisms and a planet-wide circulatory system), an *atmosphere* (blanket of gasses), a *geologic system* (surface and interior of earth), a *hydrosphere* (circulating water systems), and an *energy system* (energy that powers all earth systems—sun, wind, water, volcanic). Our planet is a living breathing entity with its own soul. Get acquainted. Solutions to how progressive societies can help instead of harm the natural world will depend on your willingness to buck the system. Cutting-edge organizations and facilities that explore life energy, Earth energies, and devices to assist with mind-over-matter already exist.[14] Join one. Take classes.
- *Rediscover the power of water.* Water will surprise you. Its main ingredient, hydrogen, is spread throughout the galaxies and, in the form of ice, is found in the dust clouds of outer space. What

you can do with it, how it spins, self-organizes, and recharges itself is a model for how interstellar space ships can travel.[15] As of 2003, the hard science exists to prove that water retains the memory of a substance dissolved in it, even if that substance is diluted to the point that not a single molecule is left. This validates homeopathy for medical use. The Japanese scientist Masaru Emoto has shown that expressing love or gratitude near or above water will restructure the water molecule to look like a lovely crystal. A similar thing happens when you clean water. But curse or speak hatefully, or pollute it, and the water molecule pulls in, clouds, and takes on the appearance of a cancer cell.[16] Water, like Earth, is alive, intelligent, and possessed of memory and feeling. It responds to care with equal caring; even the quality of your thought affects it.

- *Invent, invent, invent.* Don't wait until you're grown up. Start now. A seven-year-old has created a line of jewelry she markets from her bedroom computer; a boy of eleven has obtained a patent on a single card to replace all the credit cards people usually carry; a youngster invented a foot scanner to fast-check people's shoes at airport security; a teen created a political Web site that puts talk show screamers to shame.[17] The unsung heroes of science have always been backyard tinkers and those who dare to challenge consensus. That's how we got a plastic bag that dissolves in water and mycelial networks (fungal strains from wild mushrooms) that build and retain soil and filter out pollutants, even on road surfaces.[18] And that is how we will solve the energy crisis. "Peak oil," that point at which demand exceeds supply, is here. We have options: wind power, batteries that never need recharging, heat from colossal greenhouses to turn turbines for electricity, a device that taps energy from the vacuum of space and converts it to AC current, "over unity" machines (those that produce more energy than they use), hydrogen, and cold fusion.[19] The problem with energy is not supply, but cash to pay for new development, conversion, and distribution. The roadblock this creates will continue until a global disaster intervenes and forces action.

- *Pass it on.* If you saw Mimi Leder's 2000 drama *Pay It Forward*, you understand the pledge to make the world better by doing something nice for complete strangers. If you didn't see the film, you still know in your heart that sooner or later kindness is always passed on. Growing numbers of today's children take this seriously by joining peace movements, instigating projects through global Web sites, sponsoring fund raising drives, and starting up kid clubs to benefit one another.[20] This is no fad. It is a character trait of ascended blues. Most are born knowing what the Rev. Dr. Margaret Stortz often says, "Service is love in work clothes."

- *Become a planetary citizen.* The truth is that 250 people control more than 50 percent of the world's wealth. Some are responsible stewards, and others are "commercial fascists" whose goal is to buy up the sources of people's needs so they can control the very necessities of life—like good water and grain seeds. Since most of the world's population is afraid of freedom, as it requires too much personal responsibility and guarantees too little protection, many of these plutocrats and their companies go unchallenged. No longer. You new ones possess the greatest genius ever recorded and you're not intimidated by giants. You've already proved what you can do with smart mobs. Now try this: Organize and produce a blizzard of small joint ventures that create jobs and improve living standards globally. This alone will loosen the economic stranglehold that now exists. No country, heritage, race, or tradition can honestly claim you, so call yourselves what you are: planetary citizens, as much at home in Dublin as Sydney or Seattle, Calcutta, or Johannesburg.[21]

- *Beware of the dark side.* Terrorism casts a dark shadow on all of you, tricking those untrained in reasoning skills to believe that violence solves problems or pleases God. Nothing could be further from the truth. Terrorism appears in many guises:

religious fervor, genocide, family honor killings, identity theft, global epidemics and plagues, child labor, any form of slavery, even in the form of some spiritual types and channelers who have little more than false empowerment and foolish fantasies to offer. As ascension picks up and light increases, so will darkness. Yet hostile people and nasty conditions can be our best teachers. Even the dark side has a place in the overall scheme of things.

16

The Great Shifting

Time is the measure that man gives to passing events. The only power in time is what man imparts to it.

CHARLES FILLMORE

Mystical traditions say that the new children are reincarnated Lemurians and Atlanteans, advanced beings from an elder land surviving as memory in dream and myth. (*Lemuria* "once located in the Pacific Ocean" and *Atlantis* "in or near the Atlantic.") A few modern psychics predict that an even more advanced group of souls, called "those who will not be named," is due to be born about a decade hence; after them, still more unique and unusual souls. Special ones like this will come and go for centuries. Their job is to keep the ascension of the fifth world on course with the right people in place at the right time. Few of us will ever encounter any of them, as they enter without fanfare and are not part of any particular root race. They serve the great plan.

Of themselves, the ascended blues are well equipped to challenge society and upset consensus without extra help. Our planet, though, has its own destiny. The life cycles of the human family and those of Earth are colliding. Earth changes of biblical import, which began in the late eighties, accelerate daily. The time of the great shifting has arrived. Regardless of age or intent, we're all in this together.

A correlate to our situation is the numbers of children and teens I have met who have no sense of a personal future. Many of our young adults are bypassing career pursuits as well, in favor of travel or small jobs in small places, "hanging out," so to speak, with smiles on their faces, completely content, satisfied with the inner knowledge that when it is time for them to be elsewhere doing something else they will know or be guided to know. Those I interviewed appeared to be without ambition or concern. Their reply, as if in chorus, was "I don't see a future for myself, and it's okay." I did what I could in the way of counseling, trying to convince each one that with a little effort and planning not only could they have a wonderful life, they could help others by investing in social and political change. The results of my efforts were wrinkled noses, big grins, and a polite "No thanks."

The puzzle of children happy to be here, happy to be who they are where they are, but with no interest in a future, does not make sense unless you factor in the will of the soul. That's what we are, you know, souls. Souls come to Earth, take on bodies, develop personalities, experience positive and negative opportunities to learn and grow, launch missions or have jobs, and then return to Source through death's doorway. Groups of souls, however, can agree to do things differently, to cluster and combine their energies for the purpose of creating or participating in events, specific ones, that lead to consequences of a higher order. I witnessed a striking version of this when, in spirit-form, I went to ground zero on and after September 11, 2001 to do what I could to help the souls of those who were killed or injured in the attack on Manhattan's twin towers. I recorded what I discovered there in a memorial I later wrote about the tragedy.[1] An excerpt from that memorial follows:

"Each person involved in the tragedy, regardless of who, victim or perpetrator, had agreed before birth to be part of this event—to be there at that location, at that time, as that person. They had not committed as souls to be killed or to kill, necessarily, but, rather, to be present and accounted for, to ensure that the energy needed for the emergency to occur and have the effect it did would be available. It was only as time neared that final decisions were made as to outcomes, that is, who would do what. It was their purpose as souls to create this great 'wake-up call,' one so horrendous that it would shake up the entire earthplane, affecting every government and every religion, every man, woman, and child, and the environment as well."

I share this with you to make a point: Not every tragedy is quite what it appears, nor is every crowning affair as glorious. We have individual will. We also contend with the will of family, community, government, corporation, religion, and state. There are levels and networks, inter connections and interweavings—all manner of intent—that influence us to produce what happens in our world and our history, both personal and collective. But there's a higher will present throughout creation and within all created things, possessed of another agenda than what seems obvious or expected. And on occasion, this will supersedes ours. Of the children I interviewed who weren't interested in the future, the majority had an energy pattern similar to those at ground zero. They already knew or sensed that their present lifespan would be short, their function to serve as bridges, not builders.

Predictions of catastrophic Earth changes soon to occur are no longer an abstraction. They've begun. Proof lies in government reports that somehow miss the evening news.[2] A sample list of catastrophic changes includes:

New and dangerous viruses and bacteria are growing in our warming oceans. The percentage of people using marine beaches who have developed ear infections, sore throats and eyes, respiratory or gastrointestinal disease has risen sharply. The same holds true with ocean life.

Shellfish are dying in the Gulf of Mexico in a patch as big as New Jersey. But not just shellfish. Every living thing. Dead zones like this are spreading rapidly. Nitrogen runoffs and fertilizer from farmlands in the Mississippi River Basin are the suspected cause. Little is being done to solve the problem.

The Earth's magnetic field is disappearing near the poles. If it

reaches zero, a magnetic reversal will occur. These happen peri-
odically. The last one was seven hundred thousand years ago.
A magnetic pole reversal establishes a new polarity on Earth
while exposing the planet to a fuller impact of charged solar
particles. Satellites in low-Earth orbit over southern Africa are
already finding evidence of radiation damage there, suffered as
a result of the Earth's magnetic field having weakened.[3]

Birds are disappearing suddenly and by the hundreds of thousands. Migratory birds in North America are not returning to
their nesting grounds; neither are salmon seeking the spawning
grounds of their past. Sea mammals are losing their way or
beaching in unprecedented numbers. The near collapse of the
Earth's magnetic field is the suspected reason.

Overall volcanic activity on earth has increased 500 percent since
1975; natural disasters are up 410 percent since 1963.

Solar flares and plasma outbursts on the sun are of greater intensity today than in the past thousand years and are increasing.
Earth's temperature has risen dramatically in the last thirty
years, while solar brightness has dimmed somewhat. The last
period of warmth similar to what we are now experiencing
occurred during the time of the Vikings (Middle Ages, 1100 to
1250 C.E.).

Earth's light, or "earthshine," is dimming, down 10 percent since
1950. The most appreciable loss occurred after the year 2000.

At the current rate that land is being cleared for commercial
farms, 30 percent of the Amazon will be gone by 2006. If this
isn't stopped, the world's weather and oxygen ratios will be
drastically affected.

The Colorado River is lower now than during the Dust Bowl. The
western states are experiencing the worst drought in more than
five hundred years.

In 2004, for the first time in history, tornadoes spinning the
wrong way were spotted. There are places in Mexico where
the ground temperature is heating up in excess of 200 degrees.

During a seven-day period in early July there were 772 earthquakes recorded off the California–Nevada border, near Mammoth Lake, and on May 31 the jet stream from the upper atmosphere touched the ground (no record exists of this happening before).

The ice sheet covering Greenland is melting; the same is true in the Antarctic. Sea levels have risen appreciably because of this. The concentration of carbon dioxide in the lower atmosphere is at its highest level in 420 thousand years. Permafrost throughout Scandinavia is also melting, releasing methane gas from the peat bogs (a more potent form of greenhouse gas than carbon dioxide).

A bulge almost a half mile long has developed under Yellowstone Lake. Portions of the park had to be closed in 2003 because ground temperatures reached 200 degrees; 2004 was equally "difficult."

Other major fault lines besides the San Andreas (which stretches for 700 miles along the Pacific Coast) are becoming active. These are Cape Ann near Boston, New Madrid in Missouri, Meers in Oklahoma, and the one at Charleston, South Carolina.

From Eric Yensen, Ph.D., biology professor and ecologist:[4] "We now have good evidence of rapid past climate changes. Global warming appears to be capable of melting polar ice too rapidly. This puts too much fresh water into the sea off Greenland. This fresh water would not sink, which would stop the great ocean conveyor belt (also known as global thermohaline circulation), which goes from the surface to the deep ocean off Greenland. This would reduce oceanic distribution of heat to the poles, increasing the potential of severe storms and possibly switching us into an ice age. The climatologists think this could happen as rapidly as within the span of a decade. Climate changes of this magnitude would create environmental and economic chaos. The Pentagon Climate Report in October 2003 indicated that the most serious threat to the country is not terrorism but global climate change, although apparently this report is not convenient news for the Administration and it has not received much attention. The future of civilization depends upon our reaction to this threat."

The "great conveyor belt" is a mammoth river within the oceans that flows in a three-dimensional figure eight, propelled by the sinking of cold, salty waters from the North Atlantic. This creates a void that pulls warm, salty Gulf Stream waters northward. The Gulf Stream gives up its heat to the atmosphere above the North Atlantic, where prevailing winds carry the heat eastward to warm Europe. Should the great conveyor belt lose the salt it needs to operate (which has happened before in the distant past and is happening again now, with the fresh water flush assailing it from polar melt), an abrupt and dramatic cooling would occur throughout the North Atlantic region, where some 60 percent of the world's economy is based. The first blow is a food blow, affecting the United States, Canada, Europe, and Russia. A domino effect of weather reversals would spread worldwide.[5] The 2004 Roland Emmerich movie *The Day After Tomorrow*, even though it exaggerates the domino effect, depicts how truly unstable the world's climate really is.

What can we do about this? Well, we know that the ozone layer can repair itself. Thanks to the Kyoto Accord and other eco-friendly policies, limiting fluorocarbons in the air has made a measurable difference. Forty years ago, one car emitted the same quantity of pollutants as do twenty cars today. Levels of airborne lead, a major air pollutant, are down 98 percent since the 1970s. If corporations, businesses, and farmers wake up to the devastation caused by their manufacturing and farming processes and lack of wise land management and waste disposal, much of the damage already done can be repaired, further damage considerably lessened. Yet the big question remains: can we do this in time to save the great conveyor belt? Yes, to slowing down the salt sink; no, to preventing its eventual stoppage, as such occurrences have happened before and will happen again.

Everything I've mentioned thus far makes up but a portion of what's happening on the earthplane. Add to these changes what our government is doing with the installations of HAARP (High Frequency Active Auroral Research Project) and GWEN (Ground Wave Emergency Network). The former pulses extremely low frequency (ELF) waves that mimic the Schumann Resonance (the ELF waves that naturally exist in the earth's electromagnetic cavity, that space between the ground and the ionosphere). GWEN consists of transmitter towers that bathe the entire United States in an artificial magnetic field at the same frequency spectrum as human brain waves. Both of these installations are meant to protect our country from being surprised by enemy weaponry. Improperly used, they can interfere with weather *and* human behavior. People who live near such installations report feeling dizzy and disoriented and experience a sensation of burning much of the time; some claim to experience depression and lethargy, as if drugged.[6] The government denies any negative effects but offers no explanation for the anomalies that plague site operations.

Ours is not the only country experimenting with forces that have a direct bearing on the symbiotic balance between nature and humankind. Experimentations of this order, no matter where conducted or by whom, generate effects that actually accelerate the great shifting. Still, what is happening on Earth is but a reflection of what's happening in outer space.[7] Our entire solar system is changing. The universe we thought we knew is taking on a whole new appearance and vibrancy. See for yourself:

Our moon is growing an atmosphere as it continues its spin away from us.

Just since 1997, the structure of Earth has shifted from being slightly egg-shaped (elongated at the poles) to being pumpkin-shaped (flattened at the poles). Gas is forming in Earth's upper atmosphere that wasn't there before, and this is not related to global warming or fluorocarbon emissions.

Magnetic fields and the brightness of the planets are changing. Venus is markedly brighter and glows in the dark. Jupiter's magnetic field has more than doubled from 1992. It has such a high energetic charge now that a visible tube of ionizing radiation has formed between it and its moon, Io.

Both Uranus and Neptune show signs of recent magnetic pole shifts. Their atmospheric qualities have altered, especially on Neptune's moon Triton, which has exhibited a sudden jump in pressure and temperature that is comparable on Earth to a rise of 22 degrees Fahrenheit.

The sun's magnetic field is more than 230 percent stronger than it was in 1901. Overall energetic activity has substantially increased, leading to a recent frenzy that defies predictions.

The ice caps of Mars recently melted, causing a 50 percent change in surface features. Atmospheric density on Mars has risen 200 percent since 1977. Microbe fossils have been found in rocks from there, proving that Mars once supported life.

Saturn's polar regions have noticeably brightened, its magnetic field increased. Pluto has experienced a 300 percent increase in atmospheric pressure from 1990, while becoming considerably darker in color.

The glowing plasma at the leading edge of our solar system has recently increased 1,000 percent.

A loud WOW! would be appropriate at this point, followed by a soft "uh-oh" in recognition of the repercussions. Admittedly, any change alters our sense of order and safety to some degree. That's human nature. But big changes, significant ones, impact all of society, as well as the course of history. Simon Winchester's unnerving book, *Krakatoa: The Day the World Exploded, August 27, 1883*, reminds us how unexpected repercussions can be.[8]

Krakatoa's eruption destroyed 165 villages, killed 36,417 people, and created the loudest sound in human history—heard three thousand miles away—the sound of an entire island being blown to bits. According to Winchester, Krakatoa so terrified and dispossessed the Islamic people of the East Indies, whose screams for help went virtually unanswered, that it turned a relaxed and tolerant faith into a fiercer form of Islam fused with anti-colonialism. This ferocity still seeks "death revenge" today. Conversely, the first expression of a global village emerged from this disaster. Because telegraph and undersea cables existed, everyone everywhere suddenly knew what had happened. The world ceased to be a collection of isolated individuals and events, but instead became a network of interconnections among people and mutual occurrences. With the ending of one world, another began.

We've come close to experiencing other disasters of this severity, some even worse, since Krakatoa—violent storms, floods, fires, winds, plagues, genocides, crime and terrorism of unprecedented cruelty, earthquakes, several asteroid near-misses. Example: The huge earthquake (9.0 on the Richter Scale) that struck the island of Sumatra in the Indian Ocean on December 26, 2004, ruptured the longest trail ever recorded on the ocean floor, and created a tsunami wave that swept a path of destruction from Sri Lanka to Thailand. Nearly 300,000 people lost their lives or vanished. The sheer force of the quake altered Earth's rotational axis and spin, moved the location of the North Pole somewhat, and changed the length of our days. Water wells in the state of Virginia sloshed in rhythm to the quake, half a world away.

Mayan lore warned that the fifth world would end in huge movement shifts as fifth world ascension began. Even though most experts agree to the end-date of December 21, 2012, the Mayan calendar highlights many dates, especially a period between June 8, 2004 and June 6, 2012, as the "time of preparation," of trials and testing, when light (good) and dark (evil) will engage one another in unchecked struggles of equal fierceness.

The Mayan calendar is based primarily on the orbit of Venus. Ah, you must have read the newspaper: Venus crosses between Earth and the sun twice in an eight-year period every 105 and 120 years. Called a Venus eclipse, the next twin events are . . . June 8, 2004 and June 6, 2012. We're right there, smack in the eight-year lapse between Venus eclipses, the time of preparation. Always a period of sweeping changes in society and with the Earth, this particular twinning consists of unusually intense, powerful energies. A few predictions for this span based on interpretations of the calendar by experts in its study:

- Start of World War III ("War of Armageddon")
- Collapse of the American and Russian governments (which become dictatorships)
- Bankruptcy of stock market, banking, and reserve systems (Bretton-Woods Treaty dissolved or replaced)
- Shift of financial center to China
- Extraordinary leaps in genome and medical research, robotics, communication devices

Additionally, native peoples around the world have begun their last rituals, sensing that we've run out of time—that what was prophesied will now occur. "We can only prepare," they say, and to that extent they discourage pregnancy. Twin adjectives for the current twinning time: spectacular and horrific. I do not believe in doomsday, nor do I accept the dire messages flooding the Internet of late. I have long since learned that what you see depends on where you stand. A catastrophe to one person can be a miracle to another, and our attitude is what determines our sense of comfort and safety. I've lived through far too many tragedies to fall prey to the purveyors of fear. There is no denying, though, that events on the scale of Krakatoa, 9/11, and the Indian Ocean tsunami dot our horizon; disaster has already paved the path we tread. As long as we hold in consciousness the truth of what is happening—a shift of worlds, of energy frequencies, of landscapes, priorities, and measures, a house cleaning of sorts—we can deal with it, we can help each other, we can participate in finding and implementing solutions. However rocky the road ahead, *success is assured!*

If I learned nothing else from the near-death phenomenon, I learned this: Death does not end life, it only changes the perspective by which we view and value life. Believe me when I say that I, for one, am looking forward to what the future holds.

Since the more we understand the less we fear, let's turn to timetables other than Mayan for a better grasp of specifics. Astrology can be helpful with this, as it enables us to focus on smaller segments of time, to scale down the grandiosity of changing worlds to the immediacy of changing lives.

The planet Uranus symbolizes, among other things, the qualities of rebellion, humanitarianism, eccentricity, idealism, and enlightenment. Its energy equates with sudden upsets, visionary perspectives, the new and the different, the march of science. Uranus moves from one zodiac sign to another in seven-year cycles. Its passages appear as if a strike of a lightning bolt or the beam of a giant flashlight, in terms of how unexpectedly behaviors and issues relating to the sign the planet is in are highlighted, then illumined. For this reason, Uranus functions as an awakener.

If you study Uranian cycles throughout history, you will recognize that each overspreads the length of a social age or revolution—turnarounds in society that are significant and long term. Here are some examples (beginning and ending years for each cycle will vary depending on the Uranian orbit):

CYCLE	SOCIAL AGE
1975 Uranus entered the sign of Scorpio	The sexual revolution, counterculture, psychotherapies, drugs and crime, hospice
1981 Uranus entered Sagittarius	The New Age movement, charismatic churches, merger mania, foreign exchanges, gambling issues
1988 Uranus entered Capricorn	The political revolution, death of Communism, "earthquakes" on all levels, hostile takeovers, "greed is good"
1995 Uranus entered Aquarius	The information explosion, global Internet, high technology, computer commerce, "the quick fix"
2003 Uranus entered Pisces	The religious revolution, spiritual technologies, meaning-making, creativity and imagination, ethics, "the conceptual age"

If you have any doubts about the social age we're now in, you haven't been keeping up with the news, going to the movies or bookstores, or paying any attention to the death toll around the world, between Islamic terrorists and just about everyone else. We are in a time of religious fervor, with adherents too busy clashing with each other to honor the sacred space all share, the spiritual core of "soul breath"—the same human family from the same Source breathing the same air on the same planet. We cannot divide what exists together without denying God.

Our information explosion wore us out, to the degree that more people live alone today than ever before—with fewer kids, fewer friends, fewer committed relationships. Loneliness, fatigue, and a sense of isolation top the list of client complaints with therapists. Collectively, the need to belong is fueling the current trend of rebuilding neighborhoods and forming communities. The urge is to find meaning, to reassess motives and actions, to slow things down. This meaning-making is behind the nationwide switch of people going from psychologists to philosophers and pastoral care for assistance, along with a hunger for the arts and creative, imaginative endeavors. All are examples of the heavenly lightning bolt of Uranian energy splashing down into the watery sign of Pisces, where energy naturally diffuses and boundaries cease. Daniel Pink terms this shift in consciousness the "Conceptual Age" in his timely book *A Whole New Mind.*[9]

The social age in which we now find ourselves is unique in history in that throughout the full seven years, Uranus shares its cycle with Neptune in Aquarius. Neptune is considered to be the ruler or planetary correspondent to Pisces; Uranus has its home base in Aquarius (the sign it functions best in, which is why the last cycle was so frenzied. Uranus in Aquarius—what a trip!). The two have traded places, crisscrossed, you might say (called a "mutual reception" in astrological terms). If this seems confusing, just know this: Mutual receptions intensify energy way out of proportion and to extremes. In this case, the technological revolution from the last cycle jumps to an even higher octave (Neptune in Aquarius), at the same moment that our mental health, our psyche, our soul are screaming for attention (Uranus in Pisces). The polarization that is occurring is so extreme that we are being forced to accept the only solution that will work . . . a holon, the principle feature of fifth world ascension.

A holon, if you recall, occurs when opposing forces coexist as mutual benefactors; each one, although different, works together to achieve better results. How do you get warring factions to even listen to each other, let alone cooperate? Find the radical middle. We're moving that way in politics; we must, or only dictatorships will survive. And we're moving that way in human relations. Just look at what happened in South Africa with apartheid (the separation of one race from another, blacks from whites). What made the difference in healing the cruel legacy of apartheid was *reconciliation*, achieved through compromise and forgiveness.

Reconciliation makes holons possible. Reconciliation is the highest form of forgiveness, forgiveness in action. We are now living in the days where the sacred is being reborn, the true self rediscovered, where spiritual technologies—meditation, prayer, affirmations, visualization, contemplation, worship, philosophy, service, compassion, yoga, dance, music, art—outperform hard logic. Let's take full advantage of these opportunities while we have a chance, because we will need this grace in the times to follow:

CYCLE		SOCIAL AGE
2010	Uranus enters Aries	The age of challenge, opposing worldviews on the increase, war threats, new discoveries, flights to Mars, the Mayan calendar ends
2018	Uranus enters Taurus	The age of Earth and climate changes, security and safety issues; fortunes change hands, global economies switch
2025	Uranus enters Gemini	The Age of Aquarius dawns, healing of opposing worldviews, transformation and transmutation, outer space issues

The generational signatures of the new children through these cycles are important to know and cross-compare. Here's a reminder of their positive and negative signatures:

GENERATIONAL SIGNATURES

GENERATION	POSITIVE SIGNATURE	NEGATIVE SIGNATURE
Millennials (1982–2001): The Fixers	Tolerance	Anger (a peculiar impatience)
9/11s (2002–2024): The Adapters	Adaptability	Fear (insecurity)
Aquarians (2025–2043): The Universalists	Humanitarian	Instability (crisis)

At the end of their book, *Generations: The History of America's Future, 1584 to 2069*, the authors Neil Howe and William Strauss conjectured about future time frames and what generational patterning might reveal about the challenges that lie ahead and the people who will face them.[10] They isolated a time between 2013 and 2029 as when our country will face the greatest upheaval in American history. To understand the significance of this period, Strauss and Howe asked us to recall the eras of greatest upheaval—the Glorious Revolution of 1688, the American Revolution, the Civil War, the Great Depression, and World War II. "How will this crisis end?" they wondered. Then they offered this comment:

> Three of the four antecedents ended in triumph, the fourth (the Civil War) in a mixture of moral fatigue, vast human tragedy, and a weak and vengeful sense of victory. We can foresee a full range of possible outcomes, from stirring achievement to apocalyptic tragedy.

In my research with child experiencers of near-death states, about 20 percent said they were here in this lifetime for "the changes," that the

Earth and all the peoples on the Earth would go through great shifts that would alter the world. Of course none could give me dates, so I asked them to describe or draw what they would look like when the changes occurred. The resulting scenarios pictured them as parents with older children or grandparents. I grabbed my handy calculator and projected from their age at the time of their near-death episode to the time when their age might match what they described. Yup, every one of them wound up in the same time frame, 2013 through 2029. An exact match with the time frame projected by Strauss and Howe.

We pass through the Mayan portal under the aegis of Aries, "the god of war." The millennials will be the heavy lifters by then, their signature—tolerance and anger. Many will become soldiers. The 9/11s, haunted by subconscious fears, will follow in a struggle to physically change things. Skilled adapters and pragmatic realists, I believe they'll actually remold "the changes" by acting as spiritual warriors, committed to transforming the warlike drive of Arien energy into more effective and positive means.

The Great Ages

*And I saw a new heaven and a new earth; for the first
heaven and the first earth had passed away.*

REVELATIONS 21:1

I said the Aquarian Age dawns in 2025, when astronomically it doesn't
start until around 2375 and ends about 4535. (Astrology predicts it will
come sooner than that, more like 2133.) I also said that 1981 was the
time the New Age movement began, when in fact it began in 1899. Am I
nuts? I don't think so, but I do know that in calculating dates for grandi-
ose events you have to make allowance for the "harbinger effect"—that
condition whereby coming events always cast a shadow—the bigger
the event, the greater the lead time. We feel what's coming before it
physically manifests, as if it were somehow being "announced," and
act accordingly. Readying ourselves, then, for the age of Aquarius (and
singing its title song for more than 30 years) has been a fun game we
have played with each other. Yet, true Aquarian energy, that visionary,
humanitarian, eccentric, globe-trotting, rabble-rousing lift, has managed
to seep into every aspect of society since as long ago as 1899 and is
growing in significance. By 2025, we'll get a heavy dose of the stuff, and
it will feel as if the age of Aquarius has finally arrived (note my use of the
word "feel"). The crossover or overlap period between ages is approxi-

mately 200 years. During this overlap (energy acceleration), the opposite sign actually has the larger influence. For us, that means Leo (the ruling class; generous and engaging if unchallenged, stubborn control freaks otherwise, they desire wealth, admiration, and attention). Leo traits read like today's headline news, don't they?

The great ages of the zodiac last about 2,160 years apiece. Each is considered a month in a cosmic year of the great wheel. As important as the crossover from the age of Pisces to the age of Aquarius is, that's not what's been creeping into the dream life and waking hours of the world's population. The changes we're caught in right now are indicative of something far more immediate and much grander. Yes, the ages are shifting, but so is the great wheel itself.

On December 21, 2012, the ecliptic (the apparent path traveled by the sun, moon, and planets) crosses over the Milky Way near the constellation of Sagittarius. This creates a cosmic cross called "the sacred tree" by the ancient Mayans. The very center of this cross is where the solstice sun will be located on that date, completing a 25,920-year rotation of the ecliptic's great wheel around the universe's great central sun—a super huge black hole that holds a mass of about five billion suns. Twenty-seven galaxies, our Milky Way among them, rotate around this nucleus. Thousands of prophesies foretell this event as the birth of the golden age of enlightenment, which is preceded by eight years of "tribulation" (the twinning time between the two Venus eclipses). Buddhists say that this fifth turning of worlds is ruled by Venus (a fifth-ray energy in esoteric tradition), and is the time of Kuan Yin, the goddess of mercy, also known as "the Madonna of Tibet."

The great central sun is the great womb from which all stars are born and from which everything comes. The great central sun is the great mother. The changing of worlds occurring now fuses the Christ consciousness developed on Earth into the core of creation itself. *The great shifting is actually the great lifting.*

Conservative Christians term all of this "the hour of God." Their belief in the rapture, where the good will be lifted up and saved from the tribulations, fits into the sense of lifting and rapid acceleration of energy we all feel. Pop prophets have taken advantage of this belief in apocalyptic vision (biblical revelation of end times) to launch a multi-million dollar publishing spree of books detailing God's horrible wrath against evil doers, the salvation afforded by rapture, and the Second Coming of the Christ—with hardly a mention of God's forgiveness and love and the golden age now dawning.

Not to be outdone, some channelers and psychics warn of similar scenarios, except their version of the big lift involves being rescued by alien space ships and taken to a "new Earth." Apocalyptic beliefs defined the 2004 presidential election in the United States, and I believe determined the election of Pope Benedict XVI. (The Catholic Cardinals wanted a man who would steady the course and stick to church doctrine during these turbulent times; considering his advanced age at the time of his election, his steadying influence may not be felt for that long.) Even Sir Isaac Newton was quite taken with ideas of apocalypse. As his own life ebbed, he predicted 2060 as the year Babylon would fall, the Catholic church would cease to exist, and Christ would return to establish a 1,000-year kingdom of God globally.[1]

Apocalypse . . . that's what is creeping into our dreams and waking hours.

The second day I went to ground zero in spirit form to help the souls of those who were killed or injured, I was surprised to find how lucid and coherent most of the souls were, gathering as they did into the shape of a giant hand protecting the area from further assault. In addition to what I have already shared about what I learned there, I was told this: The wake-up call created by September 11 rent an etheric wound. This tear had to be big enough, violent enough, to release thousands of years of pain, suffering, and anger that had built up in the ethers from judgment errors made by humankind. All of our indiscretions, our folly, our cheating and lying and torturing and killing each other for the least of reasons, our stupidity, our greed, our empty holiness and evil scheming—all of this that is stored upon the skeins of time is now returned to us for needed healing. We cannot move as far forward as our destiny might take us if we are dragging along what has become the burdensome weight of our past sins—our mistakes.

The deeper reason for the 9/11 attack, then, is to force the world's people to face the eons of unfinished business that continue to poison mass psyche. Cleanup time began June 8, 2004 (nearly three years after the initial shock wave) and will extend as long as it takes for "we the people" to seek truth, reveal truth, and act on truth. Under the guise of apocalypse and the religious clash between Muslims, Jews, and Christians lies the only real issue—*love*—and the only real commandment—*do unto others as you would have them do unto you.* To help facilitate the needed healing, my husband Terry suggests that we reexamine the word "heal:"

Help
Everyone
Accept
Love

The missing component to understanding the 9/11 tragedy is the will of the soul. Most of us ignore or deny the presence of a will higher than our own or that there could exist a plan for Earth and the evolution of consciousness upon Earth. Yet, if truth be known, intelligence is unlimited in scope, is everywhere present, and operates from a core base of *intentionality* . . . that is both influenced and driven by awareness within its own mass, and by guidance received from vibratory and non-vibratory states of consciousness beyond human reckoning. Translation: What we think, feel, and emote does not evaporate once we have expressed it, but goes out into the air, then the ethers, and collects in something like a mass mind or group mind until it can be processed, learned from, utilized.

The concept of a mass psyche has precedence. Freud labeled it *racial memory.* Jung called it *collective unconscious.* De Chardin named it the *noosphere.* Cayce dubbed it the *Akashic record.* Of late, various scientists have posited that research in the new field of vacuum physics shows that a zero-point field does indeed exist, and that it holds the constant and enduring memory of the universe, literally a record of all that exists, has ever existed, and is yet to occur. This field is an ocean of subatomic vibrational waves that occupies the space "in-between" things.[2] Everything collects there and returns from there.[3]

We live in an informed universe because of this field, wherein every molecule, atom, thought, and emotion knows itself, where it came from, and what it's for. We are interconnected and intertwined, devoid of the secrets we think are hidden. Who sees what of this unseen reality is determined by the sensitivity one has attained. Events like 9/11 demand that we confront the myriad aspects of darkness, what we don't want to see or admit, to discover what's really there.

Believe it or not, the great central sun is without what we call light. It consists of a darkness so deep, so black, that light is lost to its depths. Whereas a significant portion of the universe is composed of dark matter, 90 percent of all creation and created things consists of dark energy—*dark energy is the zero-point field!* All that begins comes from darkness. All that ends goes back to darkness. What child experiencers of near-death states name "the darkness that knows," is the alpha and the omega . . . the secret soul of the universe.

Yet for most of us, any thought of darkness threatens our comfort zone; we fear a loss of boundaries and clarity. References to tribulation trouble us even more, as if we are somehow fated to walk the knife's edge betwixt global war and global climate and Earth changes, each step bringing us closer to destruction. Yes, the worst can happen, but so can the best. By focusing on the light released by uplifting energy, the inspiration we need to convert negatives into positives is revealed. We may not be able to stop the changes, but we can alter how they play out and to what extent. Light molds and shapes darkness and gives it the luster of volition, that creative shine only our free will can supply. Diversity is light's child in that the ability to vary, guaranteed by free will, is what fulfills God's great plan.

And that inspiring, uplifting light is exactly what heaven is sending. Get this: Maria Esperanza de Bianchini, recognized by Pope John Paul II as a genuine visionary, saw "rivers of light" streaming to Earth before she died in August 2004.[4] She predicted:

When the light arrives, it comes with supernatural light and God will allow us to feel His Presence deep in our hearts—the Divine spark that will awaken our conscience, to help us realize that God is everything and we are nothing without Him. When we get this light, we will be able to feel God in our hearts again. We will feel Him all the time with us.

Light is cosmic action, the photon its ultimate unit. As we move further into the fifth world, we are literally entering an age of light. Electrons, the workhorses of the modern age, are incapable of keeping up with the growing demands of society—so our scientists are turning to photons that can carry *the equivalent of more than 11,000 encyclopedias in one second over one tiny pipeline of fiber*.[5] In the United States "photon valley" is the name given to a nationwide collection of thousands of companies, all racing to bring photonics to the information super highway—that is, to a computer near you. And their progress is nothing short of spectacular.

We are being flooded with light, natural and supernatural, the harnessing of the photon amidst the blessings of divine revelation. This explosion of light, and the fact that people are seeing it, using it, feeling it, has spawned more inventors and visionaries than ever before in history and in every country. Yup, you guessed it, the schematics have been completed for a computer made of DNA threads that is so unbelievably fast that, with just twelve atoms, it is slated to outperform the mightiest of the mighty—light— *and beyond.*[6]

The challenges of tribulation are worth its risks. Frenetic energy, that hyper-urge currently overwhelming populations everywhere, is the signal that ascension is at our front step, ringing the doorbell. We're not leaving the planet via some kind of rapture or in space ships. Consciousness is rising right where we are, and we are meeting that rise—our destiny—as a collective. Clarissa Pinkola Estes, esteemed author of several books, puts the situation before us into perspective:[7]

We have been in training for a dark time such as this, since the day we assented to come to Earth. For many decades, worldwide, souls just like us have been felled and left for dead in so many ways over and over brought down by naïveté, by lack of love, by being ambushed and assaulted by various cultural and personal shocks on the extreme. We have a history of being gutted, and yet remember this especially—we have also, of necessity, perfected the knack of resurrection. Over and over again we have been the living proof that that which has been exiled, lost, or foundered can be restored to life again.

The Mayan calendar outlines the great plan on Earth in detail, giving us a sense of stages and levels, helping us to identify with almost pinpoint accuracy the where and when of happenings. But the yugas, or world ages of Vedic tradition, give the great plan perspective in a "flow form" that is extraordinary. In his book *The Holy Science*, Swami Sri Yukteswar translated this ancient material and described as he did the yugic calendar.[8] For the purpose of simplifying Yukteswar's words, I designed the chart of evolutionary ages which follows, used here with permission of the Self-Realization Fellowship, which holds the reprint rights to his work. Yukteswar, for those who don't know, is the mentor to Paramahansa Yogananda, one of the most beloved purveyors of Eastern philosophy, mysticism, and the science of spirituality to reach Western shores.

Notice in this chart how, at the halfway mark of the great wheel's rotation around the great central sun, the energy on Earth switches in the direction of its flow. The Vedic understanding of this phenomenon is that in the process of developing consciousness, both darkness and light are necessary to refine what emerges; the fullness of one carries within it the potential for the other. This potential or "seed" insures that the two flow into each other and back out again, continuously, until the dance of opposites becomes the flow of complements. Ages repeat in this manner, pivoting from ascending energy to descending, descending to ascending, so as to create and sustain the spiraling motion necessary for all aspects of developing consciousness to reach transcendence—to reunify with God.

Directional sweeps fold over each other twice, at the lowest point of the Iron Age and the highest point of the Golden Age. The most powerful messiahs emerge during iron ages, supplying the spiritual light and

EVOLUTIONARY AGES

DESCENDING

Golden Age 11,500 B.C. to 6,700 B.C.   lasts 4,800 years
Satya Yuga, advanced mentally and spiritually, 100% brain capacity (Lemuria)

Silver Age 6,700 B.C. to 3,100 B.C.   lasts 3,600 years
Treta Yuga, not as advanced but still high intellect achievements, 75% brain capacity (Atlantis)

Bronze Age 3,100 B.C. to 700 B.C.   lasts 2,400 years
Dwapara Yuga, inventive but more materialistic, 50% brain capacity (Egypt and India)

Iron Age 700 B.C. to 500 A.D.   lasts 1,200 years
Kali Yuga, humankind at its lowest ebb mentally and spiritually, 25% brain capacity (Messiahs)

ASCENDING

Iron Age 500 A.D. to 1,700 A.D.   lasts 1,200 years
Kali Yuga, humankind still at low ebb, slow improvements, 25% brain capacity

Bronze Age 1,700 A.D. to 4,100 A.D.   lasts 2,400 years
Dwapara Yuga, understanding different forms of energy, technology, interplanetary travel, 50% brain capacity

Silver Age 4,100 A.D. to 7,700 A.D.   lasts 3,600 years
Treta Yuga, humankind as a whole develops telepathy/mental power, 75% brain capacity

Golden Age 7,700 A.D. to 12,500 A.D.   lasts 4,800 years
Satya Yuga, technology is superfluous as mental/spiritual powers fully manifested, 100% brain capacity

loving encouragement necessary in times of darkness (great struggles). The golden ages are when humans are the most like the Creator, virtually godlike and possessed of great knowing. Neither the highs nor the lows last. Everything cycles. "End times" only change the environment of what we're used to; they do not alter God's plan. "Graduation," our reunion with Source as co-creators with the Creator, usually requires a bit of doing to integrate and perfect before it occurs. This need not be so. We as souls do not have to stick with any calendar of events to rejoin Source. Unfinished business slows us down, certainly, but learning the lessons of love and forgiveness sets us free—to become as custodians of the great plan, not victims of it.

What the Mayan calendar illustrates, the evolutionary ages of the yugas illuminate.

Look again at the chart. Note that we are presently not quite halfway through the ascending pattern of the Bronze Age, a time when different forms of energy are discovered, technology reigns, and there is interplanetary travel. Brain capacity, according to Vedic understanding, has the possibility of reaching 50 percent by 4100 C.E. Although the Mayan calendar and the evolutionary ages of the yugas seem to be out of sync with each other, I suggest that the opposite is true. In the Vedic tradition, somewhere around the middle of any ascending age (give or take a few hundred years) the quotient of available energy jumps—a breakout or quantum leap is said to occur. This jump intensifies markedly with each year thereafter.

The yugas, at least to my way of thinking, show how consciousness evolves and why history records the anomalies it does: lengthy "down times" (iron ages), and almost unbelievable achievements (the "forbidden history" of golden ages, where the only evidence that remains confounds scientists so much they refuse to comment on it—like finding a sandal print of a right foot stepping on trilobites that dates back more than six million years, or the discovery of diamonds in meteorites that existed *before* the sun). One thing is for certain: the notion of end times quickly fades when you consider evolutionary ages and how cyclic they are.

Actually, if you study evolution, the idea of gradual change based on genetic mutations, you run smack into missing links that are so numerous they defy explanation. For example, how can you explain the origin of flowering plants? You can't using the theory of natural selection espoused by Charles Darwin.[9] Biochemistry and the knowledge of DNA did not exist in Darwin's time. Using today's science for cross-checking, we find that the theory of evolution is fatally flawed—transitional fossils do not exist to back up his claims. New thinking and new models are finding that intelligent design or extraterrestrial intervention more accurately accounts for what happened with the beginnings of life on Earth and the emergence of humans. Creation's story is cyclic, with giant strides of steady growth followed by bone-chilling decline, up again then down, again and again. And always, there are Noahs, survivors to seed the next cycle.

Who is our Noah for this change of worlds? I submit to you that it is Nelson Mandela of South Africa. Out of the horrors of apartheid, he gave us *reconciliation*—the only solution to the survival of reason, tolerance, civility, and progress in the times in which we live. Who will be our Adams and our Messiahs for this next cycle? We will know when it is right for us to know.

In the meantime, the esoteric teachings of theosophy tell us that we have several more mutations of the physical body to go through before the indigo children can appear in appreciable numbers worldwide and there is clear evidence of the sixth root race as a presence on the earth-plane. The few indigos who are popping up now are precursors to what is to come. It is the job of the ascended blues to lead us through the Mayan portal, and into the ascension of the fifth world and the energy jumps within the Bronze Age as it, too, ascends.

Already DNA strands are altering to accommodate the new harmonics.

Some psychics predict that in the times ahead the number of DNA strands will increase to twelve, cloning will be perfected, all manner of genetic manipulation will become commonplace (including choosing the genes we want our babies to have), and the extraterrestrial question will be settled—in other words, proof that intelligent beings are alive and well on other planets and in the places in-between what we call space will be found.

Cautions abound, though, when it comes to messing with genes. Hopi elders fear that children will be created (cloned) who are soulless and have "no life force in their eyes." These children and their mothers, they say, will be shunned because they are unnatural; there will be "confusion between sexes, and children and their elders." The Hopi talk about the twinning time as the days of the Red Kachina, who brings purification to the Earth and her creatures. "Those who return to the ways given to us in the original teachings, and live a natural way of life, will not be touched by the coming Purifier. They will survive and build the new world."[10]

Jeremy Rifkin, author of *The Biotech Century: Harnessing the Gene and Remaking the World*, shares the Hopis' fear.[11] He warns:

> The new gene-splicing technologies allow us to break down the walls of nature, making the innards of the genome vulnerable to a new kind of human colonization. Transferring genes across all biological barriers is a technological tour de force, unprecedented in human history. We are experimenting with nature in ways never before possible, creating unfathomable new opportunities for society and grave new risks for the environment.

In the Book of Revelations we are told that the major shift ahead of us will happen "in the twinkling of an eye." In the book *Last Cry: Native American Prophecies and Tales of the End Times* by Dr. Robert Ghost Wolf, Hopi elders are quoted as saying:[12]

> We will receive many warnings allowing us to change our ways from below the Earth as well as above. Then one morning in a moment, we will awaken to the Red Dawn. The sky will be the color of blood, many things will then begin to happen that right now we are not sure of their exact nature. For much of reality will not be as it is now. No thing living will go untouched, here or in the heavens. The way through this time it is said is to be found in our hearts, and reuniting with our spiritual self.

Grave messages. And there are plenty more on the Internet. Dooms-day is a hot topic that is quickly becoming hotter. What I take heart from, what inspires me and fills me with courage during this span of predicted apocalypse, is the work of J. R. R. Tolkien and *The Lord of the Rings* trilogy.[13] I have been a fan of his for almost thirty years and have read all his books, including *The Silmarillion* and what has been released of the letters he penned.

You could say that his popular trilogy on death and immortality presaged World War II and the rise of Hitler. Tolkien himself fought in the trenches of World War I and was felled by a deadly fever. While hospitalized he began what he later considered to be his most important work, *The Silmarillion*. This book, in essence, is the bible of Middle Earth, from creation through the evolution of the first and second worlds and the beginning of the third. His children's book, *The Hobbit*, fleshes out the third world and introduces us to its inhabitants. The intricacies and intrigues of this world are expanded in the masterpiece epic *The Lord of the Rings*.

This epic delves into the great shift in Middle Earth from the third world to the fourth and the apocalyptic battle that takes place between the forces of good and evil. During the apocalypse, the races of dwarves, elves, wizards, hobbits, ents, and such fade from Earth to make way for "the race of men," a turning from the innocence of mysticism, magic, and spirituality to the mental gymnastics of invention, commerce, and nation building.

Tolkien clearly stated in his letters that he never invented the stories of Middle Earth; thus, they are not fantasies.[14] Rather, he entered this world (grid) as a reporter, witnessed what happened there, and returned to record what he experienced. Thanks to his careful attention to detail, we have today a work so realistic and so personal it can be used as a template to help us pass from the fourth world to the fifth—that next jump in the great ages of Earth, from the mental exercises exclusive to humankind to the abstractions of ascension, where masculine and feminine, left-brain and right-brain, and science and spirituality join together in holons (the balanced use of energy).

The major themes from this template that speak to us now are:

The glory in ordinary events reconnects us with universal spirit.
Each age requires heroes to take a stand on an issue.

The common man and woman serve as heroes.

Perseverance in the midst of hardship is necessary, for sacrifice provides the raw substance for the making of heroes.

People must have the courage to travel back to Source and undo what has gone astray.

All races must cooperate to find peace and freedom, and not be swept along by malevolent forces.

Empty words dehumanize language and strip culture of its power.

The struggle between good and evil never results in a permanent victory for either side.

Evil occurs only when events become unbalanced and run to extremes. The profound mystery of evil is that in a higher sense, in the long run, it serves the good.

The relationship of the mythical past to present and future reality is necessary in order that all aspects of knowledge can be fully integrated.

The real ending to this drama never appeared in the movie version of *The Lord of the Rings* trilogy directed by Peter Jackson, because Jackson didn't like it. What bothered Jackson is that, when the conquering heroes returned home, remnants of the evil forces they had just defeated had nearly destroyed the countryside and enslaved the people. Emboldened by their previous victories, the heroes taught others how to fight and devised successful strategies to overcome this final effrontery to peace. The resurrection that followed speaks powerfully to the soul.

Jackson completely missed one of the most important (and least liked) themes of apocalypse: *No one emerges unscathed*. There are no innocents in the great shifting. All are affected, directly or indirectly.

Fifth chakra energy spreads throughout the masses during the Fifth World, accelerating in its development as ascension continues, and challenging the way we handle power. This is the energy that opens the door to the highest states of consciousness possible to attain in human form. We shift with the five. The time is now.

Moving into Now

*There is always a door that opens in childhood
to let the future in.*

BARTON GREGORIAN

Synchronicity . . . the fluid dynamics of mind on the move.

The same message is popping up everywhere, telling us what we need to know when we need to know it. For example:

Happened during the same time frame: Three films—*The Passion of the Christ* (about God's Son), *Hellboy* (about Satan's son), and *The Lord of the Rings* (the template for understanding the great shift we are now experiencing and how to survive and thrive in spite of threats to the contrary)—representing the extreme right, the extreme left, and the third way (the middle path), all highlight through in-your-face, here-and-now imagery issues of global import impossible to ignore. *Synchronicity.*

Happening during the same time frame: Worldwide abandonment and drugging of children is occurring at rates never before seen; religious and cultural butchery and racial genocide are subjecting children to a constant mix of fear and violence. We are meeting our past and throwing away our future—just when the most intelligent, intuitive, inventive, volunteer-minded, and spiritually oriented children in history are entering the earthplane by the millions. *Synchronicity.*

Happening during the same time frame: Scientific discoveries show that the universe operates more like a great thought than a giant machine, that observation is necessary for the universe to fulfill itself, that consciousness is no accident, and neither are humans, just as other scientists, impressed with experiments (for example, the one showing that the spoken word can structurally change water) are proving that thoughts, feelings, words, and intention physically shape not only body function and health, but the environment of our lives. Molecular biology is establishing that the body-mind link is primary; one experiment after another demonstrates the same thing, that our mind is linked to group mind, universal mind, Greater Mind (Source). *Synchronicity.*

The best and the worst and the way in-between. All of it happening NOW.

NOW, at this particular moment in history where mind meets matter, when apocalypse looms and the world turns, people are awakening to their own point of power . . . the NOW moment.

NOW, that moment of clarity, of awareness and perfection, of oneness, is the doorway to power. You find it by being silent, and resting in the silence, you find within that perceived "center of being" at the core of you, your heart of hearts. By allowing the past and who you think you are, the present and how things seem to be, and the possibilities of a future yet to manifest—all of it—to drift by your gaze and into nothingness, by meditating or contemplating or merging into union with whatever is highest and best to you, at the moment identity ceases as identity and all that exists is breath and pulse . . . truth surfaces.

It takes practice to quiet the body and the mind, but when you do, if only for a single moment, internal systems begin to click into place and the mind self-corrects. You awaken to what is true about you and the world around you in the silence. No spell, no ritual, no exercise, no technique, no teacher, guru, minister, imam, nor priest is more powerful than the silence at the core of you, in your heart of hearts. Mystics and visionaries of yore told us that in the silence you meet your soul. They were right . . . God is within.

I discovered this in death and so did Don Miguel Ruiz, a fellow experiencer of multiple near-death states.[1] He witnessed that:

> The whole of humanity is just one organ of a bigger living being, which is the planet earth. The planet earth has different organs. Humanity is only one organ, the animals are another organ, the forest, the oceans. And everything is working together in a perfect metabolism, because the planet earth is alive. At the same time, the planet earth is like an atom going around the nucleus, which is the sun. Then, we can see the whole chain and it will tell us that there is only one living being. The whole universe of the universe of universes is only one living being.

We are awakening as a people to what the ancient adepts held as sacred knowledge: The entire solar system is the university of the soul.

We are starting to recognize that at this NOW moment in time, consciousness itself is becoming self-aware. The whole is awakening.

As this occurs, humankind moves closer to the realization that together we create what happens in the world by projecting into it our perceptions of truth (not necessarily what really is true). As we accept the responsibility for what we alone have done, we move into the rhythm of NOW, that natural synchronicity that vibrates at forty cycles per second—the brain wave pattern termed "high beta" or the "Zen of mergence," where that which resonates together joins together. The power of NOW, in simple terms, is a return to the natural state of conscious awareness and clarity, where polarities fuse and holons result.

The new children, most of them, are born with this knowledge intact. They move easily with the rhythm and pulse of collective consciousness, collective memory, collective dreaming, collective thought, concerns, voices—like cell clusters of a larger brain that is part of a universal brain that is part of a mind so vast no language exists to name or describe it. And we ARE that, all of us, one with the One.

Try to explain this to the new kids and they'll just squeal with laughter. I did with one young boy and he chortled, "Why can't you see what your mind knows?"

Chris Van Cleave, an exceptional balladeer who performs widely, wrote a song about these youngsters I was lucky enough to hear performed. Here is the first stanza to his composition "The Children:"[2]

> *We are the people being saved by the children*
> *Witness how they show us on the way*
> *We are the generation, so say the children*
> *To be the one to pass through night to day.*

Studying the march of generations enables us to glimpse the path of evolving consciousness as it moves through the human experience. It's a way of reducing large tracks of information into bite-sized chunks we can wrap our heads around. To that end, let's do a final generational review.

Generation X is the crossover group that moved us from traditional values to the introduction of global values. They're the ones who were on the ground floor of the information explosion and were imprinted with its quick-click method of circumnavigation. (For the most part, this generation covers those born between 1961 and 1981.)

The millennial generation represents the first truly global emergence of a mindset that transcends borders. Not only do they supply muscle for the passage of humankind through the Mayan portal, but they also possess the energy that enables large, pivotal events—both positive and negative—to occur worldwide. In China, millions of these young people are joining the Communist Party; well-educated and socially oriented, they are dedicated to helpfulness and caring as a collective. In the predominately Muslim countries, just as many are becoming fighters or supporters of conflict, equally dedicated to their belief that force is the only answer to their problems. (This generation is generally associated with those born between 1982 and 2001.)

9/11s, imprinted by the violence of terrorism, are the ones who will be called upon to find the solution to terrorism and participate directly in the transformation of Islam as it is presently practiced—and of any religious body, dictum, or creed that nullifies or demeans the female, children, and the freedom to choose. At the crux of all third millennium wars will be one issue—the right of individuals to think for themselves. The long-term assignment of 9/11s is to ensure that neither the enlightened nor the endarkened will dominate in the years to come. (These are the new ones born between 2002 and 2024.)

Global healing will take root and spread during the span of the Aquarian generation. Measures of this sort will be instituted before then, but the diversion of climate and Earth changes, to the degree that they occur, may slow the transformational process. Safety and survival issues always have priority. This will not prevent spectacular accomplishments in the areas of invention, communication, and travel, as well as a complete reassessment of governing bodies and national borders as they presently exist. Maps will radically change, as will the marketplace of goods and ideas. People will come to recognize as fact that evil (the darkness of negativity) cannot ever be destroyed or overpowered. The only way to disarm evil and that which seems evil is through the simplicity of open-heartedness. Nothing else has ever or will ever work. This generation will bear the brunt of "power over" or "power to"—the most important challenge the ascended fifth world will encounter. (In all probability, this generation will span the years 2025 through 2043.)

The time span of 2013 through 2029 concerns me the most. This is when generational statisticians and a percentage of children who underwent near-death experiences say the greatest challenges will occur in our country and around the world, generating anything from "stirring achievement to apocalyptic tragedy" (as Strauss and Howe so aptly put it). No matter how strong the millennials may be, fatigue weakens. Anyone of any age is sorely challenged to think straight when confused, bone-tired, hungry, or overstressed. For this reason, I want to talk a little bit more about the energy of ascension . . . as it can trick the mind.

People have physical reactions to the pressure of intense, spiraling energy (animals do too). A sampling of possible effects includes migraines, a sense of tiredness interspersed with sudden spikes of energy, electrical sensations in the limbs and spinal column, muscular cramps, flu-like symptoms, intense visions and dreams, digestive upsets and bloating, irritability, unusual mood swings, psychic "downloads" of information, a sense of isolation, and feeling heavy, light, fast, and slow all at the same time.[3]

Other weird things can happen, too. Some say they hear soundless music or infrasound. Infrasound—an extreme bass—is what elephants hear. It is produced not only by spiraling energy, but also by storms, seasonal winds and weather patterns, and earthquakes. Infrasound is usually present at genuine hauntings. High pitches, on the other hand, are electrical in nature and heard most frequently by birds, dogs, and cats. They can accompany extraterrestrial or angel sightings, and may "chime" at sacred sites or during sacred ceremony. Soundless sound (low-pitched or high) is quickly becoming commonplace.

Possession already is.

Does that surprise you? Any time you're not grounded you can be subject to a broad range of possession experiences, in which, for example, a bodiless being can slip into your body and take control. Abusing drugs and alcohol automatically weakens natural defenses, which invites psychic invasion. Such takeovers are most often temporary, but they can be long-term, leading to personality disorders and mental illness. Also, during wars and especially with explosions and violent weather, the Earth's crust as well as the ethers can get ruffled up or excessively shaken. This releases anything that rests, from dust particles and pollens to emotional artifacts, psychic residue (leftover bits of our energy), and "hangers-on." Hangers-on are essentially psychic mischief, like curses, negative thoughts, or passions that only serve to taunt or drain energy. After the attacks of 9/11, my doctor reported having to deal with a bombardment of hangers-on that were affecting his patients' health. Exorcising them is not difficult. Prayer and meditation usually do the trick, as well as positive affirmations, a healthy diet, exercise, and sunshine.

What is much more harmful is trickster energy. Trickster energy of itself simply refers to the times we are fooled by people or events into thinking something is real or valuable when it isn't. The test is one of clarity and discrimination. But tricksters may also be full-blown manifestations, such as the sudden appearance of a seeming angel, saint, alien, animal, demon, or any type of otherworldly being that knows exactly how to appeal to your desires, needs, and weaknesses. Tricksters can take on any size or shape and act wise and knowing. As a result, channelers can mistake tricksters for valid masters; best-selling books about saintly visitors can actually be sham or exaggeration. To recognize trickster energy, be alert for a negative "hook" or controlling spin to what is offered—even if the messages drip with love and light. The goal of the trickster is to rob you of free will and make of you a follower or a know-it-all who keeps coming back for the next "revelation."

Possessors, tricksters, and hangers-on are the "dust-mites" of psychic and emotional residue and ego desires that blanket what is internal or external to us. Take a clue from this finding: Happy people seldom experience such phenomena. Yet with the stressors of ascension, even the self-realized can be deceived. Thus there is no substitute for a grounded, healthy lifestyle, good friends, loving relationships, and a work ethic of sweat, common sense, charity, and service.

"The Message Center," a guided meditation for children developed by Janet Gaddie Grimm and Patricia K. Manthey, is a wonderful story-form that inspires and uplifts the child in all of us while gently leading us away from unproductive distractions and urges.[4] The two women gave me permission to share it with you. Before using the meditation, relax your body in any manner that is simple and easy for you to do.

~

THE MESSAGE CENTER
A meditation for children by Janet Gaddie Grimm and Patricia K. Manthey

We are going to make pictures in our mind about a special place where you can talk to God and receive messages from Him. This special place is our Message Center. In order to get to your Message Center you need to walk out of your home. Imagine that when you do this, you walk away from your neighborhood and into the surrounding countryside. The air smells fresh and sweet and is very beautiful. You see that it is full of colors that swirl. There are also dashes of white light. It is always fun to start this walk, because you know that where you are going is very special.

Soon you come to a bridge and walk over it. On the other side of this bridge is a small pond. By this pond is a place where you can sit and have "quiet time." When you are at the pond you can hear it gurgling because there is a stream that feeds water into the pond. The gurgling noise is relaxing and peaceful. Every time you come to your Message Center you surround yourself with the white light of the Holy Spirit. This helps protect you and keeps you safe.

When you are in your Message Center you want to be as quiet as possible. This is your time to talk to God and also to listen back for messages. Messages can come in different ways. It may not be like a phone conversation, but ideas or feelings can come that are helpful to you. When you are at your Message Center, this is a good time to think about how you can help other people. Maybe there is someone in your family who needs help, or at school. Maybe you have an idea that would help lots of people. It doesn't make any difference if your idea about helping people is big or small. To God, all ideas about helping others are BIG. In fact, that is why we are all here on earth—to help each other. It is easy to forget this, however, with thinking about our problems or upsets in life, or if we are very busy.

When you know you are finished with your conversation with God, then be sure to thank Him for listening and for His help. Now it is time to go back home. Walk over the bridge through the grass and trees. You know the way back home. As you walk back, you feel a new lightness and are somehow softer. It is time for you to get ready for the rest of your day. Look forward to seeing at least one person that you can be kind or helpful to.

∾

The twin pillars of creation are love and law.

The twin powers of manifestation are praise and joy.

The twin realities of existence are light and darkness.

At the beginning of this book, I promised to tell you a really big story. I think you will agree that I delivered on my promise. Regardless of how you refer to the fifth world and its ascension, the time it enfolds is already here. We are in the NOW moment and we can reengineer whatever we find, now and in the years to come. We do this by creating holons—situations where opposing forces agree to cooperate with each other for mutual benefit—for the highest good of all. And we do this by finally recognizing we are all children from the same Source, headed in the same direction, participants in the same drama.

The only real issue is love.

The only real commandment is: Do unto others as you would have them do unto you.

Notes

How wonderful it is that nobody need wait a single moment
before starting to improve the world.

ANNE FRANK

INTRODUCTION

1. P. M. H. Atwater, L.H.D., *Children of the New Millennium* (New York, NY: Three Rivers Press, 1999).
2. P. M. H. Atwater, L.H.D., *The New Children and Near-Death Experiences* (Rochester, Vt.: Bear & Co., 2003).

CHAPTER ONE

1. Lecomte du Noüy, Ph.D., *Human Destiny* (New York, NY: Longmans, Green and Co., 1947).
2. There are many sources now for interpretations of the Mayan calendar. One of the most vocal and knowledgeable Westerners as concerns the Mayan calendar and its various cycles is Carl Johan Calleman, Ph.D., *The Mayan Calendar* (Albuquerque, NM: Acalan, 2003); also available as *The Mayan Calendar and the Transformation of Consciousness*, by the same author (Rochester, Vt.: Bear & Co., 2004). http://www.calleman.com. Also check out the work of Carlos Barrios and the Organization for Mayan and Indigenous Spiritual Studies at www.sacredroad.org as well as that of Ian Xel Lungold (www.mayanmajix.com, or e-mail him at Ian@mayanmajix.com).
3. One source for this material is John Major Jenkins, *Galactic Alignment: The Transformation of Consciousness According to Mayan, Egyptian, and Vedic Traditions* (Rochester, Vt.: Bear & Co., 2002). Also see www.Alignment2012.com.
4. *Intuitive Flash* is a newsletter produced by Gordon-Michael Scallion and his

wife Cynthia Keyes. Contact: Intuitive Flash, P.O. Box 367, West Chesterfield, NH 03466; 1-800-628-7493, fax (603) 256-6614; www.IntuitiveFlash .com.

CHAPTER TWO

1. Evidence for this comes from research done by the Woods Hole Oceanographic Institution as well as other prestigious scientific groups. An executive summary prepared by Peter Schwartz and Doug Randall entitled "An Abrupt Climate Change Scenario and its Implications for United States National Security" was presented to the Pentagon for review in October, 2003. The report outlined in detail what could occur throughout the world if our climate were to change as abruptly as it has in the distant past.

2. *Newsweek* magazine first broke this news to the general public on November 10, 1986 in a cover feature entitled "The Way We Were" (pages 62–72). There have been many other research breakthroughs since. One example is the discovery described in the intriguing book *The Man in the Ice: The Amazing Inside Story of the 5000-Year-Old Body Found Trapped in a Glacier in the Alps,* by Konrad Spindler, the leader of the scientific expedition that found the body. London, England: Weidenfeld and Nicolson, 1994.

3. Contact the Theosophical Society in America, P. O. Box 270, Wheaton, IL. 60189-0270; (630) 668-1571; fax (630) 668-4976; e-mail: olcott@theosmail .net; www.theosophical.org.

4. C. W. Leadbeater, *The Masters and the Path* (Madras, India: Theosophical Publishing House, 1925). This book is still available through the Society.

5. Colonel Arthur E. Powell, *The Solar System* (Madras, India: Theosophical Publishing House, 1930). This book is still available through the Society.

6. Sancta Sophia Seminary, 11 Summit Ridge Drive, Tahlequah, OK 74464-9215; (918) 456-3421; e-mail: lccc@sanctasophia.org; www.sanctasophia.org.

7. Carol E. Parrish-Harra, Ph.D., *The New Dictionary of Spiritual Thought,* Second Edition (Tahlequah, Okla.: Sparrow Hawk Press, 2002). The drawing of the root races appears on page 242.

8. The Association for Research and Enlightenment (A.R.E.) is a membership organization that offers many services, including a large publishing wing, magazine, holistic health-care opportunities, and a lending library. They sponsor study groups all over the world. Contact A.R.E., 215 67th Street, Virginia Beach, VA 23451-2061; (757) 428-3588; 1-800-333-4499; www .are-cayce.com or www.edgarcayce.org.

9. John Van Auken, Lora Little, Ed.D., and Gregory L. Little, Ed.D., *Ancient Mysteries.* This is one of various monthly publications produced by the A.R.E. Ask for it by name when you contact A.R.E. headquarters (see note 8 of this chapter).

CHAPTER THREE

1. John Van Auken is a gifted lecturer and speaker on ancient mysteries, archaeology, religion, and spirituality. Two books he co-authored are John Van Auken and Lora Little, Ed.D., *The Lost Hall of Records: Edgar Cayce's Forgotten Record of Human History in the Ancient Yucatan* (Memphis, Tenn.: Eagle Wing Books, Inc., 2000) and Gregory L. Little, Ed.D., John Van Auken, and Lora Little, Ed.D., *Mound Builders: Edgar Cayce's Forgotten Record of Ancient America* (Memphis, Tenn.: Eagle Wing Books, Inc., 2001).

2. A few of the dozens of Web sites I visited seeking more information about the Mayan sun legends: www.dartmouth.edu; http://members.aol.com/TPrinty/mexico.html (Article entitled "The July 11, 1991 Mexico City UFO's" by Tim Printy); http://wintersteel.homestead.com/files/Folklore/Quetzalcoatl.htm; www.geocities.com/Athens/4903/Mexica.html (Article entitled "Aztec Theocracy: A Social & Political Organization" by R. S. Cartwright). This material was originally a term paper and is held at the University of Idaho, Moscow, ID.

CHAPTER FOUR

1. Bahá'u'lláh lived in Iran during the 1800s. He was a gifted visionary and spiritual master in every way, and his life and death fit the messiah pattern as exemplified by Christ Jesus. The only variation from the pattern is Bahá'u'lláh's additional gift of authorship. He recorded his thoughts and revelations himself, filling numerous volumes. A religion evolved from his work, founded in 1884 as the Bahá'í Faith. It is predicated on the concept of unity in diversity. Although Bahá'í adherents downplay the importance of physical churches (they prefer to meet in people's homes), there is a large, beautiful Bahá'í temple in Wilmette, Illinois. Contact Bahá'í National Center, Wilmette, IL 60091; (708) 869-9039.

2. Caroline Myss, Ph.D., *Anatomy of the Spirit: The Seven Stages of Power and Healing* (New York: Harmony Books, 1996).

3. Gordon-Michael Scallion, *Notes from the Cosmos: A Futurist's Insights into the World of Dream Prophecy and Intuition*. Matrix Institute, West Chesterfield, NH, 1997. See also Swami Amritasvarupananda, *Mata Amritasvarupananda: A Biography*. Mata Amritasvarupananda Center, San Ramon, CA, 1988.

4. Atwater, *Children of the New Millennium*.

5. Atwater, *The New Children and Near-Death Experiences*.

6. Joseph Chilton Pearce, *The Biology of Transcendence: A Blueprint of the Human Spirit* (Rochester, Vt.: Park Street Press, 2002). Pearce is the author

of several best sellers (including *The Crack in the Cosmic Egg* and *Magical Child*). These, along with a host of other books, all of them about a child's brain development and how to raise a healthy, well-adjusted child, have established Joseph Chilton Pearce as a renowned expert in his field.

7. Paul Pearsall, Ph.D., *The Heart's Code* (New York: Broadway Books, 1998).

8. For more information about Institute of HeartMath and the research they do, contact them at P.O. Box 1463, Boulder Creek, CA 95006; 1-800-450-9111; (408) 338-8700; www.heartmath.org.

9. For more on the science of synchrony, read this book: Steve Strogatz, *Sync: The Emerging Science of Spontaneous Order* (New York: Hyperion, 2003).

10. I refer you to James Gleick, *Chaos: Making a New Science* (New York: Viking, 1987); James Gleick and Eliot Porter, *Nature's Chaos* (New York: Viking, 1990); John Briggs and F. David Peat, *A Turbulent Mirror: An Illustrated Guide to the Chaos Theory and the Science of Wholeness* (New York: Harper and Row, 1989).

CHAPTER FIVE

1. William Strauss and Neil Howe, *Generations: The History of America's Future, 1584 to 2069* (New York: William Morrow, 1991).

2. Refer to *Millennials Rising: The Next Great Generation*, Neil Howe and William Strauss, New York, Vintage Books, 2000.

CHAPTER SIX

1. Lee Carroll and Jan Tober, *The Indigo Children: The New Kids Have Arrived* (Carlsbad, Calif.: Hay House, 1999).

2. Although there are many sources of revelatory material accredited to Drunvalo Melchizedek, I summarized the particular comments that appear here from an interview with him conducted on June 22, 1999 by Diane Cooper. I wish to thank Diane for e-mailing me a copy of the text. A two-tape video by Melchizedek entitled *Through the Eyes of a Child* should be available at most video outlets, or you can obtain it from the magazine *Atlantis Rising*, P.O. Box 441, Livingston, MT 59047; order phone 1-800-228-8381; www.AtlantisRising.com.

3. Paul Dong and Thomas Raffill, *China's Super Psychics* (New York: Marlowe & Co., 1997.)

4. Twyman has written a number of books, among them *Emissary of Love* (Charlottesville, Va.: Hampton Roads, 2002). To receive *Letters from James Twyman*, sign up on list@emmissaryoflight.com.

5. In researching medical papers and articles on this subject it is possible to find some degree of verification of whatever it is you want to verify. An

article in the *Washington Post* (3/30/95) titled "Boy's Recovery from AIDS Virus is Documented" did indeed establish that a child born HIV-positive was virus free at the age of five. However, if you really dig around through the research you find again and again that specimens had been mislabeled and re-analysis did not show linkage between infant and mother. You will learn there of one physician, Dr. Lisa Frenkel, who was able to refute the notion that the immune system in infants is able to recover from HIV infections (*Science* May 15, 1998; 280: 1073–77). There are many other such reports. The fact is there is not enough evidence at this time to support the type of extravagant recovery claims being made by people who should know better than to make them.

6. Dr. Berrenda Fox published her announcement about mutations in the double helix on March 30, 2002. This paper was distributed largely through the Internet. Her clinic was the Avalon Wellness Center in Mt. Shasta, California. Several people reported that she had been jailed after it closed, yet no one has been able to confirm that or to locate her.

7. Australian channeler Susanna Thorpe-Clark has a Web site at www.hotkey .net.au/~korton/index.html. Her e-mail is korton@hotkey.net.au.

8. Twyman's admission was made in an e-mail letter dated April 8, 2003 to his "Beloved Community." The letter was entitled "Practicing What I Preach" and was written as a counterpoint to the accusations being made against him.

   Twyman's practices have generated much controversy. Many object to Twyman's excessive and misleading use of the label "Indigo," and self-promotions which have the appearance of exploiting children. His center in Oregon, where he hold retreats for members of his "beloved community," is registered as a church organization offering programs through its seminary to grant Peace Minister ordinations and a Master of Peace divinity degree. He holds large conferences featuring gifted children, which he funds through projects such as training people to bend spoons with their mind, improving children's psychic ability, and experimenting with the healing properties of a flower called "nard" (or spikenard) that he claims is rare and grows only in a small region of Nepal. The way these projects have been carried out has drawn criticism, especially as concerns spikenard. It is well known that this herb can easily be obtained throughout South America, even high grade strains, at a fraction of what he charges. His declaration of World Indigo Day, January 29, 2005, was largely seen as simply a campaign to advertise his movie *Indigo*.

   On the positive side, Twyman's efforts have certainly awakened the public to the existence of a new generation of children who are different from any other generation of record, and for that I thank him. On the negative side, his methods cause many to question his motives and intent and the effect his promotions have on the children themselves. I find myself joining this growing number of concerned people.

9. Marshall Stewart Ball touches people's hearts through a veil of silence. Although he can neither speak nor walk and depends on others for physical assistance, he is a constant source of inspiration and guidance for people in matters of the mind and heart. Having tested at a twelfth grade reading comprehension level when only nine, his capacity to think and to feel amazes all. Marshall knows the meanings and spellings of words he has never been exposed to before. Even more amazing is the powerful impact he has on those he meets. His books, *Kiss of God; Marshall Ball, Prodigy: The Wisdom of a Silent Child;* and *A Good Kiss* are available through his Web site (www.MarshallBall.com) or by writing Thoughtful House Press, P.O. Box 340045, Austin, TX 78734.

10. Mattie J. T. Stepanek died in July 2004. The condition he lived with impacted automatic functions and caused muscle weakness, breathing, digestion, and heart problems. He used a power wheelchair, ventilator, and extra oxygen when necessary. He could walk with foot braces but needed his wheelchair to tote the one hundred pounds of equipment that kept him alive. His mother has the adult form of the same disability; his three siblings previously died from it. Mattie wrote three books of poetry, all treasures. The best-known is *Heartsongs* (New York: VSP Books/Hyperion, 2001). It is possible to locate articles about him by going to Google (www.google.com) and typing in "Mattie Stepanek."

11. William T. Dickens and James R. Flynn, "Heritability Estimates Versus Large Environmental Effects: The IQ Paradox Resolved," *Psychological Review* 108, no. 2 (2001): 346–369.

12. Atwater, *The New Children and Near-Death Experiences.*

13. Pearce, *The Biology of Transcendence.*

CHAPTER SEVEN

1. Excerpted from Anna Quindlen, "Our Tired, Our Poor, Our Kids," *Newsweek,* 12 March 2001, p. 80.

2. Lori Lite has gone on to write four children's books that directly address the special needs of ascended blues. These books are *A Boy and a Turtle, The Goodnight Caterpillar, The Affirmation Web,* and *A Boy and a Bear.* Highly recommended, they can only be purchased through Lori's Web site at www.LiteBooks.net. You can reach her by phone at (770) 321-4066 or e-mail her at Lori@LiteBooks.net. "Teaching children to enhance their

lives" is her motto. As of 2004, all four books are now available on a single CD (audio version).

3. Greensboro Wonder & Wisdom, Inc. community school is located in a small rural area in Vermont. The school is run on a nonrenewable grant, several other small grants, community support, and prayer. The programs it offers are so outstanding that children's lives are being changed as their minds are challenged. For more information about the school and their amazing programs contact: Trish Alley, Greensboro, VT 05841; or e-mail her at tpalley@together.net.

4. Gary W. Hardin can be reached at dreamer@boulder.net. His book is *The Days of Wonder: Dawn of a Great Tomorrow* (Missoula, Mt.: Dream Speaker Creations, 2003). Joey Klein has his own Web site at www .joeyklein.com. Joey travels the world offering healing sessions, giving talks and workshops, and doing what he can to help those like himself who are part of the ascended fifth root race (he still identifies them as "indigos"). To reach him, contact: Health and Wellness Center, P.O. Box 44, Andover, KS 67002.

5. Cynthia Sue Larson is the author of two books: *Aura Advantage: How the Colors in Your Aura Can Help You Attain What You Desire & Attract Success* (Avon, Mass.: Adams Media, 2003); and *Karen Kimball & the Dream Weaver's Web* (Lincoln, Neb.: iUniverse, 2003)—call 1-877-823-9235 to order. She is a bio-energetic field researcher, gives talks and workshops that (like her books) are perfect for ascended blue types, and regularly publishes an Internet newsletter called *Reality Shifters*. Her work is exceptional. To contact her or to sign up for her newsletter, write: Cynthia Sue Larson, P.O. Box 7393, Berkeley, CA 94707-7393. Her Web site is http://realityshifters .com; e-mail cynthia@realityshifters.com.

CHAPTER EIGHT

1. Bobbie Sandoz wrote *Parachutes for Parents: 10 New Keys to Raising Children for a Better World* (New York: Select Books, 2004) and *In the Presence of High Beings: What Dolphins Want You to Know* (San Francisco, Calif.: Council Oak Books, 2005). Both are highly recommended. Her Web site is www.bobbiesandoz.com; e-mail her at SandozB@aol.com.

2. The first in the Harry Potter series of books is J. K. Rowling, *Harry Potter and the Sorcerer's Stone* (Scranton, Pa: Scholastic, Inc., 1998). There are now boxed sets of the various books, with more to come. This literary endeavor by J. K. Rowling has proven to be an over-the-top success.

3. Mary Summer Rain, *Mountains, Meadows, and Moonbeams: A Child's Special Reader* (Charlottesville, Va.: Hampton Roads, 1992). See note 3 of chapter 7 for material about Lori Lite and her children's books. *Fred-*

die Brenner's Mystical Adventure series by Kathy Forti, Ph.D, consists of *The Door to the Secret City, The Team Dream, An Everyday Miracle, The Great Tree House War, Looking for a Rainbow,* and *The Indian Haunting at Malibu Canyon.* Highly recommended, these books are only available via her Web site at www.FortiBooks.com; e-mail info@FortiBooks.com; or call at (310) 709-7221.

4. Judith Orloff, M.D., *Second Sight* (New York: Time Warner Bookmark, 1996). Check out her Web site at http://www.drjudithorloff.com. Henry Reed, Ph.D. and Brenda English, *The Intuitive Heart: How to Trust Your Intuition for Guidance and Healing* (Virginia Beach, Va.: A.R.E. Press, 2000). An expert in working with dreams, Reed has a great Web site and offers a host of services and ideas. Contact: Henry Reed, Ph.D., Flying Goat Ranch, 3777 Fox Creek Road, Mouth of Wilson, VA 24363; 1-800-398-1370 or (540) 579-2883; http://www.creativespirit.net; e-mail STARBUCK@LS.net. His Web site is fun for kids, too! Sonia Choquette, *The Diary of a Psychic: Shattering the Myths* (Carlsbad, Calif.: Hay House, 2003). To inquire about her online "Psychic University," e-mail her at emails@PsychicUniversity.com. See note 6 of chapter 7for information on Cynthia Sue Larson's books.

5. A.R.E. Camp has been in operation for more than forty years and currently has eleven different offerings for children, teens, adults, and families. Based on the Edgar Cayce readings, the camp is exceptionally positive, joyous, and well run. Contact: The Association for Research and Enlightenment (A.R.E.), 215 67th St., Virginia Beach, VA 23451-2061; www .edgarcayce.org/are_camp/index.html; general phone 1-800-333-4499, or for questions about camp, call (276) 686-8493, e-mail arecamp@valink .com. Rowe Camp has a long-standing reputation for excellence and offers Junior or High Camp, Young People's Camp, and New Camp. Positive and supportive. Contact: Rowe Conference Center, Kings Highway Road, Box 273, Rowe, MA 01367; (413) 339-4216; fax (413) 339-5728; e-mail RoweCenter@aol.com. Enchanted Forest Intuitive Camp is fairly new but has elicited glowing recommendations. Offers programs for kids ages two through nineteen, parents, and mentors-in-training. Joyous "lab school" training for children and families. Headed by Nancy Baumgarten and held at Enota Mountain Resort, Hiawassee, Georgia. Schedule and registration forms at www.psykids.net. To reach Nancy, call (828) 254-5880, e-mail her at nancy@celestial-dynamics.com, or write Profound Awareness Alliance, P.O. Box 16522, Asheville, NC 28816. Her motto is "Planetary harmony through global awareness, where science and spirituality meet." Geared toward highly psychic/spiritual children. Wonderful curriculum.

6. "Smart Hearts," a program for raising children's self-awareness and safety, was created by psychic crime investigator Pam Coronado. This program is now available on VHS. Her book, *Kid Safe*, can be purchased along with the video through her Web site at www.pamcoronado.com/SmartHearts .html. Contact her at iampam@earthlink.net or by calling (805) 216-4115. This program is so good it should be used by every school system.

CHAPTER NINE

1. Reverend Don Welsh is minister at the Church of Religious Science in Lancaster, California.
2. Tobin Hart, Ph.D., *The Secret Spiritual World of Children: The Breakthrough Discovery that Profoundly Alters Our Conventional View of Children's Mystical Experiences* (Makawao, Hawaii.: Inner Ocean Publishing, 2003). Hart and his wife Mary Mance Hart founded ChildSpirit Institute, a nonprofit organization dedicated to understanding and nurturing the spirituality of children and adults. Through ChildSpirit Institute, they conduct research and educational projects and sponsor annual conferences. Contact: ChildSpirit Institute, 35 Camp Court, Carrollton, GA 30117; (770) 836-8584; www.childspirit.net.
3. Neale Donald Walsch, *Tomorrow's God: Our Greatest Spiritual Challenge* (New York: Atria Books, 2004).
4. Classes in how to become a spiritual mentor are offered through Atlantic University, 215 67th Street, Virginia Beach, VA 23451-2061; 1-800-428-1512 or (757) 631-8101; fax (757) 631-8096; www.atlanticuniv.edu/mentor.
5. Just type "emergent churches" into the search engine Google (www.google .com) and a whole array of choices will pop up, from newspaper articles to the churches themselves. One leading source of information about emergent churches is www.christianitytoday.com.
6. Founded by Russell Hobbs, you can find out more about the "get your praise on" movement in an article by Arian Campo-Flores, *Newsweek*, April 19, 2004, pp. 56–57, posted on the Web at http://msnbc.msn.com/ id/4710900/.
7. Two books I suggest you read on this subject are: Lauren Artress, *Walking a Sacred Path: Rediscovering the Labyrinth as a Spiritual Tool* (New York: Riverhead Books, 1995); and E. Barrie Kavasch, *The Medicine Wheel Garden: Creating Sacred Space for Healing, Celebration, and Tranquillity* (New York: Bantam, 2002). Also inquire through: Veriditas: The Worldwide Labyrinth Project, Grace Cathedral, 1100 California Street, San Francisco, CA 94108-2209; www.gracecathedral.org.
8. There are countless books out now on feng shui; trained practitioners may even be in your area. Check for fliers at health-food stores. Among the best

books is anything by Sally Fretwell, especially her book *Sally Fretwell's Make the Ordinary Extraordinary: Homes to Live In.* To obtain a copy: phone (434) 970-1860; e-mail fengshui@pagesystems.com; on the Web at www.feng-shui-tips.net. Good sources for information on sacred geometry are also numerous, but my favorite teacher on the subject is Robert J. Gilbert, Ph.D. He and his wife operate Vesica, a school and resource center focused on the full spectrum of sacred geometry and its many components. His talks and classes are outstanding. Contact: Vesica, Spirit and Science Resources, P.O. Box 27, Asheville, NC 28802; (828) 296-8324; e-mail info@vesica.org; www.vesica.org.

9. Two of the many new seminaries springing up globally are OneSpirit Interfaith Seminary, 330 West 38th St., Suite 1500, New York, NY 10018; (212) 931-6840; www.onespiritinterfaith.org.; and The New Seminary, PMB 344, 2565 Broadway, New York, NY 10025-5657; (212) 222-3711; fax (212) 864-8355; e-mail info@newseminary.org; http://newseminary.org.

10. Deborah Koff-Chapin first came out with *Soul Cards* in 2000, quickly followed by her book *Drawing Out Your Soul.* All of her work is published by The Center for Touch Drawing, Langley, Wash.; www.touchdrawing. com. Paul Ferrini came out with *Wisdom Cards* in 2002, along with his book *Everyday Wisdom.* All of his work is published by Heartways Press, Greenfield, Mass.; www.paulferrini.com; 1-888-HARTWAY. Rowena Pattee Kryder created *Vibrational Medicine Cards: A Sacred Geometry of the Self* in 2000. She has authored several books along the same order, including *Sophia's Body: Seeing Primal Patterns in Nature* and *Source: Visionary Interpretations of Global Creation Myths.* All of her work is published by Golden Point Productions, Crestone, Colo. P. M. H. Atwater discovered the ancient goddess runes and "the way of a cast" in 1978. A historical set dating back to the matriarchal societies of Old Europe, these "group runes" or "family runes" became the therapy she used after surviving death three times in 1977 and having three near-death experiences. She found them to be an effective tool to help develop whole brain functioning and healthy life approaches (uniting left and right brain hemispheres). She wrote two books about them; the second one, *Goddess Runes,* has been reissued as *Runes of the Goddess* by Galde Press, P. O. Box 460, Lakeville, MN 55044-0460; 1-800-777-3454; phyllis@galdepress.com. Check her Web site for links to the new publisher. The *Goddess Runes Instruction Booklet* and the CD entitled *The Adventure Begins* can both be purchased directly from Atwater's Web site at www.cinemind.com/atwater or www.pmhatwater. com. Send postal queries to: P. M. H. Atwater, L.H.D., P.O. Box 7691, Charlottesville, VA 22906-7691.

11. For more wisdom on spiritual discernment, refer to: Elizabeth Lesser, *The Seeker's Guide: Making Your Life a Spiritual Adventure* (New York: Random House, 2000).

12. Edie Jurmain, "Searching," *Science of Mind* November (2003): 58. I am grateful to both Edie and the magazine's editor for allowing me to reprint this wonderfully creative material.

CHAPTER TEN

1. In the article "Culture of lies is rubbing off on our children," Susan E. Tifft, professor of journalism and public policy at Duke University, coined the phrase "Pinocchio culture" to explain the peculiar American habit of making celebrities of the fallen. She notes that the young people of today, although more conservative in many ways than their elders, are surprisingly blasé about shading the truth. Her commentary first appeared in the *Los Angeles Times*. The reprint I read was dated June 29, 2003, in *The Daily Progress* newspaper, Charlottesville, VA.

2. Ron Taffel, *Parenting by Heart* (Boulder, Colo.: Perseus, 1993).

3. See the article "Helping Depressed Kids" by Mary Carmichael, *Newsweek,* April 5, 2004, 65–66.

4. Neil C. Warren, *Make Anger Your Ally: Harnessing Our Most Baffling Emotion* (Garden City, NY: Doubleday, 1983). This book is as valid today as when it was first written.

5. Frank DeMarco, *DreamHealer: His Name is Adam* (Charlottesville, Va.: Hampton Roads, 2004).

6. Amy Z. Rowland, *Essential Reiki for Our Times* (Rochester, Vt.: Healing Arts Press, 1998). A reiki master teacher who specializes in working with children, teaching them the fundamentals of the reiki system of healing and how to use the techniques in a healthy way, every day, is Ellen Louise Kahne. Her success rate is amazing. Write or call Ellen Louise Kahne, Reiki Peace Network, Inc., P.O. Box 754217, Forest Hills, NY 11375; 1-877-432-5638; e-mail HealNet@aol.com; www.ReikiPeaceNetwork.com.

CHAPTER ELEVEN

1. Daniel G. Amen, M.D., *Change Your Brain, Change Your Life* (New York: Three Rivers Press, 1998).

2. "Ritalin may cause long-term brain change" according to a report that appeared in *USA Today,* November 12, 2001, concerning findings by chief researcher Joan Baizer at the University of Buffalo. Also see: "More Kids Receiving Psychiatric Drugs," an article by Shankar Vedantam originally appearing in the the Washington Post that appeared in *The Daily Progress,* January 14, 2003; "Illegal drugs help kids? Cannabis considered for

ADHD," by Claudia Pinto, *The Daily Progress,* May 11, 2004. On the Internet, refer to International Coalition for Drug Awareness, www.drugawareness.org.

3. Atwater, *The New Children and Near-Death Experiences,* p. 94.

4. There are numerous books out now about this subject. Begin with Neil Z. Miller, *Vaccines, Autism, and Childhood Disorders: Crucial Data that Could Save Your Child's Life* (Santa Fe, N.M.: New Atlantean Press, 2003).

5. Thom Hartmann, *The Edison Gene: ADHD and the Gift of the Hunter Child,* (Rochester, Vt.: Park Street Press, 2003), 121.

6. Some excellent books on the subject: Doris Rapp, M.D., *Is This Your Child?* (New York: William Morrow, 1991); Doris Rapp, M.D., *Is This Your Child's World?* (New York: William Morrow, 1991); Michael Lyon, M.D., *Healing the Hyperactive Brain* (Calgary, Alberta: Focused Publishing, 2000); Michael Lyon, M.D. and G. Christine Laurell, Ph.D., *Is Your Child's Brain Starving?* (Coquitlam, B. C., Canada: Mind Publishing, Inc., 2002); William Shaw, Ph.D., *Biological Treatments for Autism and PDD* (Lenexa, Kan.: The Great Plains Laboratory, Inc., 2002)

To contact Autism Network for Dietary Intervention, visit www.autismndi .com. For the latest updates on autism, refer to www.theautismperspective .org.

New information about the autism spectrum is available at http:// williamstillman.com. Stillman has written some important books on autism, with more to come. You may contact him directly at billstillman2@aol.com, or write to him at P.O. Box 167, Hummelstown, PA 17036-0167; (717) 566-5538. His latest research, "Autism and the God Connection: Divine Experiences of Exquisitely Sensitive Beings," is due out in spring 2006, from Sourcebooks, Chicago, IL. And for an eye opener, get Marcia Angell, *The Truth about Drug Companies: How They Deceive Us and What to Do About It* (New York: Random House, 2004). Refer to her article by the same name on http://www.nybooks.com/articles/17244.

7. "TV may weaken capacity to focus," Associated Press, Chicago, dated April 5, 2004. See also the online journal of Pediatrics at www.pediatrics .org.

"Groups link media to child violence," a joint statement from the American Medical Association, the American Academy of Pediatrics, the American Psychological Association, and the American Academy of Child and Adolescent Psychiatry, dateline: Washington, D. C., released nationwide by the wire services July 26, 2000. See also *The Angry Child,* Tim Murphy, New York: Crown Publishing, 2001. Dr. Murphy made additional comments about the harm to children from overexposure to media coverage in

USA Today, March 2003. Refer also to the works and workshops of Joseph Chilton Pearce.

8. Marie Winn, *The Plug-In Drug* (New York: Penguin Books, 1977). Also refer to Keith Buzzell, M.D., *The Children of Cyclops: The Influence of Television Viewing on the Developing Human Brain,* available from Association of Waldorf Schools of North America, 3911 Bannister Road, Fair Oaks, CA 95628.

9. See Atwater, *The New Children and Near-Death Experiences,* and the case of Alice Morrison-Mays on pages 135–136. The stress in this case was caused by Alice's mother receiving news of her father's death. Instead of grieving to release the stress, she held it in until her child was born.

10. The best references on the work of Barbara McClintock are on the Internet. I recommend www.cshl.org/public/mcclinock.html and www.wisc.edu/dysci/usex/brochures/brochures/addproceedings98.pdf.

11. Hartmann, *The Edison Gene: ADHD and the Gift of the Hunter Child* (Rochester, Vt.: Park Street Press, 2003).

CHAPTER TWELVE

1. Neil Howe and William Strauss, *Millennials Rising: The Next Great Generation* (New York: Vintage Books, 2000).

2. Christine Gorman, "The New Science of Dyslexia," *Time* 28 July 2003, pp. 53–59.

3. Sharon Begley, "The IQ Puzzle," *Newsweek* 6 May 1996, pp. 70–72.

4. Dickens and Flynn, "Heritability Estimates Versus Large Environmental Effects," 346–369.

5. Soleira Green, "Quantum Intelligence, Beyond IQ, EQ and SQ. . . The Evolution of Intelligence," published on her Web site. As a visionary, she is actively involved in producing conferences that address such issues as "corporate soul" and "global transformations." She moves around a lot in her work, so the best way to reach her is via e-mail at Soleira@SOULutions.co.uk, or through www.AlchemicalCoach.com or www.CorporateSOULutions.com. My thanks to Soleira for her generosity in allowing me to quote at will from her Web site article.

6. Pearce, *Biology of Transcendence.*

7. Educational Kinesiology Foundation, 1575 Spinnaker Drive, Suite 204B, Ventura, CA 93001; 1-800-356-2109 or (805) 658-7942; e-mail at edukfd@earthlink.net; www.braingym.org.

8. Pegasus Group, P. O. Box 1455 Stn. Main, Winnipeg, MB, Canada R3C 2Z4; (204) 298-3584; e-mail at pegasusgroup@shaw.ca. The founder and president is Carolynne Gladstone.

9. Martha Loving (Orgain), 3685 Dots Drive, Charlottesville, VA 22903;

(434) 295-5706 or (434) 996-5766; e-mail at lovingcolor@aol.com; www
.lovingcolor.org.

10. Helen Garabedian, *Itsy Bitsy Yoga: Poses to Help Your Baby Sleep Longer,
Digest Better, and Grow Stronger* (New York: Fireside Books, 2004). Her
Web site is www.itsybitsyyoga.com.

11. Refer to Cleve Backster, *Primary Perception: Biocommunication with
Plants, Living Foods, and Human Cells* (Anza, Calif.: White Rose Millennium, 2003).

12. Candace B. Pert, Ph.D., *Molecules of Emotion: Why You Feel the Way You
Feel* (New York: Scribner, 1997).

13. Lynne McTaggart, *The Field: The Quest for the Secret Force of the Universe*
(New York: Quill, 2003).

14. Russian advances in researching junk DNA are many and on several fronts.
A name to be aware of is Konstantin Korotkov, Ph.D., Professor of Bio-
physics in St. Petersburg, Russia. His scientific analysis of the human energy
field and his invention of the gas discharge visualization camera (which
is an improvement over Kirlian photography, a well-known modality for
photographing energy fields), is well worth studying. His Web site is www
.Korotkov.org. You may also refer to Forum for Border Science at www
.fosar-bludorf.com. Recent DNA discoveries by Grazyna Fosar and
Franz Bludorf are chronicled in their book, *Vernetzte Intelligenz* (ISBN
3930243237; not yet translated from the German). Their Web site is www
.fosar-bludorf.com. Another reference is http://noosphere.princeton.edu/
fristwall2.html.

15. Sara Lyara Estes is the author of *Operation Terra: Messages from the
Hosts of Heaven, a New Revelation on Earthchanges, ETs, the End Times
and the Journey to the New Earth, Terra* (1999–2002) and *Operation
Terra: Messages from the Hosts of Heaven* (2001–2003). Oroville, WA:
Celestial Cooperatives. Both books can be ordered from her Web site at
www.operationterra.com.

CHAPTER THIRTEEN

1. Diane Ravitch, *The Language Police: How Pressure Groups Restrict What
Children Learn* (New York: Knopf, 2003).

2. Thomas L. Friedman, "In Pakistan, it's Jihad 101," *The New York Times*,
13 November 2001. This piece was published broadly in many of our
nation's newspapers.

3. I urge you to explore the research and ideas of Daria M. Brezinski, Ph.D.
She is soon to come out with a book that digs even deeper into how modern educational systems were formed, and what can be done to turn them
around so they are relevant to the needs of our children. Contact: Dr. Daria

M. Brezinski, P. O. Box 3017, Charlottesville, VA 22903; 1-877-PRO-KIDS; e-mail dr.daria@earthlink.net.

4. For more information refer to these books: *Frames of Mind: The Theory of Multiple Intelligences*, Howard Gardner (Basic Books, New York, NY, 1983; revised edition 1993). And *In Their Own Way: Discovering and Encouraging Your Child's Personal Learning Style*, Thomas Armstrong (Tarcher/Putnam, New York, NY, 1987).

5. Jane Healy, Ph.D., *Endangered Minds* (Topeka, Kan.: Sagebrush Education Resources, 1999). Also refer to Clare Cherry, Douglas Godwin, and Jesse Staples, *Is The Left Brain Always Right? A Guide to Whole Child Development* (Carthage, Ill.: Fearon, 1989).

6. Linda Kreger Silverman, Ph.D., *Upside-Down Brilliance: The Visual-Spatial Learner* (Denver, Colo.: Deleon Publishing, 2002).

7. Benay Dara-Abrams, Ph.D., is CEO and Chairman of BrainJolt, a development company that designs and implements "multi-intelligent online learning" programs aimed at delivering "anyone, anyhow, anywhere, anytime" learning. They adapt content to the individual (anyone) through the educational methodologies they find to be the most conducive to that person's own learning style (anyhow) at a convenient place (anywhere) and time (anytime). Contact her at: BrainJolt, 961 Andover Way, Los Altos, CA 94024; (650) 964-6094; e-mail benay@brainjolt.com; www.brainjolt .com.

8. Bronwyn Fryer, "Meet Generation Net," *Newsweek*, Spring 2000. This special issue of *Newsweek* featured the entire Dara-Abrams family. The full impact of what it was trying to convey didn't dawn on me until I met Benay Dara-Abrams later on and was able to converse with her. That spring issue was amazing enough—what is now happening in the field of e-schools is utterly breathtaking! See www.dara-abrams.com/news/newsweek-score.html for the complete text of the article.

9. To learn more about the work of Dr. Linda Kreger Silverman, contact Institute for the Study of Advanced Development, 1452 Marion Street, Denver, CO 80218; 1-888-443-8331 or (303) 837-8378; fax (303) 831-7465; www.gifteddevelopment.com.

10. Carla Hannaford, *Smart Moves: Why Learning is Not All in Your Head* (Alexander, N.C.: Great River Books, 1995). Also see the Great River Books Web site at http://www.greatriverbooks.com. This independent publisher is producing some of the best books and materials available on approaches to human development and learning for all ages at any setting. Contact them directly at 161 M Street, Salt Lake City, UT 84103-3877; (801) 532-4833; e-mail info@greatriverbooks.com.

11. The sleep kit called "My Little Angel Helps Me Go To Sleep," was created by medical intuitive Caroline Sutterland. Other kits are "My Little Angel Tells Me I'm Special," "My Little Angel Helps Me and My Family," "My Little Angel Helps Me in the Hospital," and "My Little Angel Loves Me." To obtain the kits, contact her at Sutherland Communications, 816 Peace Portal Drive, Box 199, Blaine, WA 98230; 1-800-348-0404 or 1-800-575-6185; fax (360) 332-4174; e-mailcomments@carolinesutherland.com; www.angels4kids.com.

12. For starters, refer to Debra Keller, *Feng Shui: For the Classroom* (Kansas City, Mo.: Andrews McMeel Publishing, 2004).

13. For more information about the Center for Well Being, call (631) 907-5555.To learn more about the Ross School, navigate their Web site at www.rossinstitute.org.

14. Linda Redford was told in her near-death experience to help God's children. Guided to use her Cherokee heritage, it took her many years to develop and test the Adawee Teachings. Her dedication and spiritual calling are readily apparent in this powerful yet simple school enrichment program. For more information, contact her at Honor Kids International, 11672 Rochester Ave., Apt. 302, Los Angeles, CA 90025-2388; e-mail HonorKids7@aol.com; www.honorkids.com.

15. The "freeze-frame" techniques were developed by the Institute of HeartMath, and are readily available. Contact: HeartMath, 14700 W. Park Avenue, Boulder Creek, CA 95006; (831) 338-8500; e-mail info@heartmath.org; www.heartmath.org.

16. The web address of Edutopia Online is www.glef.org. George Lucas has long been concerned about the critical shortage of teachers predicted for the second decade of the twenty-first century. Through his educational foundation and this Web site, he is reaching out to form a community of teachers who are prepared to handle this challenge in new ways.

17. Begin by contacting Association of Waldorf Schools for North America (AWSNA), 3911 Bannister Road, Fair Oaks, CA 95628; (916) 961-0927; e-mail awsna@awsna.org; http://www.awsna.org. Inquire about schools near you. Steiner's teachings cover the entire human life span, from the cradle to the grave, and constitute the most extensive collection of work from one individual. You may also wish to explore information about Sunbridge College (www.sunbridge.edu), Biodynamic Farming and Gardening Association (www.biodynamics.com), and Anthroposophical Society in America (www.anthroposophy.org). All of these are areas covered by Steiner's teachings.

18. Maria Montessori, M.D., noticed that in an atmosphere of acceptance and trust, of freedom within limits, a child's natural love of learning would

flourish. All Montessori instructors are well-schooled in a holistic curriculum that encompasses both verbal and nonverbal modes of learning. To inquire about schools near you, begin with The Montessori Group, 1240 Banana River Drive, Indian Harbour Beach, FL 32937; (321) 779-0031; fax (321) 777-9566; www.montessorischools.org.

19. The Mead School follows the teachings of its innovative founder, Dr. Elaine de Beauport. A bit pricey, the community-based system is located in Stamford, Connecticut. Query them at 1095 Riverbank Road, Stamford, CT 06903; (203) 595-9500; fax (203) 595-0735; e-mail mschool@optionline. net; www.meadschool.org.

20. Contact the main organization directly: Greensboro Wonder & Wisdom School, Inc., P.O. Box 300, Greensboro, VT 05841. A nonprofit organization, the school's goal is to inspire passion for life-long learning by sharing community wisdom and the wonders of life through imaginative programming, for people of all ages. Their Beyond School Enrichment Program is for kids grades one through four (Wonder Kids), and grades five and six (Senior Trotters). Trish Alley is to be congratulated for her vision in creating this small-town treasure.

21. What has transpired globally because of iEARN is almost beyond belief. Contact them and learn about the ways newer aspects of education are seeking to transform this world and how you can participate: iEARN, 475 Riverside Drive, Suite 540, New York, NY 10115; (212) 870-2693; fax (212) 870-2672; e-mail iearn@us.iearn.org; www.iearn.org.

22. I cannot speak well enough of Schumacher and St. James educational programs, and I am gratified that they are expanding their reach to other countries, including many areas of the United States. The central contact in England is: Schumacher College, The Old Postern, Dartington, Totnes, Devon TQ9 6EA, U.K.; phone (011) 44 1803-865934; fax (0) 1803-866899; e-mail admin@schumachercollege.org.uk; www.schumachercollege.org.uk. In the United States, contact St. James Schools, 12 East 79th Street, New York, NY 10021; (212) 744-7300; fax (212) 744-5876. This educational system holds that every subject leads the human soul to freedom. In that regard, the concept that undergirds their offerings is based on spiritual principles.

23. For more information, contact: Union Institute & University, 440 East McMillan Street, Cincinnati, OH 45206-1925; 1-800-486-3116 or (513) 861-6400; fax (513) 861-3218; e-mail admissions@tui.edc; www.tui.edu.

24. Laura L. Sawyer received her Ph.D. in Transformative Learning from Union Institute & University in 2004. Her dissertation entitled "Fostering Transformative Learning, Development, and Spiritual Growth in Higher Education: A Case Study," is on file at Union (refer to note 23 of this chapter).

25. Bobbie Sandoz, *Parachutes for Parents: 10 New Keys to Raising Children for a Better World* (New York: Select Books, 2004). Sandoz is highly intuitive, has many "out-of-the-box" educational ideas that are well grounded in actual experience, and on occasion sponsors educational conferences for teacher enrichment.

26. Jeffrey Mishlove, Ph.D., is well-known as host of the long-running television program *Thinking Allowed*. His work in the field of consciousness research resulted in several best sellers, including Jeffrey Mishlove, Ph.D., *The Root of Consciousness: The Classic Encyclopedia of Consciousness Studies* (Tulsa, Okla.: Council Oak Distribution & Books, 1993). His Web site is www.Mishlove.com.

CHAPTER FOURTEEN

1. Murray Milner, Jr., *Freaks, Geeks, and Cool Kids—American Teenagers, Schools and the Culture of Consumption* (New York: Routledge, 2004).

2. Howard Rheingold, *Smart Mobs: The Next Social Revolution* (Cambridge, Mass.: Perseus, 2002).

3. Susan Linn, *Consuming Kids: The Hostile Takeover of Childhood* (New York: The New Press, 2004).

4. There are many sources for good advice. The ones I recommend are: Hugh and Gayle Prather, *Spiritual Parenting: A Guide to Understanding and Nurturing the Heart of Your Child* (New York: Harmony Books, 1996); Johanna van Zwet, *Parent's Toolbox for Spiritual Growth* (Virginia Beach, Va.: A.R.E. Press, 2001). Joan Bramsch's Web site address is www.EmpoweredParent.com. *The Empowered Parenting Journal* and just about everything else she has to offer constitute a valuable source for parents who could use a little help. To view a sample copy of her journal, the web address is http://epjournalapril2004.blogspot.com/. Begin with that date, and explore from there; the site is updated on occasion.

5. For a brochure that describes the best of Paula Underwood, contact: A Tribe of Two Press, P. O. Box 133, Bayfield, CO 81122; 1-800-995-3320; www.tribeoftwopress.com. I have followed the work of Paula Underwood for several decades and find it to be authentic and extraordinary in every way.

6. MRT, or moral reconation therapy, is a cognitive-behavioral treatment applied in group settings for substance abusers and those with anti-social personalities (which is most of our prison population). Since large numbers of people never receive training in morals as a child, they grow up not knowing that a moral code exists, that there is something within that prevents the average person from acting out negative thoughts, dreams, and fantasies. Begin with the Web sites www.moral-reconation-therapy.com and www.ccimrt.com for more information about this successful prison program.

7. Don Miguel Ruiz, *The Four Agreements* (San Rafael, Calif.: Amber Allen, 1997).

8. It's hard to avoid statistics such as these in today's news, from the Katie Couric special on teen sex on NBC in early 2005 to a plethora of magazine and newspaper articles nationwide. I've attended numerous talks and workshops on the subject. Here is a sample of articles I have collected:

"Unsweet Thirteen," an interview by Michele Hatty with actress Evan Rachel Wood who was appearing in a movie that explored the darker side of adolescence, in *USA Weekend,* September 12–14, 2003.
"The Sex Lives of Kids," by contributing editors Dr. Drew Pinsky and Dennie Hughes, *USA Weekend,* August 23–25, 2002.
"Choosing Virginity," by Lorraine Ali and Julie Scelfo, *Newsweek,* May 10, 1999, 61–71.
"How Well Do You Know Your Kid?" by Barbara Kantrowitz and Pat Wingert, *Newsweek,* May 10, 1999, 36–48.
"This Could Be Your Kid," by Suzanne Smalley, *Newsweek,* August 18, 2003, 44–47.
"Vatican Disapproves of Gender Ambiguity," Associated Press wire services, *The Daily Progress,* August 1, 2004.
"Beyond the Birds and Bees," by Karen Springen, *Newsweek,* April 25, 2005.

I wish to thank Glenn Mingo and his "Notes from a Hermit" (a private news service) and my daughter Natalie DeGennaro, who keeps me constantly updated on the latest news nationwide.

9. Net Gen is presently a software product from Microsoft. A popular spin-off is threedegrees (same company).

CHAPTER FIFTEEN

1. Paul H. Ray and Sherry Ruth Anderson, *The Cultural Creatives: How Fifty Million People are Changing the World* (New York: Harmony, 2000).

2. Mark Satin, *Radical Middle: The Politics We Need Now* (Boulder, Colo.: Westview Press, 2004).

3. Jee Kim, Mathilda de Dios, Pablo Caraballo, et al., eds., *The Future 500: Youth Organizing and Activism in the U.S.* (New Orleans, La.: New Mouth from the Dirty South, 2002). William Upski Wimsatt is also one of the many contributors to this book.

4. "How to Build Global Community" is the title of a postcard and poster created by the Syracuse Cultural Workers, a group of young activists determined to help change this world for the better. Write to them at P.O. Box 6367, Syracuse, NY 13217, or access their Web site at www.syrculturalworkers .org. I thank them for allowing me to use their material.

5. Walter Isaacson, *Benjamin Franklin: An American Life* (New York: & Schuster, 2003).

6. Movie producer Stephen Simon has created a Web site called Moving sages Media (also known as Spiritual Cinema Circle), where he reviews movies that are uplifting and contain mystical or spiritual content. Acknowledging that movie makers are finally going in the direction of spiritual cinema, he offers classes via his Web site in how to interpret and benefit from these movies. He also travels to different cities, and through special showings, helps people to rediscover inner wisdom and divine power via the silver screen. To learn more about this new genre and the services he offers, access his Web site at www.SpiritualCinemaCircle.com; 1-888-447-5494.

7. Riane Eisler, *The Power of Partnership: Seven Relationships that Will Change Your Life* (Novato, Calif.: New World Library, 2002).

8. For ideas, refer to *Natural Home Magazine,* Interweave Press, 201 E. Fourth Street, Loveland, CO 80537-5655; (970) 669-7672; e-mail webmaster@ naturalhomemagazine.com; on the Web at www.interweave.com and www .naturalhomemagazine.com. Also consult International Institute for Bau-Biologie, 1401 A Cleveland Street, Clearwater, FL 33755; (727) 461-4371, fax (727) 441-4373; http://buildingbiology.net/.

9. Information about feng shui practitioners in your area can usually be found on health-food store bulletin boards or at your favorite vitamin shop. Do-it-yourself books are popular, such as: Angi Ma Wong, *Feng Shui: Do's & Taboos* (Williamstown, Mass.: Storey Books, 2000). Although there are many books and sources on dowsing, the best place to begin is still with the headquarters of The American Society of Dowsers, P.O. Box 24, Danville, VT 05828; (802) 684-3417; fax (802) 684-2565; e-mail ASD@dowsers.org; www.dowsers.org. This is a membership organization with a museum and bookstore.

10. Among the best sources of information about permaculture and ecological design is The Permaculture Activist, P.O. Box 1209, Black Mountain, NC 28711. They put out a small catalogue that is excellent, and free. To speak with a permaculture expert, contact: Lee Barnes, Ph.D., P.O. Box 1303, Waynesville, NC 28786-1303; (828) 452-5716; e-mail lbarnes@primeline. com (his area of expertise is the Katuah Bioregion/Southern Appalachian Mountains). For classes, seminars, and workshops, visit the Earthaven Ecovillage. Contact: Culture's Edge, 1025 Camp Elliott Road, Black Mountain, NC 28711; (828) 669-3937; e-mail culturesedge@earthaven.org. These people can refer you to permaculture groups elsewhere in the United States or globally.

11. Many universities now teach natural systems agriculture or courses similar to it. One in particular is given at the University of Northern Iowa. A

book that examines the mistakes of chemical agribusiness operations and presents viable alternatives to the practice is Andrew Kimball, ed., *Fatal Harvest: The Tragedy of Industrial Agriculture* (Washington, D.C.: Island Press, 2002).

12. To learn more about the Eden Project, contact: The Visitor Centre, Bodelva, St. Austell, Cornwall PL24 2SG, United Kingdom; phone (011) 44 1726-811911; fax (011) 44 1726-811912; www.edenproject.com.

13. The most successful co-creative gardening with angels and fairies has been accomplished at two facilities, Findhorn and Perelandra. From these two places and the people who pioneered them have come a teaching and a technique that can be applied anywhere on Earth. Contact: The Findhorn Foundation, The Park, Findhorn Bay, Forres IV36 0TZ, Scotland; phone (011) 44 1309-673655; www.findhorn.org; and Perelandra, P.O. Box 3603, Warrenton, VA 20188; 1-800-960-8806 and (540) 937-2153; fax (540) 937-3360; www.perelandra-ltd.com.

14. Orgone Biophysical Research Laboratory continues the work of Wilhelm Reich on the science of life energy. Contact: Orgone Biophysical Research Laboratory, Greensprings Center, P.O. Box 1148, Ashland, OR 97520; (541) 552-0118; e-mail demeo@mind.net; www.orgonelab.org. U.S. Psychotronics Association, a membership organization, experiments with energy devices and "mind-over-matter." Contact: U. S. Psychotronics Association, P.O. Box 45, Elkhorn, WI 53121; (262) 742-4790; fax (262) 742-3670; e-mail uspa@elknet.net; www.psychotronics.org. Vesica Spirit & Sciences Resources centers around the work of Dr. Robert J. Gilbert and the Science of Sacred Geometry and Biogeometry. See note 8 of chapter 9 for contact information. Dr. Gilbert offers a large and dynamic choice of classes and workshops, and training not only in Sacred Geometry but in the heart and soul of spiritual mystery. Paul Devereux's investigation of Earth energies, fairy paths, and spirit roads deepens and broadens the subject (as do any of his books). Refer to Paul Devereux, *Fairy Paths and Spirit Roads: Exploring Otherworldly Routes in the Old and New Worlds* (New York: Sterling, 2003).

15. Viktor Schauberger, an Austrian forest warden, had a lot of ideas about water a century ago that most people ignored. When I discovered his work, I was amazed at how advanced his concepts were, and how relevant to the future of life on Earth. I recommend this small book as an introduction to his work: Olof Alexandersson, *Living Water: Viktor Schauberger and the Secrets of Natural Energy* (Lower Lake, Calif.: The Great Tradition, 1990). The book was published in Swedish in 1976.

16. Masaru Emoto, *The Message from Water* (Tokyo: Hado Publishing, 1999). The book is available in English in the United States.

17. The clever young man is Andre Hilliard and his Web site is www
.blacksheepnews.com.

18. A leader working with fungal strains of wild mushrooms is scientist Paul
Stamets. He's part of a network of innovative researchers, inventors, and
thinkers who examine the intricate workings of nature in search of ground-
breaking and effective models for solving environmental, social, and economic problems. For more information about these "bioneers," contact:
Bioneers, c/o Collective Heritage Institute, 901 West San Mateo Road, Suite
L, Santa Fe, NM 87505; 1-877-246-6337; www.bioneers.org.

19. Some online sources I can point you to include: www.enviromission.com.
au (information about trapping greenhouse heat) and www.seaspower.com
(information on tapping energy from the vacuum of space). For more on cold
fusion, refer to the U.S. Navy report entitled "Technical Report 1862, February 2002. Thermal and Nuclear Aspects of the Pd/D20 System," written by
Dr. Frank E. Gordon. A giant in the field of alternative forms of energy was
the late Dr. Eugene F. Mallove. A book of his was nominated for a Pulitzer
Prize, and that book concerned cold fusion: *Fire from Ice: Searching for the
Truth Behind the Cold Fusion Furor* (Concord, N.H.: Infinite Energy Press,
1991). For more on hydrogen, refer to Jeremy Rifkin, *The Hydrogen Economy: The Creation of the Worldwide Energy Web and the Redistribution
of Power on Earth* (New York: Tarcher/Penguin, 2002). For more information about alternative energy technologies, access http://whitetiger511.tripod
.com. This is the Web site of White Tiger Organic Farm and Techno Eco
Village (TEV), the contact person is Greg O'Neill, Spokane, WA. Also refer
to *Infinite Energy* magazine (for information on new energy, new science):
New Energy Foundation, Inc., P.O. Box 2816, Concord, NH 03302-2816;
(603) 228-4516; fax (603) 224-5975. Another excellent source of cutting-
edge information and activity on many fronts is Institute for Frontier Science,
6114 LaSalle Avenue, PMB 605, Oakland, CA 94611; (510) 531-5767; fax
(510) 531-7224; e-mail brubik@earthlink.net; www.concentric.net/~explore.
The Institute is presently headed by Beverly Rubik, Ph.D. Queries welcome.

20. Some excellent Web sites of people and groups working together to make a
difference:

www.payitforwardfoundation.org
www.WantToKnow.info/resources#community
www.Kidscare.org
www.treemusketeers.org
www.gregorysmith.com
www.callforpeace.org
www.planusa.org/index.php

Also, for a book about one youngster who is making a huge difference helping those in need, read Craig Kielburger and Kevin Major, *Free the Children: A Young Man Fights Child Labor and Proves that Children Can Change the World* (Glenville, NY; Perennial, 1999).

21. Some Web sites along this line of planetary citizenship: http://allianceforthenewhumanity.org;www.sfcg.org(SearchforCommonGround); www.globalexchange.org;   www.newdimensions.org;   http://worldwatch.org; www.globalissues.org; www.ips-dc.org (Institute for Policy Studies); and www.centresa.ch (Center for Social Architecture). An organization to consider joining is Global Heart Foundation, 3251 West 6th Street, P. O. Box 75127, Los Angeles, CA 90075; (213) 388-2181; fax (213) 388-1926; e-mail touching@globalheartfdn.org. An organization that offers a spate of spiritually oriented classes and workshops is The Center for Visionary Leadership. East Coast: P.O. Box 2241, Arlington, VA 22202; (202) 237-2800; West Coast: 369 3rd Street, #563, San Rafael, CA 94901; (415) 472-2540. Joint e-mail cvldc@visionarylead.org. Joint Web site www.visionarylead.org. They produce an e-zine called *Soul Light*. Two magazines of outstanding quality and content are *Utne* (1-800-736-UTNE, or write Utne Subscriber Service, Box 7460, Red Oak, IA 51591-0460; www.utne.com) and *Ode*, based in the Netherlands (Ode International, 101 West 23rd Street, PMB 2245, New York, NY, 10011-2490; www.odemagazine.com. Two books geared to this topic: Howard Gardner, Mihaly Csikszentmihaly, and William Damon, *Good Work: Where Excellence and Ethics Meet* (New York: Basic Books, 2002) and Thom Hartmann, *The Prophet's Way: Touching the Power of Life* (New York: Three Rivers Press, 2001).

CHAPTER SIXTEEN

1. *The Challenge of September 11, A Memorial* is available as a free download from the Web site of P. M. H. Atwater at www.cinemind.com/atwater or www.pmhatwater.com. For more in-depth material on the soul, the soul's will, soul cycles, and much more, refer to Atwater's books *Future Memory*, (Charlottesville, Va.: Hampton Roads Publishing, 1999) and *We Live Forever: The Real Truth about Death* (Virginia Beach, Va.: A.R.E. Press, 2004).

2. I study and analyze a broad range of reports to keep apprised of this kind of information. A sample list of my sources includes: the National Solar Observatory in New Mexico, U. S. Geological Survey, British Geological Survey, World Transformations at www.worldtrans.org, Volcanoes.com (a site maintained by the University of North Dakota), Environmental News Network at www.enn.com/news, the Discovery Channel's Earth Alert at www.discovery.com/news/earthalert/earthalert.html, Centers for Disease

Control at www.cdc.gov/od/oc/media/news.htm, and Envirolink at www
.envirolink.org.

3. "Satellites in low-Earth orbit over southern Africa are already showing
signs of radiation damage," by Bonny Schoonakker, in the South Afr-
can newspaper *Sunday Times,* accessed on the Web at www.sundaytimes
.co.za/2004/07/18/news/news14.asp.

4. From a personal e-mail from Dr. Yensen to the author, dated April 29,
2004, affirming the preceding listing of earth changes and clarifying the
current situation of the great conveyor belt in the Atlantic.

5. You can obtain a copy of the executive summary of the Pentagon Climate
Change Report over the Internet. The report by Peter Schwartz and Doug
Randall is entitled "An Abrupt Climate Change Scenario and Its Implications for United States National Security." Access www.ems.org/climate/
pentagon_climate_change.html#report.

6. For more information about HAARP, refer to this book: Nick Begich and
Jeane Manning, *Angels Don't Play This HAARP—Advances in Tesla Technology* (Eagle River, Ark: Earthpulse Press, 1995).

7. In addition to my previous sources for information about changes in our
environment, I turned to Russian scientists for more clarity and up-to-date
findings concerning the universe. The most active in providing such reports
is Vernadsky Institute Laboratory for Comparative Planetology in Moscow,
and the most vocal of their scientists is Dr. E. V. Dmitriev. One of his papers is
"When Mars was simliar to Jupiter." Vernadsky Institute and Brown University in Providence, Rhode Island, participate regularly in symposiums through
Brown's Planetary Geo Sciences Group. At their 49th symposium held October 11–13, 2004, in Moscow, Dmitriev presented the paper "New Tasks on
Mars Investigation in Interest of Cosmogony, Planetology, and Verification of
Jordano Brunoöf Hypothesis about Great Number of Inhabited Worlds." To
read this paper visit www.geokhiru/-planetology/program. Brown's Web site
for this material is www.planetary.brown.edu. The findings I present in this
section come from Dmitriev's studies and those of his colleagues. To reach
Dmitriev directly, e-mail him at deva1001@mtu-net.ru.

8. Simon Winchester, *Krakatoa: The Day the World Exploded, August 27,
1883* (New York: Harper Collins, 2003).

9. Daniel Pink, *A Whole New Mind: Moving from the Information Age to the
Conceptual Age* (New York, Riverhead Books, 2005).

10. Strauss and Howe, *Generations* (see chap. 5, n1).

CHAPTER SEVENTEEN

1. Sir Isaac Newton, *Observations Upon the Prophecies of Daniel, and the
Apocalypse of St. John* (Cave Junction, Ore.: Oregon Institute of Science
and Medicine, 1991). Originally published in 1733.

2. P.M.H. Atwater, L.H.D., *Future Memory* (Charlottesville, Va.: Hampton Roads, 1999). I examine the "in-between" at length in this book.

3. An excellent book on this subject is Ervin Laszlo, Ph.D., *Science and the Akashic Field: An Integral Theory of Everything* (Rochester, Vt.: Inner Traditions, 2004).

4. "Death of Famous Mystic Raises Questions about Prophecies Pertaining to the Year 2004," article by Michael H. Brown found at www.spiritdaily.org. The quote I use here was sent to me by a friend who was greatly moved by that particular passage. For a further investigation of Maria Esperanza de Bianchini and her gift of prophecy read the book *The Bridge to Heaven: Interviews with Maria Esperanza of Betania,"* by Michael H. Brown, Lima, PA, Marin Communications, 1994.

5. "Photons: Coming Even Faster to a Computer Near You," by Patricia King, *Newsweek,* April 20, 1998, 13.

6. Israeli scientists devised the DNA computer. Although the computer can perform 330 trillion operatios per second, more than 100,000 times the speed of the fastest PC, so far it can only handle rudimentary tasks. Research is ongoing. For more information see *National Geographic's* daily news Web site at news.nationalgeographic.com.

7. Clarissa Pinkola Estes, Ph.D., is known for penning the best seller *Women Who Run with the Wolves: Myths and Stories of the Wild Woman Archetype* (New York: Ballantine Books, 1992). This book turned out to be a paradigm shifter in how it encouraged women to embrace all aspects of themselves, including that which is wild and free, strong and independent.

8. Swami Sri Yukteswar, *The Holy Science* (Los Angeles: Self-Realization Fellowship, 1990). I wish to thank the Fellowship for considering the chart I designed based on Yukteswar's lengthy work and for giving me permission to publish it.

9. Richard Milton, *The Facts of Life: Shattering the Myths of Darwinism* (Rochester, Vt.: Park Street Press, 1997).

10. From the article "Hopi Prophecy Fulfilled," sent to me March 19, 2004 by Glenn Mingo, who operates the private news service "Notes from a Hermit." No author's name was shown. The article does refer to this Web site: www.wolflodge.org/bluestar/bluestar.

11. Jeremy Rifkin, *The Biotech Century: Harnessing the Gene and Remaking the World* (New York: Tarcher/Putnam, 1999).

12. Dr. Robert Ghost Wolf, *Last Cry: Native American Prophecies & Tales of the End Times* (Victoria, British Columbia: Trafford Publishing, 2003).

13. J. R. R. Tolkien, *The Lord of the Rings* (London: George Allen and Unwin Ltd., 1954, 1955) The trilogy was published over a two-year period. Hough-

ton Mifflin Company in Boston is the American publisher, there have been various editions since the middle 1960s. A classic. *The Hobbit* was originally published in 1937. *The Silmarillion* was published in 1977 by George Allen and Unwin Ltd; it is currently available through Houghton Mifflin.

14. Humphrey Carpenter, *The Letters of J. R. R. Tolkien* (Boston: Houghton Mifflin Company, 1981).

CHAPTER EIGHTEEN

1. Don Miguel Ruiz, *The Voice of Knowledge: A Practical Guide to Inner Peace* (San Rafael, Calif.: Amber Allen Publishing, 2004). This is his newest book; see also note 7 of chapter 14.

2. "The Children" by Chris Van Cleave will soon be on one of his CDs. You can avail yourself of his offerings via www.vancleavemusic.com, or by e-mailing seebeyond@mindspring.com. He can be reached through his agent, Carolyn Amundson, Amundson Initiatives, 1045 Selma Blvd., Staunton, VA 24401; (540) 885-7439; e-mail initiatives@mindspring.com.

3. Many psychics have listed "ascension symptoms" on their Web sites. Of those that are the most helpful, I suggest exploring the material of Karen Bishop. What she has to offer can be downloaded at http://whatsuponplanetearth.com/index.html.

4. "The Message Center" was developed by Janet Gaddie Grimm and Patricia K. Manthey as a guided meditation for children. Its purpose is to help further "children in compassionate action." My thanks to both of them for allowing me to use their material.

Web Site of
P. M. H. Atwater, L.H.D.

www.pmhatwater.com

The "Notes" section on pages 206–231 of this book includes expanded information and extensive listings of resources that might be of interest to readers. However, there was no way to include in those pages everything that might be beneficial. Hence I have added a special section to my website (which is one of the most extensive on near-death experiences). It includes updated information on the topics covered in this book: additional ideas, suggestions, books, and websites. Look for "Beyond the Indigo Children Extras" to access that page.

Other resources recommended on the Web site for near-death experiencers apply to the new children as well. They range from types of therapy that really work to hospitals with a heart. You will also find my schedule, e-books, services, talks and workshops listed on the site.

Pay a visit to the Marketplace on the Web site, too. It's chock-full of people, services, products, ideas—all geared to those who prefer holistic ways of living. The Marketplace is offered as a public service.

There are many surprises on the Web site—enjoy.

Additional Books to Consider

*Life is not measured by the number of breaths we take, but
by the moments that take our breath away.*

GEORGE CARLIN

The books listed here are meant to supplement those described in the text
and listed in the notes. There are real treasures in the notes. Please, don't miss
them.

KIDS' STUFF

The Birth Called Death, Kathie Jordan (Ashland, Ore.: RiverWood Books,
2003).

Children of Light, Jan Royce Conant (Dryden, N.Y.: Ithaca Press, 2005). Available online at Books@IthacaPress.com. Or www.JanRoyceConant.com.

The Children of Vision-Peace, Arupa Tesolin (An Intuita.com Publication, available through www.intuita.com)

The Children's Illustrated Encyclopedia of Heaven, Anita Ganeri (Boston: Element Books, 1999).

Dream House, Fu-Ding Cheng (Charlottesville, Va.: Hampton Roads, 2000).

*The Element Illustrated Encyclopedia of Mind, Body, Spirit & Earth: A Unique
Exploration of Our Place in the Universe*, Joanna Crosse (Rockport, Mass.:
Element Books, 1998).

Herman's Magical Universe, Becky McCarley (Charlottesville, Va.: Hampton
Roads, 1999).

The Kids' Book about Death and Dying, Eric. E. Rofes and The Unit at Fayer-
weather Street School (Boston: Little Brown, 1985).

Little World, Mary Duty (Xlibris Corporation). Contact: Orders@Xlibris.com.

The Magic Seed, Sharon Price (Del Mar, Calif.: PowerPartners USA Inc., 2002).

Penny Bear's Gift of Love, Penny Wigglesworth (Marblehead, Mass.: Penny Bear Publishing, 2003). Check with www.pennybear.org.

Sonny's Dream, Noriko Senshu (Charlottesville, Va.: Hampton Roads, 2001).

A Spirited Alphabet, Morgan Simone Daleo and Frank Riccio (Charlottesville, Va.: Hampton Roads, 1999).

The Sunbeam and the Wave, Harriet Elizabeth Hamilton (Unity Village, Mo.: Unity Books, 2000). A Wee Wisdom book.

A Walk in the Rain with a Brain, Edward M. Hallowell, M.D. and Bill Mayer (Scranton, Pa.: Regan Books, 2004).

What's Happening to Grandpa?, Maria Shriver (New York: Little, Brown, 2004).

What's Wrong with Timmy? Maria Shriver. (New York: Little, Brown, 2001).

TEEN STUFF

Conversations with God for Teens, Neale Donald Walsch (Charlottesville, Va.: Hampton Roads, 2001).

The Energy of Money, Maria Nemeth, Ph.D. (New York: Wellspring/Ballantine, 2000). For all ages, but especially teens.

Fire in the Heart: A Spiritual Guide for Teens, Deepak Chopra, M.D. (New York: Simon & Schuster, 2004).

The Laws of Money, the Lessons of Life, Suze Orman (New York: Free Press, 2003). The new kids are into money and business, big time.

Natural Capitalism: Creating the Next Industrial Revolution, Paul Hawken, Amory Lovins, and L. Hunter Lovins (New York: Little, Brown, 1999).

Planetary Citizenship: Your Values, Beliefs and Actions Can Shape a Sustainable World, Hazel Henderson and Daisaku Ikeda (Santa Monica, Calif.: Middleway Press, 2004).

The Primal Teen: What the New Discoveries about the Teenage Brain Tell Us About Our Kids, Barbara Strauch (New York: Doubleday, 2003).

Teen Psychic: Exploring Your Intuitive Spiritual Powers, Julie Tallard Johnson (Rochester, Vt.: Bindu Books, 2003).

There is Nothing Wrong with You—For Teens, Cheri Huber (Mountain View, Calif.: Keep-It-Simple, 2001).

The Thundering Years: Rituals and Sacred Wisdom for Teens, Julie Tallard Johnson (Rochester, Vt.: Bindu Books, 2001).

MORE FOR PARENTS AND TEACHERS

Clark Smart Kids, Clark Smart Parents, Clark Howard (New York: Hyperion, 2005).

The Family Virtues Guide: Simple Ways to Bring Out the Best in Our Children and Ourselves, Linda Kavelin Popov (New York: Plume Books, 1997).

From Magical Child to Magical Teen: A Guide to Adolescent Development,
Joseph Chilton Pearce (Rochester, Vt.: Park Street Press, 1985). Reissued.

The Gift of Fear, Gavin DeBecker (New York: Dell, 1998).

Guiding the Gifted Child: A Practical Source for Parents and Teachers, James
T. Webb, Ph.D., Elizabeth A. Meckstroth, M.S.W., and Stephanie S. Tolan,
M.A. (Scottsdale, Ariz.: Gifted Psychology Press, 1994).

Mind Power for Children: The Guide for Parents and Teachers, John Kehoe and
Nancy Fischer (Vancouver, British Columbia: Zoetic, Inc., 2002).

Parenting the Enlightened Child, Alyce Bartholomew Soden (Chapel Hill, N.C.:
Professional Press, 1997).

Parenting Well in a Media Age: Keeping Our Kids Human, Gloria DeGaetano
(Torrance, Calif.: Personhood Press, 2004).

A Practical Guide for Crisis Response in Our Schools, Mark D. Lerner, Ph.D.,
Joseph S. Volpe, Ph.D., and Brad Lindell, Ph.D. (Commack, N.Y.; American
Academy of Experts in Traumatic Stress, 2004).

The Soul of Education, Rachael Kessler (Alexandria, Va.: Association for Supervision and Curriculum Development, 2000).

THE WORLD OF INTUITION AND SPIRITUALITY

Abraham: A Journey to the Heart of Three Faiths, Bruce Feiler (New York:
Perennial, 2004).

Animals as Guides for the Soul, Susan Chernak McElroy (New York: Ballan-
tine/Wellspring, 1998).

Animal Speak: The Spiritual and Magical Powers of Creatures Great and Small,
Ted Andrews (St. Paul, Minn.: Llewellyn, 1997).

The Art of Forgiveness, Lovingkindness, and Peace, Jack Kornfield (New York:
Bantam, 2002).

Awakening Intuition: Using Your Mind-Body Network for Insight and Healing,
Mona Lisa Schulz, M.D., Ph.D. (New York: Three Rivers Press, 1999).

*The Beethoven Factor: The New Positive Psychology of Hardiness, Happi-
ness, Healing and Hope,* Paul Pearsall, Ph.D. (Charlottesville, Va.: Hampton
Roads, 2003).

Behaving as if the God in All Life Mattered, Machaelle Small Wright (Warrenton, Va.: Perelandra Ltd., 1997).

The Best Guide to Meditation, Victor N. Davich (New York: St. Martin's Press,
1998).

Children of the Earth . . . Remember, Schim Schimmel (Minnetonka, Minn.:
North Wood Press, 1997).

Dear Children of the Earth: A Letter from Home, Schim Schimmel (Minnetonka,
Minn.: North Wood Press, 1994).

Healing the Hurts of Nation—The Human Side of Globalization, Palden Jen-kin (Glastonbury, United Kingdom: Gothic Image Publications, 2003). Also available in the United States.

Dogs That Know When Their Owners are Coming Home, Rupert Sheldrake (New York: Crown, 1999).

Enchantment of the Faerie Realm, Ted Andrews (St. Paul, Minn.: Llewellyn, 1993).

Excuse Me, Your Life is Waiting—The Power of Feelings, Lynn Grabhorn (Charlottesville, Va.: Hampton Roads, 2000).

How Psychic Are You? 76 Techniques to Boost Your Innate Power, Julie Soskin (New York: Penguin Books, 2002).

The Mind of the Soul, Gary Zukav (New York: Free Press, 2004).

Lake of Memory Rising: Return of the Five Ancient Truths at the Heart of Religion, William Fix (San Francisco: Council Oak Books, 2000).

The Last Ghost Dance: A Guide for Earth Mages, Brooke Medicine Eagle (New York: Wellspring/Ballantine, 2000).

The Magic Formula, Michael J. Roads (Cleveland, Ohio: Silver Roads, 2003).

Messiah's Handbook, Richard Bach (Charlottesville, Va.: Hampton Roads, 2004).

Natural Born Intuition: How to Awaken and Develop Your Inner Wisdom, Lauren Thibodeau, Ph.D. (Kansas City, Mo.: New Page Books, 2004).

A New Christianity for a New World: Why Traditional Faith is Dying and How a New Faith is Being Born, Bishop John Shelby Spong (San Francisco: Harper San Francisco, 2002).

One River, Many Wells, Matthew Fox (Los Angeles: Jeremy P. Tarcher, 2004).

Opening the Inner Eye, William H. Kautz (Lincoln, Neb.: Writers Club Press (iUniversecom), 2003).

The Power of Intention: Learning to Co-Create Your World Your Way, Wayne W. Dyer, Ph.D. (Carlsbad, Calif.: Hay House, 2004).

The Power of Now: A Guide to Spiritual Enlightenment, Echart Tolle (Los Altos, CA; New World, 1999).

Practical Intuition: How to Harness the Power of Your Instinct and Make It Work for You, Laura Day (New York: Broadway Books, 1996).

Practical Psychic Self-Defense: Understanding and Surviving Unseen Influences, Robert Bruce (Charlottesville, Va.: Hampton Roads, 2002).

Prayers: A Communion with Our Creator, Don Miguel Ruiz (San Rafael, Calif.: Amber Allen, 2001).

Prayers to an Evolutionary God, William Cleary and Diarmuid O'Murchu (Woodstock, Vt.: Skylight Paths, 2004).

The Quantum Self, Dana Zohar (New York: HarperCollins, 1991).

The Quantum Society, Dana Zohar (New York: William Morrow, 1994).

The Second Coming of Christ: The Resurrection of the Christ Within You, Paramahansa Yogananda (Los Angeles: Self-Realization Fellowship, 2004).

The Sense of Being Stared At: And Other Unexplained Powers of the Human Mind, Rupert Sheldrake (New York: Three Rivers Press, 2004).

The Sixth Sense of Children, Litany Burns (New York: New American Library, 2002).

The Soul's Religion, Thomas Moore (New York: Perennial, 2001).

Stories and Poems for Extremely Intelligent Children of All Ages, Harold Bloom, ed. (New York: Scribner, 2002).

Talking with the Animals, Patty Summers (Charlottesville, Va.: Hampton Roads, 1998).

Teaching Children to Love: 80 Games & Fun Activities for Raising Balanced Children in Unbalanced Times, Doc Lew Childre (Boulder Creek, Calif.: Planetary Publications, 1996).

Thinking from the Infinite, Carell Zaehn (Marina del Rey, Calif.: DeVorss, 2004).

Thinking with Your Soul: Spiritual Intelligence and Why It Matters, Richard N. Wolman, Ph.D. (New York: Harmony, 2001).

The Third Appearance: A Crisis of Perception, Walter Starcke (Boerne, Texas: Guadalupe Press, 2004).

Totems: The Transformative Power of Your Personal Animal Totem, Brad Steiger (San Francisco: Harper San Francisco, 1997).

Venture Inward: A Guide to the Doorways to Inner Exploration, Hugh Lynn Cayce (Virginia Beach, Va.: A.R.E. Press, 1995).

The Wise Child: A Spiritual Guide to Nurturing Your Child's Intuition, Sonia Choquette, Ph.D. (New York: Three Rivers Press, 1999).

The World Café: Shaping Our Futures Through Conversations That Matter, Juanita Brown and David Isaacs (San Francisco: Berrett-Koehler, 2005).

BEFORE THIS LIFE, REINCARNATION, AND GHOSTS

The Afterlife Experiments: Breakthrough Scientific Evidence of Life After Death, Gary E. Schwartz, Ph.D. (New York: Pocket Books, 2002).

Babies Remember Birth, David Chamberlain, Ph.D. (Los Angeles: Jeremy Tarcher, 1988).

Children's Past Lives: How Past Life Memories Affect Your Child, Carol Bowman (New York: Bantam, 1997).

Cosmic Cradle: Souls Waiting in the Wings for Birth, Elizabeth M. Carman, Ph.D. and Neil J. Carman, Ph.D. (Fairfield, Iowa: Sunstar Publishing Ltd., 1999).

Old Souls: The Scientific Evidence for Past Lives, Tom Shroder (New York: Simon & Schuster, 1999).

Relax, It's Only a Ghost: My Adventures with Spirits, Hauntings and Things That Go Bump in the Night, Echo Bodine (Boston: Element Books, 2000).

Remembering Your Life Before Birth, Michael Gabriel, M.A. and Marie Gabriel (Fairfield, Conn.: Aslan Publishing, 1995).

Return from Heaven, Carol Bowman (New York: Harper Collins, 2001).

Return of the Revolutionaries: The Case for Reincarnation and Soul Groups Reunited, Walter Semkiw, M.D. (Charlottesville, Va.: Hampton Roads, 2003).

Many Mansions: The Edgar Cayce Story of Reincarnation, Gina Cerminara (New York: Signet Books, 1990).

THE CHAKRAS, HEALTH, AND HEALING

Chakra Therapy: For Personal Growth and Healing, Keith Sherwood (St. Paul, Minn.: Llewellyn, 1988). Reissued.

Eastern Body, Western Mind: Psychology and the Chakra System, Anodea Judith, Ph.D. (Berkeley, Calif.: Celestial Arts, 2004).

Energy Medicine, Donna Eden (New York: Putnam, 1999).

Essential Musical Intelligence: Using Music as Your Path to Healing, Creativity, and Radiant Wholeness, Louise Montello (Wheaton, Ill.: Quest Books, 2002).

The Healing Energies of Water, Charlie Ryrie (Boston: Tuttle Publishing, 1999).

The Healing Power of Light, Primrose Cooper (York Beach, Maine: Weiser Books, 2001).

How People Heal: Exploring the Scientific Basis of Subtle Energy in Healing, Diane Goldner (Charlottesville, Va.: Hampton Roads, 2003).

Prayer is Good Medicine, Larry Dossey, M.D. (San Francisco: Harper San Francisco, 1997).

Secret Teachings of Plants: The Intelligence of the Heart in the Direct Perception of Nature, Stephen Harrod Buhner (Rochester, Vt.: Bear & Co., 2004).

Wheels of Life: A User's Guide to the Chakra System, Anodea Judith, Ph.D. (St. Paul, Minn.: Llewellyn, 1987). Reissued.

Yoga Baby, DeAnsin Goodson Parker, Ph.D. (New York: Broadway Books, 2000).

QUESTIONS OF OUR ORIGINS AND GENETICS

Adam's Curse, A Future Without Men, Brian Sykes (New York: W. W. Norton, 2004).

The Genesis Race: Our Extraterrestrial DNA and the True Origins of the Species, Will Hart (Rochester, Vt.: Bear & Co., 2003).

Gods, Genes, and Consciousness: Nonhuman Intervention in Human History, Paul Von Ward (Charlottesville, Va.: Hampton Roads, 2004).

Hidden History of the Human Race, Michael A. Cremo and Richard L. Thompson (Badger, Calif.: Govardhan Hill, 1994).

Lost Book of Enki: Memories and Prophecies of an Extraterrestrial God, Zecharia Sitchin (Rochester, Vt.: Bear & Co., 2002).

Watermark: The Disaster That Changed the World and Humanity 12,000 Years Ago, Christy Vitale (New York: Pocket Books, 2004).

A LITTLE MORE ON THE STORY OF CREATION

The Dreaming Universe, Fred Alan Wolf, Ph.D. (New York: Touchstone, 1995).

Forbidden Archeology, Michael A. Cremo and Richard L. Thompson (Badger, Calif.: Govardhan Hill, 1993).

Forbidden Science, Jacques Vallee, Ph.D. (Berkeley, Calif.: North Atlantic Books, 1992).

Genesis of the Cosmos: The Ancient Science of Continuous Creation, Paul A. LaViolette, Ph.D. (Rochester, Vt.: Bear & Co., 1995).

The Living Energy Universe: A Fundamental Discovery That Transforms Science & Medicine, Gary Schwartz, Ph.D. and Linda Russek, Ph.D. (Charlottesville, Va.: Hampton Roads, 1999).

Matrix of Creation: Sacred Geometry in the Realm of the Planets, Richard Heath (Rochester, Vt.: Inner Traditions, 2004).

Maya Cosmogenesis 2012, John Major Jenkins (Rochester, Vt.: Bear & Co., 1998).

The Synchronized Universe: New Science of the Paranormal, Claude Swanson, Ph.D. (Tuscon, Ariz.: Poseidia Press, 2003).

Index